Bye Balham

Warming Up Vol 1

Richard HERRING

© Richard Herring, 2008

Published by Go Faster Stripe Ltd
21 Hanover Street, Canton, Cardiff CF5 1LS
www.gofasterstripe.com

We are not just books – we are mostly DVDs in fact.

First Edition

ISBN 978-0-9560901-0-2

Book design, cover photo and proof reading by Chris Brown
Printed by Bell and Bain, Glasgow
Thanks to: Chris Evans, Chris Brown and Rob Sedgebeer

To the people of Balham. The cool ones who lived there before it got all poncey. And not the ones who live in Sistova Road.

One day in November 2002 I was at Waterloo, waiting for a train to take me to Hampshire to see my girlfriend. With some time to kill, I popped into McDonald's for a cup of coffee. I may have bought some sneaky fries as well. I was engrossed in my newspaper, when I became aware of a slight kerfuffle behind me. I turned to see a pigeon, which had found its way inside from the station concourse, flapping and panicking overhead. The other patrons of this fine restaurant gasped and laughed as the bird flew over their heads. Suddenly these disparate commuters were united in joy or amazement at this oddly surreal spectacle. There was something strangely fascinating about this juxtaposition of bird and burger bar. Even though the sky-rat was a dirty grey, it still brightened the room, our humdrum lives suddenly filled with unexpected excitement. In this previously dreary and unexceptional place, this flurry of feather and fluster somehow symbolised hope.

Two hapless employees of the global conglomerate, like Dastardly and Muttley were doing their best to catch that pigeon, presumably to release it back to the relative outdoors of Waterloo Station. But the bird, perhaps fearful that it would be plucked and served up in a burger (wrongly fearful of course, McDonald's only use the finest ingredients, KFC on the other hand…), was trying to elude its benefactors, causing them to trip and tumble into each other, much like their cartoon predecessors.

And the bird's continued freedom was giving the rest of us untold pleasure. Because as well as symbolising hope, it also represented hopelessness, an irresistible combination to the patrons of this fine establishment. I am sure we were all thinking the same things –

"Like the bird we are supposedly free, and yet are all imprisoned in our daily routine."

"How I wish I could fly and soar away from the grasping hands of capitalism."

"I hope it doesn't poo in my food…. Not that it would make much difference."

We were willing it to get away. The bird swooped low, almost brushing my left ear, then soared upward to the roof before coasting majestically into a high internal window above the staircase. Then cartoon-like it slid down the pane, disappearing out of sight into some drab foliage in a window box. All of us were united in sympathy and pain, having anthropomorphised the creature . Again the same ironies no doubt popped into our minds -

"How tragic. Its literal flight from its oppressors is over."

"Our hopes, like its bird brains are dashed."

"I feel a little queasy… and for once it's not because of the food."

But then, to our further amazement, the pigeon's head popped above the foliage, a little battered, comically confused, but basically unharmed. The diners cheered, the piped music seemed to swell triumphantly, people of different races and creeds embraced and kissed one another. At least it felt like they should have done, because our hero was still alive, if not in the mood to fly anywhere for a while. Best of all he had fallen out of reach of his pursuers. The rebellion continued.

At which point I had to leave to get my train and so can pretend to myself that the bird remained free and undefeated forever.

*   *   *   *   *   *

This might seem like an insignificant, if charming, incident and not something that would prompt anyone to do anything, except find somewhere more salubrious to have their coffee, but it made me think. In a world obsessed with major historical events and the deeds of politicians and celebrities, billions of supposedly insignificant events are unrecorded and forgotten.

At the time I was going through a period of what some call writer's block, but in this case might have been writer's laziness. Since becoming a professional writer and comedian in 1990 I had been fairly prodigious. Along with Stewart Lee, I wrote hours of radio and TV comedy in the 1990s. I had created over a dozen shows for the Edinburgh Fringe, including sketch shows, stand up and plays. The latest, Talking Cock, a male riposte to The Vagina Monologues, had not only been the most critically successful, it was also being translated into over ten European languages and I had been asked to write an 80,000-word book about the purple-headed womb broom (most of them would be taken up with such colourful euphemisms). I had spent 2001 and 2002 writing thirty-seven episodes of the sitcom Time Gentlemen Please with Al Murray, which was not only exhausting, but also (for the first time in my life) rather lucrative. Perhaps I felt I had earned a breather.

And for once things seemed to be coming together for me. In August I had got together with a fantastic woman who unbelievably thought I was fantastic as well and I had enough money in the bank to think about moving from my pokey flat in Balham to a swanky house that wasn't in Balham. My girlfriend (S) even had a small baby (P) from a previous relationship, which meant I had a ready-made family, without all the palaver of having to have sex. Bonus! So confident was I in my new love that I had asked S and P to move in with me. At thirty-five maybe at last I had grown up. Maybe at last I was going to be happy.

Perhaps contentment and relative wealth had dampened my creative zeal. I was worried about my recent lack of impetus on the writing front, as well as my slow progress on the book, despite rapidly approaching deadlines.

On top of this I had also just been reading The Salmon of Doubt, a collection of articles and funny bits and bobs by the late, great Douglas Adams, another notorious sufferer of writer's block. As brilliant as this book was it also made me slightly sad that in the periods of bleakness and blankness Adams hadn't written more of this stuff. He was a man who could turn mundanity to hilarity and was so eloquent about the things that fascinated and appalled him. Given how unfairly short his life was to be, it felt like an additional waste, in spite of his marvellous self-justifying observation, "Why do writers spend all day in the pub? Because they can!"

But he knew more than anyone that writing is hard. It's the hardest job in the world (read the entry for 11th March to see just how hard)!

So maybe if I wrote about something every day then I would not only help to record the minutiae of every day life, but might also warm my brain up so I could get on with the work that was ahead of me. I decided to that if I put it up on my new website (www. richardherring.com) it would be an incentive to keep going. I didn't really know what a blog was at this point, but that, it seems, was what I was starting. I did not realise that over five years later I would still be writing it and not have missed a single day in the interim. Or that it actually wouldn't prove to be much use for "Warming Up" (as I had called it), more often than not being the only constructive thing I achieved with my day.

It began at an interesting point in my career: I was suddenly going it alone and having to reinvent myself. I had worked with Stewart Lee since meeting him at University in 1986. In the decade after leaving college, we worked our way through BBC Radio before getting our own BBC2 series, Fist of Fun which ran for two series. After a brief hiatus where a controller who liked us was replaced by one who didn't, who in turn was replaced by one who did, we returned for two series of the live Sunday afternoon show This Morning With Richard, Not Judy. Both of these shows had a loyal, cultish following, but by 1999 I thought we were really starting to get somewhere interesting with the relationship and were on the cusp of creating a show that might be more universally popular. At which point evil Jane Root, the enemy of laughter, became Controller of BBC2 and cancelled the show. But because I worked intensively with Al Murray over the next couple of years, it was only in 2002 that the dust started to settle and I had time to think about what I was going to do next. After coming so close to TV success it was almost like starting over. And I had no idea what direction I should be going. I didn't have a solo stand up act and had little compunction to have another go at that. For a couple of years in the early 90s I had tried out at the various comedy clubs on the circuit, but with massively varying degrees of success. It hadn't been an experience I had enjoyed and after one particularly rowdy student gig where I had ended up taking down my trousers on stage I decided that the medium was not for me, that I was much better when working with others. Now, some ten years later I was performing solo again for the first time, but in one-man shows in theatres and arts centres, and it was not what I would call stand up comedy. I was too much of a chicken to try that again.

But I didn't really know what I was any more. Was I a writer or *a performer? And where was my career going? Was I washed up and dried out? Or would one of my new projects bring me the success that I had been within a hair's breadth of achieving just a few years before.*

My personal life was clearly also at a bit of a turning point, though I was not planning to write about that in Warming Up. I didn't want to turn it into a personal confessional, or list every single boring thing I had done each day; rather I would concentrate on one incident and try to explore its comic possibilities and hidden poetry. That was the theory, but of course it became difficult not to discuss the people around me, as well as to disguise my mood when I was tetchy or depressed or happy. And things ended up being a lot more revealing than I had intended. Looking back at it, it gives quite an insight into the life of a jobbing writer/comedian: the empty theatres, the endless procrastination, hope raised and then hope smashed into a pane of glass, sliding down into a window box.

*   *   *   *   *   *

So, Bye Bye, Balham is a collection of most of the blogs from the first six months of this ridiculous enterprise, ending as you might infer from the title with my move from South London (where I had lived in various houses for the previous ten years) to Shepherd's Bush. I have expurgated a small amount of the more boring entries, just for economy of space and because a few of them are embarrassingly sparse and rubbish (though if you are desperate to see them they are all still up on the website). I wrote Warming Up very much as it occurred to me, in both senses of the word. Very rarely did I go back over my daily brain dump to edit or improve it. I thought I would have to tidy things up a bit, out of respect to you, the paying customer, but beyond the tiniest occasional tweak, I have left it pretty much in its original state. I think it is the ramshackle nature of the writing that is part of its half-arsed charm, but I am also quite impressed with how neatly some of the entries are put together. Despite my inclination not to reveal too much of my personal life to complete strangers, with the passage of five years that kind of secrecy no longer seems necessary, so I have added some background detail at the start of each monthly chapters and where relevant after certain entries. In fact with the additional benefit of hindsight I have been able to make sense of things that, at the time, I was clearly quite clueless about.

I have found the exercise of going back over my past life and being able to sarcastically comment on my own stupidity or predictability quite enlightening. It's also slightly disconcerting that nearly all my concerns and obsessions are the same now as they were then and to be forced to acknowledge how little I have moved on. But though it's taken me half a decade to understand what a twat I was back in 2003, I would still recommend this as an exercise. It probably takes us five years to get things into perspective and understand our mistakes, but it's good to finally do so, even if it is too late to do anything about it.

This whole process of retrospective self-mockery reminded me of my very first diary. In 1975 I was given a Disney diary, which I filled in every day and I have to be honest, it wasn't very interesting. To cut myself some slack I was only eight. I would mainly list what subjects we had studied at school, which meant that, due to there being a timetable, one week's entries were more or less identical to the next. Even though there was only space for maybe forty or fifty words, some days I still struggled to think of anything to write. And there were a fair few entries saying, "I did nothing today" (which is something I often wish I could do on Warming Up, because there are still so many days that feel like that – back then I didn't have so many past experiences to draw upon and write about to fill the void).

Anyway, about five years later I remember going through the diary and mocking my lack of imagination, essentially acting as a teacher, passing comment on each entry with such sarcastic remarks as "Really, how very interesting?" or "You did nothing? Surely you must have done something, even if it was just breathing." The sophisticated thirteen-year-old me, satirised the stupid eight-year-old me, without the self-knowledge to realise that the eighteen-year-old me would look back at those comments with a more world-weary eye and be able to pull them apart in turn.

But this is almost exactly what I find myself doing now – five years on, correcting my mistakes, trying to work out where my relationship went wrong, with hindsight able to spot where I screwed things up, even though I thought I was so correct at the time.

And even now I have no concept of the fact that in 2013 I will read back over this entry, merrily chuckling to myself about how stupid I used to be and ruing the many mistakes I am surely making now in my life without even knowing it. Life is a cruel trick, but nevertheless a diverting one. I am enjoying mocking the thirty-five-year-old me as much as the thirteen-year-old me, delighted in picking apart the eight-year-old me. But I have a sneaking feeling that the uncynical and literal eight-year-old me was probably the best version of this lumbering lunk of meat that I call myself, which declines every five years, but manages to convince itself that it is somehow improving.

* * * * * *

I hope that you enjoy this self-indulgent journey – the two or three thousand regular visitors to the website seem to like it. In truth I think it accidentally gives some insight into my world and the strange hinterland I occupy, mainly concerned with the mundane, but occasionally mounting a foray into the odd and exclusive world of celebrity. I might be failing to hobnob with Elton John and his friends one week and then be hanging out with old school Dr Who fans the next, all the time stressing and procrastinating about a broken fence that I don't have the wherewithal to fix, due to my uselessness in anything remotely practical. It is the diary, not quite of a nobody, but nor is it a diary of a somebody. It is the diary, it might be argued of a slightly jammy bastard who sometimes doesn't appreciate how fortunate he is to live this jet-setting life of relative inactivity. I rather like the fact that with a blog life just rolls onwards, not reaching any kind of denouement. It is the fact that it is written at the time, without the benefit of hindsight or any sense of what will be coming next that, I think, makes it fascinating. This book ends with me moving into my new house and more or less finishing the book I had been writing, but nothing is resolved and the blog moved onwards. Same shit, different day. Life is not as neat as a novel and there's a part of me that believes that this reality and mundanity makes this the ultimate art form. I am not saying that I am better than Shakespeare, Michelangelo and Mozart combined. That is for other people to say.

To keep things interesting for those who have been here before,

I have also written a few exclusive, new entries, containing material that I considered too personal for the blog. I don't quite understand why being in book form makes it any more acceptable, but probably it's more to do, once again, with the passage of time. I see them as being the Warming Up version of those late night editions of Hollyoaks – After Dark episodes that they sometimes do. And there is no higher benchmark that I can hope to aspire to.

I had lived in my one-and-a-half bedroom flat in Balham for about five years, but had decided it was time to move on and had started house hunting in West London in the autumn. I was looking for somewhere big enough to house myself and my ready-made family and also included a room I could use as an office and another room that I could have a pinball machine in. S, my girlfriend, was much too busy with her proper journalist job and young child to come and help in the search, which in hindsight was a bit of a stupid mistake as, of course, she would have to live in the place and it would have been preferable to have her input and her blessing. I had met S in July, when she interviewed me about my Talking Cock show and we had a fun afternoon chatting and getting drunk together. It wasn't until we met again in Edinburgh though that love blossomed. She was only there for a few days, but on her second visit to the Fringe we fell quickly and completely for each other. I was convinced she was the one that I had waited half my lifetime for and the fact she had a baby was not an issue for me. When she asked me one afternoon in bed whether her son wasn't a problem for me, I replied, "He's just more of you to love." It came out instinctively and it gave even me a jolt as I realised that I was sincere. I was smitten. The minute I finished my last show that year I got in my car and drove to Hampshire, stopping only to sleep briefly at a Travelodge, Hell-bent on seeing this woman as soon as I could. Friends advised caution, but I was crazy about this amazing woman and was sure it was going to work.

The fact that within two months I had asked her to move in with me demonstrates what an effect she had had on me. Despite one attempt in my mid-20s (where my then girlfriend and I were ripped off by a bogus estate agent who stole our deposit and prevented us from living in sin – for which I should probably be grateful to him, as things turned out), I had never lived with a girlfriend before.

This was a massive step and we were rushing into it headlong, not thinking, nor properly discussing what we both actually wanted or needed. I think she really hoped to stay living in Hampshire and I had considered this for a weekend, before for the first time contemplating, with a slight chill in my marrow, what this would mean if we broke up. That fleeting reality check may have been the beginning of the end for us, but at the time I was pretty much oblivious. Happy, in love, full of hope.

Monday 25th November

As the tube was about to pull out of Balham station, two Australian backpackers jumped in as the doors were closing. The bloke got in fine, but the girl got her bag caught in the door, with her still outside.

She was laughing.

Neither of them tried to pull open the door, which is what you have to do. For a second they seemed bamboozled and then she said, "Oh, press the button," still laughing.

She indicated the open door/close door buttons to her friend.

I thought, "That's not going to work now. You have to pull the door – it takes a bit of effort – and then jump in quickly. Because they're tourists, they don't know that."

The fella pressed the button. The door opened.

I never knew that. So much for me and all my London knowledge.

They were both still laughing. You know when you're abroad and on holiday and in love, everything is fun. Even travelling on the underground.

I was reading my paper and tuned out. When I tuned in again, the tube was at either Clapham Common or Clapham North, they both look the same. I was aware of a slight commotion. I assumed it must be the Aussies as it was coming from where they'd been standing. But when I looked up there was a fat, slurring English woman drinking a can of Special Brew through a straw. It was an unusual and slightly shocking image, even to my jaded London-weary eye.

Though Special Brew is famously the beer of tramps, I don't think she was homeless. But as it was four o'clock in the afternoon, and given that she chose to drink beer through a straw, and that her beer of choice was Special Brew, I guessed she was an alcoholic. She looked middle aged, but then so would anyone if they drank Special Brew through a straw on Monday afternoons.

She was arguing with a man she was with who, like her, was fat and white. He seemed younger. He was wearing a baseball cap and oddly inappropriate sports gear. Probably inappropriate because he had clearly not done any sport at any point in his life. He was also drinking Special Brew. He also chose to use a straw. Saves on any of that strenuous lifting of the can to your lips. He was drunk and lairy, red-faced and petulant.

I don't know where they came from. Possibly they'd got on at Clapham South, maybe they'd been seated further up the carriage and had just got up to get off the train. Their conversation was personal, but self-consciously and showily confrontational (performed publicly in order to intimidate the rest of us). I only heard the dregs of it.

"You should get a life," said the fat woman drinking Special Brew through a straw at 4pm. Mind you, she was saying it to a fat bloke drinking Special Brew through a straw at 4pm, so she had a point.

"I don't need to get a life," he slurred, "I've got a life. I'm my own boss. I do what I want. I've got the best fucking life in the world."

Hey, maybe he had a point too. He was drinking Special Brew through a straw. It beats working.

I presume they were lovers, but they seemed more like mother and son. Though that was possibly only because of the man's strangely inappropriate and juvenile clothing and her premature ageing. They staggered off the train and the man cleverly parodied the announcement being made over the intercom. "Mind the Gash!" he leered to no-one in particular. Even he seemed to get no pleasure from his joke.

The Aussie tourists were still standing there, pretending not to watch. No longer laughing. I felt a bit ashamed to be British and the train headed north.

Tuesday 26th November

I seem to be more confrontational in my old age.

A couple of weeks ago at the Michael Moore gig at the Roundhouse, there was a big queue for the toilet during the interval, so I set out to urinate in the makeshift car park at the back. As I unzipped my fly, a large shaven-headed bouncer shouted at me, "Oi! Are you pissing on my car?"

I should have realised that it was extremely unlikely that it actually was his car. I should also have been aware that he had been standing by a Portakabin, waiting for someone to urinate in the car park. It was clearly his job to stop it. He could have stopped me earlier as I crossed in front of him, but he was going for a theatrical effect. The man's job was preventing people from urinating in a car park. That must be a hard thing to accept about yourself. You would have to compensate for the loss of ego by acting like a tough man, as if he was a detective arresting a murderer. I wish I'd said, "Is this your car? What an amazing coincidence. I wonder if you could recite your number plate for me."

Instead I said, "I'm wasn't going to piss on it. I was going to piss behind it."

This fact momentarily confused him.

He advanced towards me, all macho, trying to stand too close to me, to intimidate me, make me scared. But I wasn't really scared. I thought it was amusing.

"Why are you pissing in the car park? It's disgusting, you animal!"

"There's a big queue for the toilet..."

"So what. You will fucking queue up with everyone else. Pissing in the car park. Disgusting!"

Now I admit that it is quite unpleasant of me to piss in the car park (although it is in fact more a patch of waste-land, with the cars parked on mud and grass) and if everyone did it then it would created a fetid and unhygienic quagmire, so I can understand why the Roundhouse employ one of their staff to stop people doing it. I think if the bouncer had chosen to point that out to me politely, probably as he saw me heading into the car park, rather than waiting to catch me 'in the act', then I would have immediately apologised and gone and queued up.

But because he was being such a dick I tried to talk to him about it, and managed, at the time at least, not to be too perturbed by his aggression. We both knew he couldn't hit me. I hadn't done anything. I hadn't even pissed a bit.

He continued to take out his frustration at being an anti-piss monitor, calling me names and swearing at me and asking me what I thought I was doing. He instructed me to go and wait like everyone else, all the time playing to the queue, who were in earshot, provided he projected his voice a little. Trying to humiliate me. But I wasn't humiliated. I am not embarrassed that I tried to urinate al fresco. I believe that every man in that queue had done something similar. He called me a "muppet" (or it might have been a "mop-head", I wasn't quite sure, but either option amused me). I asked him if he had never weed outside. He claimed that he never had, whilst re-iterating how animalistic and disgusting I was. I expressed astonishment at this lie. Then I queued up with the others and actually didn't have to wait very long at all. I had been wrong to try and wee in the car park, but as Jesus said, "Let he who is without sin, wee the first wee."

Afterwards I did feel a little shaken, partly through the delayed shock of being threatened by a much bigger and stronger man, but mainly because I wished I had come back with wittier and more sarcastic retorts to the big monkey. I would truly have loved to point out to him the nature of his job. I think he might have hit me.

The incident that happened today was on the tube. I was waiting to get on the Bakerloo line north at Oxford Circus. As the train pulled in I stood by one of the doors. I was first in the queue. But the bloke behind me was standing much too close, forcing me to stand in front of the door. I asked him to move back so people could get off. He said, "You move, I was here first". Now from my perception he had sidled up well after I had. I think maybe the train shifted a little bit, so my prime position became a blocking one. I am pretty sure he sidled, but I may be wrong. In any case, I refused to move for him. Which is what interests me, because when I was younger I would have backed down, but I tend not to now. It became a stupid, macho face-off like before. He kept badgering me. I told him to fuck off. He said, "Don't tell me to shut up."

I said, "I didn't. I told you to *fuck off.*"

He called me a "shabby cunt". My hair is long at the moment and I had grown my beard for an acting part. I found this quite amusing again, and in hindsight was quite flattered that he didn't call me a "fat cunt" – the diet is clearly working. But I didn't rise to it any further nor did I choose to make a sarcastic comment about the sophistication of his clothing.

We sat almost opposite each other until Paddington, each ignoring the other, though I tried to look as if I was mental to try and intimidate him. Within about two stops I had realised how pathetic we were both being and was laughing to myself about our attempts to be the alpha male over something so trivial (hopefully the laughing to myself made the mental act more convincing). I realised that I wasn't even sure who was right about the positions we were standing in as the tube arrived. I thought about making a reconciliatory, mutually piss-taking comment as I got off, but wasn't sure he'd find it as amusing as me.

He wasn't a big twat like the Roundhouse ape, but it is fascinating to observe men's battles for status (even over the most humiliating and unimportant of issues), especially when one of the men is me, so I can really view that stupidity from inside.

Thursday 28th November 2002

I was talking to my girlfriend the other day about number plate-based games I used to play in the car, as a child, to pass the time. Some involved making words out of the three main letters (eg KPG – could be "keeping". The letters had to remain in order, but the longer the word the better and I think there was some bonus for using less vowels or something).

I also played a game where you had a list of numbers 1-999 and had to cross them off when you saw a car with that number. Amazing how you could be tricked by parents into being quiet.

But the most annoying variant which I found in a book of travel games was that you had to spot the numbers 1-999 in numerical order. So first you had to see a car with the number 1, then 2, then 3. If you saw a 3 before the 2 you couldn't count it. Now clearly this is an extremely difficult game, (especially as I refused to accept personalised or foreign number plates), as statistically you would have to see 1000 cars for every progression, and a total of 999,000 cars to complete your task[1].

I remember I did take it quite seriously for a period of months when I was around 12. After all that time I had got to about 45 and then, not surprisingly gave up. The book had tricked me. Even then, I could see that.

But to illustrate to my girlfriend how hard it was I decided to

---

[1] *This isn't, in fact, mathematically accurate, but you take the general point.*

play it on the drive from her house in Hampshire to mine. The game is even harder these days as in the last year the number-plate system has changed and only a few two-figure numbers are used in the new system. One of these is '02' which is quite handy for early in the game, but it means that around one in twenty cars (maybe more) are now not going to be any use. As the years pass, the game will become even more difficult.

On that journey I got up to 2. The frightening thing is that I have continued playing over the last week. Frightening because I know it is a both a pointlessly anal and Herculean (Hercu-anal) task. More frightening because I am doing it when I am driving too. I'm not the most attentive driver at the best of times and yet however much I chastise myself I can't help trying to look at the number plates of other cars on the road and ones that are parked in the hope of catching sight of the next number. I have got up to 3. Saw a 5 yesterday, but what good is that to me now? Oh how the numbers mock me. I would have liked to start from where I stopped off as a child, but cannot be sure of what number I had actually reached and so must begin again.

It is slightly worrying that I should become obsessed with this again and I think it may signal a descent into nervous breakdown. But I think a part of me wants to do it to avenge the child me who was so cruelly tricked. To stand up to that book of travel games and say, "Oh, you thought it was impossible did you. You were laughing up your sleeve at me and all the other kids who you were putting through this Hell. Well screw you, pal, because I've done it. It's taken me years. I've crashed my car forty times, but I have completed the task. Clearly there's now way for me to prove that I've done it, and I don't know who you are and have no way of finding you. But the important thing is I've done it. No-one can say my life was pointless or had no meaning. I have seen all the numbers on car licence plates, in numerical order. They said it couldn't be done."

If anyone knows anyone with a number 4 number plate could you please send me their address?

My obsession with this game continued over the next couple of years and interestingly (given my mention of Hercules in

this entry) became the central driving point of my stage show
The Twelve Tasks of Hercules Terrace *(available on DVD from*
www.gofasterstripe.com). So that others might join in I created
some deliberately over the top anal rules for the game, which
can be seen in the Appendix at the end of this book.

Saturday 30th November

Being eleven months old must be a bewildering and amazing
experience. All the new information to process and understand, and
you're just reaching a point where some of it is making sense, when
the babbling of adults begins to form into coherent ideas.

A lot of it has got to be annoying and frustrating, but wouldn't
be great to be back to a point where you started to understand
why things were funny, but nearly every funny thing you saw was
completely new to you. "Oh, I see. You are jiggling me up and down
whilst singing a song about something or someone called 'Tigger'.
Hilarious. Let's do it again. For much too long. For me it is the
ridiculous number of repetitions that makes it amusing."

S's baby, P, has the fortune or misfortune to be about eleven
months old. He has begun to recognise various statements and can
do 'tricks'. If you say "Clap Hands" he usually will do so. "Put your
hands in the air!" will also elicit the required response. (He knows
this pleases me, so sometimes when I am not paying him attention
he will put his hands in the air without being asked.) Occasionally
he gets confused. Sometimes he claps when he should be stretching
and vice versa.

But the trick he does that makes me wonder is to point at Martin
Amis.

OK, I'll explain.

At the bottom of S's stairs she has a large, framed photo of
Martin Amis and every time she carries P past it (and often when
we are just sitting in the room at the bottom of the stairs), she will
ask him "Where's Martin Amis?". This is obviously a sort of a joke.
A ridiculously complicated and irrelevant question to ask an infant.
However, P will usually look over at the picture. Recently he has
begun to point and say "Der!" which may or may not mean "there".

As with the hands thing, he occasionally gets crossed wires and will look at a picture of a duck or Winnie the Pooh, both of which he also usually recognises.

Martin Amis is the most important one. Martin Amis is the one he is most commonly asked to identify. I just wonder what affect this will have on his life. Will he over-estimate the importance of Martin Amis in this world? Will Martin Amis become a Santa-like figure to him, or perhaps a God? Will he be confused as to why none of the other kids at school talk about or even recognise Martin Amis? Perhaps he will be bullied at school for his obsession with Martin Amis. Possibly in later life he will seek out the man who caused him so much suffering and strangle him with his bare hands. Maybe he'll just be more keen to read his books.

To be honest, I have nearly thirty-five years of experience of life than P, but he knows almost as much about Martin Amis as I do. I think if I was in a room with a picture of Martin Amis in it and someone said "Where's Martin Amis?" I could almost certainly point at the picture and say "There!" But that's mainly because I have been to S's house and she's told me who the picture is of. Six months ago, if there had been ten pictures of different middle-aged men on the walls of the room I might have to have taken a guess.

So it's not like the eleven-month-olds have a monopoly on the "information to process and understand" front.

I was later to attempt to read Yellow Dog *by Martin Amis, but thankfully it committed suicide by falling into a running bath, when I was out of the room. As I write this I have just finished reading,* Money, *which I found slightly hard going to begin with, but was worth persevering with.*

 lthough I had been house hunting in Chiswick, I had been getting a little frustrated by how expensive and clean it was. It was also just full of middle class families and I didn't think I really fitted in – though S was perhaps understandably concerned when I complained about it being so family friendly. In December one of the estate agents asked me if I'd be interested in seeing a couple of properties in Shepherd's Bush and I was amazed by how much more I got for my money and also felt more comfortable with the place. It was more multi-cultural, more real, more dirty and dangerous. In the last couple of years there had been a fatal shooting within yards of one of the houses I viewed. That beats boring old Chiswick. Even more understandably S was not so keen on bringing up her son somewhere so potentially dangerous, but I was pragmatic and also slightly insulted by her objections. I was buying a house for her and her son to live in. She should be grateful to me, shouldn't she? Maybe if she had helped with the search then she could have more of a say. I had seen a couple of places I liked and was at the stage where I was thinking of making an offer. She wondered whether it wouldn't be better to wait until we were sure what was going on between us and what we needed. But I'd been trying to move for over a year now and didn't want to wait for house prices to get even more expensive, so I pressed on, making an offer on a house that was big enough for a family, but which over half of the family weren't really keen on. Looking back at this it seems obvious that this was a dumb mistake, but at the time I thought I was doing the right thing for everyone.

Sunday 1st December

Amazing how paranoia can get to you. Was having slightly weird dream. I was walking up Poynders Road in Clapham and there was an extremely lanky, black youth cycling in circles in the middle of the road, on a racing bike that was too small for him. He was more comic than threatening. But slightly further up the road was a small, ginger-haired, white girl. "Do you want to buy a racing bike?" she scowled. For some reason her general demeanour was terrifying. Despite her being a small, ginger-haired girl. Her face went a bit like the way Bilbo Baggins' does when he gets possessive about his ring in the film. I know it doesn't sound very frightening. But it was.

So much so, it woke me up with a start. And I did that thing that happens in films, but never (I thought) in real life, where you sit up sharply as you wake going, "Argh!"

For some reason I was convinced there was someone in the house. Every noise seemed to confirm this, but I knew I was being stupid, so tried to ignore it. Just as I was drifting off again I thought I heard a big bang, like a door being kicked in. (if it was actually real, it was probably my girlfriend's baby kicking out against his cot)

By this time I had invented a scenario where a professional hit-man paid to kill me or my girlfriend had gained access to the house (in a fairly bumbling fashion for a pro as I'd heard him crashing around like a bull in a shop containing nothing as fragile as china, but that still made a dull thud when it fell on the floor. Maybe a bull in a bookshop. But a bookshop that only sells paperbacks). I was even imagining how knowing he was there, I could anticipate him bursting into the room and leap on him unexpectedly, disarming him in the process. Possibly I would die, but the resulting commotion would alert the neighbours (who had probably slept through the soft-backed bibliophile bull-like behaviour, but were bound to be roused by the disarming and the fatal gunshot) and at least my girlfriend and her baby would be spared. I would be a hero and the church at my funeral would be full of weeping women, who had secretly loved me all through my life, all dressed in black (though slightly inappropriately revealing) clothing, and dabbing at their faces with white, lace handkerchiefs, who would then all lez up... in honour of me.

I had honestly thought it through to this extent.

I knew there was nobody in the house, but also knew I wouldn't sleep unless I went down and checked. Like if there had been someone that me going down and checking was going to do any earthly good: "Ah yes, there you are. Oh good shot!" Let's not even get into who would be prepared to actually pay this slapstick assassin to murder me or S. But there are dark forces....

I looked in all the rooms, was momentarily spooked by my jacket hanging on the back of a chair in the dark kitchen, but amazingly the assailant was no-where to be seen. Perhaps he had glimpsed me coming down the stairs and realised he and his guns and knives would be no match for a naked, overweight bloke who hadn't even thought to pick up so much as a coat-hanger to protect himself with.

I still wasn't ready to sleep. I sat downstairs and played on my Gameboy and read before finally going back to bed at around 1.30am.

My girlfriend slept through the whole thing. If only she could have known how brave I was on her behalf she would have been very flattered. As long as no-one told her about the funerary lesbian action.

Monday 2nd December

If you live in London, experience tells you not to engage in conversation with anyone you don't know. Because if they want to talk to you, a stranger, then the only explanation is that they are mental. It is a sad state of affairs, but one that I participate in as willingly as the next man. It is so accepted by everyone that it has actually become true. Only the eccentric will speak to you when they don't have to.

In Sainsbury's yesterday there was a sweet, small old man. Both he and his suspiciously black hair were thin, he had the bizarre, gnarled giant ears that come with age, but he was dressed in a suit and tie and was 'chipper' personified. He was one of those fellas who fake tap dances everywhere. He was chatting to everyone and everyone was signally ignoring him. Some people out of his eye-line (like me) smirked at his antics, but anyone he addressed simply pretended he didn't exist.

But he wasn't mad. He was trying to be friendly in a slightly heavy-handed, old-fashioned fashion, and possibly had a couple of marbles missing from his collection, but was more like a borderline batty grandfather than a menace. If anyone had replied to him I doubt that he would have cut their throats.

"It's good to be young," he laughed to a little boy. "I'm old now. I look it, don't I?" Not complaining. Enjoying life's ironies.

He tried to pass down the queue but an Asian lady with a pram was in his way. "Make way for a little one," he chirruped. And as she stepped aside, not looking at him or acknowledging him in any way, he nudged her lightly and with a twinkle in his eyes said, "We are ships that pass in the night." She didn't get it. She didn't laugh. But I think he was aware of the ridiculousness of him flirting with this woman, as he was of the ridiculousness of him being old. Yeah, OK and he was a Nectar point short of a reward, but not someone that the rest of us couldn't have humoured, if we weren't all complicit in this London no-talking rule. It wouldn't be a problem if the sane amongst us started to act like normal human beings and communicated. But we won't do that. Because we are afraid of a tiny, weak old man with gnarled ears.

The extent of Londoners' fear of communication is highlighted by a tiny incident that happened minutes earlier. I was approaching the chilled cabinet holding the *Be Good To Yourself* microwave meals for one – willingly and with some anticipation which is the sad thing. They're quite good, they're easy to make and they're low calorie. And I am digging the hole of my own sadness even deeper. There was another bloke on his own, about my age, looking at them, trying to make a choice. I thought "Ha. Saddo!" I got engrossed in deciding whether I would be having Chiang Mai style chicken noodles or possibly chicken biryani that night. Suddenly he asked, "What's the date?" Out of nowhere. Now that's not a ridiculous request. He obviously wanted to know so he could work out how long it would be before his chosen dish had passed the sell-by date. But I still felt a bit shocked that he had talked to me, just like that, in London. I looked up to see that another bloke, presumably his friend had joined him. They were shopping together. So even in this trifling case the stranger hadn't even been talking to me. That's how stupid it gets. But I told him the date anyway – it was the 2nd, so was the sell-by date. "I'll have to eat it today!" he joked. It was the kind of joke enjoyed by blokes who eat *Be Good To Yourself* ready meals.

I walked away feeling slightly jealous that he was going to be eating his meal for one with a friend. That's against the *BGTY* contract of loneliness.

I have moved on. I now eat M&S microwave meals.

Wednesday 4th December

Bad news.
Diagnosis Murder is back on BBC1 just after lunch.
Not bad news because it's a bad programme (even though it sort of is). No. Bad news because I find it very hard to resist watching it. Which means that there is a danger of my lunchtime spreading out to 3pm, which is almost time for *Countdown* and before you know it, the afternoon is gone. I have always said that writing is one per cent inspiration and ninety-nine per cent procrastination (though so far no-one seems to have recognised the extraordinary wit of that statement and I am still without an entry in the *Oxford Book of Quotations*.)

Thank God that *As Time Goes By* is on after it, or no writer in the country would ever get any work done. Maybe the writer of *As Time Goes By* only wrote it in order to help all the other writers to get some work done. The writer's equivalent of jumping on a hand grenade to save your companions. Thanks to that selfless writer for his sacrifice. I've just found out it's Bob Larbey. He's written some good stuff, so that pretty much proves my hypothesis.

I don't know why *Diagnosis Murder* is so irresistible. It's not all that different from *Murder, She Wrote* (aging Disney star, caught up in unbelievable amount of mysterious murders, which they eventually solve), but Jessica Fletcher holds no such sway over me. In fact that show is as irritating as *As Time Goes By.*

I am racking my brain to think of one reason why *D M* is such a hit with me. And I can't think of a single valid reason. Except that it is an excuse not to work. Oh, and I like the way Dick Van Dyke does that goofy open-mouthed smile. Also I like his son's hairstyle. It is extremely odd. It looks like a wig, but who would buy a wig like that? Oh... and.... no, that's it.

Today I am starting work very late, due to a hangover and *D M* is on in the other room. I have resisted watching it. But I am still procrastinating by writing about it. And writing about it badly. Stooping so low as to make the "murder everywhere Jessica Fletcher goes" joke? What next? Noting that the unknown bloke who gets beamed down on *Star Trek* is going to get killed?

So I am going to stop and work. Or maybe just watch the end of the show. Yes, that's a much better idea.

> *Even now five years later I still find it hard to resist watching this show, even though I have seen nearly every episode already. For some reason it doesn't matter. There is something reassuring about it even when you know what is going to happen. And I like to look into the faces of the regular characters who are in the first couple of seasons, but then disappear in the later ones and observe their complete ignorance of their fate, as if they're thinking, "Well if anyone gets sacked, surely it will be Barry Van Dyke. I'm safe." Never underestimate the power of nepotism.*

Thursday 5th December

Sainsbury's nutcase of today.

I was planning to cut through Sainsbury's on my way home, cos it takes about forty-five seconds off my journey. As I approached the sliding doors I noticed a woman about fifteen feet away who was about to exit.

I spotted her primarily because she was walking very slowly and was holding her walking stick aloft and was waving it from side to side in what I can only describe as a Dalek-like gesture.

She was Asian and probably in her seventies or eighties and wearing a thick pair of glasses, the like of which I have only seen on Dick Emery.

Not only was she holding up a queue of perplexed people behind her, she was also blocking my way, so I decided to be gentlemanly (and not to risk being hit with her Dalek laser) and waited to one side of the door.

However when she reached me, even though it would have been much simpler for her to walk past me, she stopped and shouted "Go!"

I said, "No, no, after you."

She screeched, "Go! Go! Go!".

So I did, even though it meant crossing in front of her and having to go round.

So much for politeness.

Friday 6th December

Spending the weekend in Cheddar.

Woke up in the middle of the night (Fri night/Sat morning) to see a strange female figure to my left. Which was a surprise as my girlfriend was sleeping on my left. She was very distinctive, with brown hair, probably in her twenties, wearing a Victorian style night dress and one of those frilly night hats (which thinking about it, may actually be Victorian beach wear). Also she was floating a few inches above the bed. She was asleep.

So that would make her a ghost.

Or alternatively a dream.

I looked at her for a few seconds. It all seemed very vivid and real, and then she disappeared.

To be honest I'm not even sure if I was awake when she 'disappeared', and in my mind it was definitely just one of those realistic visions you can get when suddenly coming out of a deep sleep. (This happened on tour with Stew, when I fell asleep, exhausted on a dressing room floor and 'awoke' with a laughing old woman sitting on my chest trying to strangle me. Though that might have been Richard Thomas having a bit of a laugh!)

It interests me because it was so real (apart from the fact she was floating) and because so many people claim to see aliens or ghosts or visions of dead loved ones whilst in bed and refuse to even consider that they might have been asleep. I am sceptical about all this kind of stuff, though there is a big part of me that would love it if it were true. In this case it seems unlikely. Our house was built in the fifties or sixties and there was previously an orchard on the site, so unless this Victorian woman was sleeping in a tree, it seems odd for her to have been thirty feet in the air in her bed clothes.

If it was a ghost, it was interesting that she was asleep. I wonder if anyone has ever seen a sleeping ghost before. You rarely hear of ghosts doing very mundane stuff. Has anyone ever seen a ghost making its breakfast (with ghost toast) or reading a book or going to the toilet (things that go dump in the night)? The stereotype of them rattling chains and moaning and going on about past Christmases seems very unfair. They have to relax some time. I hope my ghost doesn't get into trouble for sleeping on the job. She still gave me a bit of a shock.

And if what I experienced was a window to a past or future reality, I wonder if a young woman woke up 'this morning' to tell her family of the strange fat, hairy, naked ghost that was in her bed, and of the strange unearthly ectoplasm he left behind him. Well it was technically the three-in-a-bed situation that I have always fantasised about. Even if both women were asleep and one had been dead for a hundred years.

Saturday 7th December

Walking past the Kings of Wessex, I realised that it is nearly eighteen years since I left school. Half my lifetime.

There's nothing like coming back to where you grew up to make you feel old. It's hardly an original observation, but fuck me, it's true.

Similarly, my eldest nephew, who held my finger with his tiny hand when he was two hours old, is now a massive, lunking, handsome youth who will be nineteen in a couple of months.

Where have the last two decades gone?

Every now and then you hear about people who fall into a coma as teenagers and wake up twenty years later, unable to grasp the fact they are now nearly forty. At least they have some kind of excuse. It's not like having experienced the intervening years that I am any more capable of appreciating the passage of time. How much time I have wasted in a self-imposed coma. All those days, weeks, months of my life I have wasted watching TV and playing computer games.

Luckily I have a job that provides some opportunities for adventure (but also more opportunity to waste time), or otherwise I would do nothing.

After the events of September 11th (by which I mean the specific event of the World Trade Towers falling over, not any of the many other events that happened in the world that day – I hate that euphemism). I realised that there was a good chance that many or all of us were likely to die in the coming months. I made a vow to myself to try and live my life to the full. To experience stuff, to get out of my flat, to at the very least read some books.

A week later nothing had changed.

I suppose I am saying that it's easy to forget that life is finite, it's easy to get caught up in the immediate deadline and not notice the bigger picture.

It's easy to say this and easy to just carry on wasting time as always. Maybe wasting time is a perfectly reasonable way of spending your time anyway.

Sunday 8th December

My dad has an advert calendar from some charity or other which, instead of having chocolate treats or pictures connected with Yuletide behind each window, has photographs of people in the Third World who have terrible eye infections.

Now I know what point they are trying to make, but I have to question if this is the most appropriate format. I can't imagine small children running downstairs, desperate to open their advent calendar, calling out "I wonder what awful infection it will be today! Conjunctivitis, hopefully. Although they usually save that for the 24th."

Yes Christmas is a time to remember those less fortunate than yourself. I'm just not sure about choosing to do that using the surprise reveal method.

I think they should take it one step at a time and maybe have traditional Christmas images behind each door, but ones that have severe ocular problems. A robin with a displaced retina, a snowman with glaucoma, a Santa with a worm that has burrowed into his eye and left him effectively blinded. Then on Christmas Eve the baby Jesus in the manger, with all the other characters around him, now cured by his miraculous powers. That's what Christmas is all about.

Monday 9th December

Christmas is great isn't it? In fact I love it so much that I'm already looking forward to Christmas 2003. I wish it could be Christmas every day. But that's mainly because my only source of income is being a Santa in a department store grotto. If it was Christmas every day, then I would make a fortune. Though to be pedantic, as a department store Santa I never actually work on Christmas Day (unlike the real fella who gets to work for one day a year and makes most of his money from merchandise and endorsements), so if it was actually Christmas Day every day, then I would have no employment and soon fall into penury. So I suppose what I really wish is that it was the fortnight before Christmas, every fortnight, though Christmas Day itself never arrived.

Imagine it, all the build-up and none of the release, no sense of closure. Like constant pornographic stimulation, but never an orgasm. On the bright side you wouldn't have to actually buy anyone any presents and on the other bright side you wouldn't be given a load of junk that you don't want, or that is similar to some of the stuff that you wanted, but not quite right. Right enough that to buy the correct thing would be wasteful and insulting to the present giver, but not right enough for you to be able to enjoy the slightly wrong thing in any way.

How much of it could people take? How long before it drove us mad, before we were slaying Santas in their sleighs, before we decked the halls with balls of reindeer, before Cliff Richard was shot in the face with a harpoon (not so close to being a pun about Christmas, but nonetheless satisfying).

And imagine how big advent calendars would have to be, and how many pictures of blind Africans would have to be taken. Charities would have to start poking out the eyes of healthy people in order to keep up with the demand.

Judging by my genuine tolerance of the Yuletide season, I estimate that a fortnight would be long enough. Some six weeks less than Christmas actually lasts at the moment.

For these reasons I doubt that my 'fortnight-before-Christmas-every-fortnight-without-it-ever-actually-becoming-Christmas' system will ever be taken up. But it is something we must be ever vigilant against.

Wednesday 11th December

Every year, around Christmas, it has become tradition for a certain group of men who I was at college with to meet up for a drink and a meal. After a furious burst of emails late last month we finally settled on a day we could all attend and it was tonight. Last year I had confidently predicted that one of us would die in the forthcoming twelve months and that there would be an empty seat around the table. As it happened Tim couldn't make it as his wife has just had a baby, so in a sense, my prediction was doubly wrong as, far from dying, one of us had created a new life.

We have been doing this for years (though I think possibly in the first couple of meetings women also attended – I know it sounds ridiculous, but we were young and foolish) and it is another firm indicator of the passing of years. I have known these men for fifteen years, since they were eighteen or nineteen. And now look at us.

The effects of a decade-and-a-half of life were put into sharp relief for me, because earlier that afternoon, Stew and me went to University College, London to be interviewed for student TV. They were all so young, so fresh-faced. I had a glimpse of Christmas past, seeing what we had all been, and then was plunged into Christmas present, with greying and receding hair, increasing stomachs and even the onset of hearing problems.

Though far from being depressing, it is also rather comforting. To have good friends who still meet up regularly, who still get on, can still laugh together and get drunk together and be foolish together and support each other through our triumphs and disasters. A rather sweet exchange of emails began on our drunken return home, and carried on to the next morning, with genuine affection expressed without any embarrassment.

Mackay had the idea of recording each year with photos from now on, something that we stupidly never thought of before, as it would be great to see concrete evidence of the toll each year has taken.

And in another fifteen years, in Christmas future, I hope we are still doing it, though families and work and death may mean some of us can't make it. Tony said if he dies he'd like the urn containing his ashes to be brought along. I added that we should put them in a pepper grinder and add some to each of our meals. Gaining strength from each other in life and death.

Unfortunately the photo of the 2002 gathering seems to have been lost, though we have managed to keep a record of every subsequent year. The tradition continues. I continue to predict the death of one of us at some point, and every year, without fail, at least one of us has procreated.

Thursday 12th December

My bicycle was stolen in the night.

I was woken up at 7.45am by my downstairs neighbour, who told me the bad news. To be honest, the loss of the bike was not a worry to me. It has been chained up outside my house for the past two years and the only time I used it recently was during the tube strike. It only cost £50 in the first place, and had gone rusty and was extremely difficult to ride. I would estimate it had a black market value of £10 maximum. If they had rung my doorbell and asked to have it I would probably have given them a tenner to take it off my hands. I am more upset about the loss of the lock, which was undoubtedly more valuable and has now presumably been cut off and thrown away.

The most annoying thing is the level of damage that the thieves have caused in making off with their booty. To release the bike and lock they simply kicked in the post it was attached to. I will need to get this repaired or replaced which will doubtless cost me over £100. I could have bought them two more brand new, non-rusty (though still fairly rubbish) bikes.

On top of that I was woken at 7.45am to be told the news. Why did she do that? It's not like getting me out of bed was going to make any difference. Did she think I was going to organise a posse to catch the varmints that had done this? Did she just want to be able to see my disappointed face? Or did she think, "A-ha! I'll wake him up early, so he can see what it's like for people who have proper jobs!"?

I would have paid another twenty quid for an extra hour's sleep.

So, what with fence, lock and loss of earnings due to tiredness I am around £200 down on yesterday.

The only positive thing is that I've got rid of that bloody awful bike.

The lesson is: don't put a lock on things you don't want to keep.

Saturday 14th December

A few months ago Stew and me appeared in an on-line Dr Who adventure called *Real Time*. We have always had a slight sci-fi crossover in our fan base and a couple of our fans were involved and got us to take part. I had my head crushed by a cyberman, but it was only an audio thing, so I had to imagine it, which was a shame.

The CD of the adventure is now commercially available[2] and we were asked to go to a shop in Barking to sign copies of it. I wish I had more time to write about this experience as it was very eventful and I am still trying to work out how the whole thing made me feel. Should I be proud or embarrassed or somewhere in between?

There were a couple of CDs being signed by various actors, one of whom was ex-Goodie Graeme Garden. Had you told the fourteen-year-old me that I would one day meet one of the Goodies, I would have been extremely excited. To be honest there was a big part of the thirty-five-year-old me that still was. The other actors were less famous, though one of them was the woman who John Cleese has sex with in front of a class of pupils in *Meaning of Life*.

I noted the coincidence that Dr Who, the Goodies and Lee and Herring are all things that the BBC no longer wants anything to do with. But then maybe that isn't a coincidence, thinking about it.

Typically the CDs of the episode we'd been in hadn't shown up, so whilst everyone else had official stuff to sign, we were going to have to sit at the end of the table and twiddle our thumbs, looking like blokes who were trying to pretend they had something to do with Dr Who. The potential for embarrassment was increasing. As it was we just signed photos of ourselves and occasional bits of artwork. Funnily enough, now that we have appeared in a Dr Who-related thing, all the stalwart fans get us to sign the books and posters that have been signed by everyone who has ever been in Dr Who.

People were queuing outside the shop when we arrived, an hour before the signing. I hadn't really expected many people to show up, but Dr Who is clearly a flourishing industry.

And as for the people who showed up.... well let's just say that the stereotype of Dr Who fans is probably the only stereotype in the world which is inaccurate, because it doesn't go far enough.

There may have been some nerds in attendance.

I have nothing against nerds, although I wouldn't let my daughter marry one. Though luckily for me and my non-existent daughter, marriage isn't something nerds have to worry too much about. In a recent Dr Who magazine I was quoted as saying something along the lines that I thought Dr Who conventions were a good thing because it got Dr Who fans off the street and away from the rest of us, plus you could just pipe in poison gas and wipe the whole lot of them off the face of the earth... This was a kind of a joke.

Seriously, there is a part of me that envies the Dr Who fans. They are not plagued by the self-consciousness that affects most of us. They are not worried about looking cool (that's for sure) or impressing anyone with their interesting opinions. They have found something that they like and they embrace it and it makes them happy. They have found somewhere that they belong, where they will always belong and it's not reliant on a fad or a trend. They don't have to worry about the thing they like going out of fashion. Because it was never in fashion. Enthusiasm is something that is frowned upon in the 'cool' world. That is a shame. Enthusiasm is a great thing.

On the flip side the things they like (whether it's sci-fi, *Dungeons and Dragons* or *Lord of the Rings*) are not actually real. The place they belong does not actually exist. Is it a refuge from reality? Isn't any hobby or interest that anyway?

Some of the people made me laugh (sometimes affectionately, sometimes at their expense, usually a bit of both) some made me feel sick, some brought tears to my eyes. As we signed photos of ourselves – that these people had only bought because we belonged to the Dr Who canon and they were anally retentive enough to collect them all – I wondered if they were being exploited for their hobby.

I didn't come out with any firm conclusions. I felt confused, part of me feeling I'd provided a service, part of me worrying that these people were being voluntarily ripped off. But then the people who run the shop were just as enthusiastic and charming as the fans. They certainly weren't riding around in gold plated Tardises. The un-self-conscious part of me really enjoyed it. Maybe just the part that wants to be cool got embarrassed and fretful.

At the end Stew got Graeme Garden's autograph and we autographed something for his son.

I guess there's a bit of nerd in all of us.

And I can't think of a nerd who ever harmed anyone.

Well maybe the Unabomber.

And I am delighted that in the intervening years that Dr Who (if not the Goodies and Lee and Herring) has enjoyed such enormous success with its triumphant return. In fact Dr Who is now properly cool again, which makes all the fans at that shop super cool because they were fans first. I am sure were the BBC to bring back Fist of Fun *they would have similar results.*

---

[2]*It's called* Real Time. *See http://www.bbc.co.uk/doctorwho/classic/webcasts/realtime/*

Sunday 15th December

Too many parties. Too many hangovers. Too many early starts.

I went out to lunch with my girlfriend. I was going to travel back with her to Hampshire, where she lives, but was too tired. So I let her take my car, so I could go home to rest.

Unfortunately I also gave her my house keys which were on the same key ring as the car key.

By the time I realised it was too late.

I had to get the train to Hampshire, just so I could pick up the keys to my house.

Made me very grumpy.

And it was all my fault.

And the fault of alcohol.

So that's my fault again.

I am looking forward to the New Year so I can give it up.

> *I include this entry, which isn't very good, partly because I don't really remember it at all – certainly if I hadn't written this then I would have no recall of it whatsoever – but mainly because it's the kind of event that I would subsequently make a lot more of. It seems a pity not to have told the story in more detail. I can only assume I was hung over again and in no mood to take part in this ridiculous daily task I had set myself. If only I had known how far it would go.*

Monday 16th December

I have been writing the intro to my book. I have been compiling a list of the answers to the question "If your penis were to get dressed, what would it wear?"

This was a question I have adapted (or stolen) from the *Vagina Monologues* (although Eve Ensler asked it about vaginas, so really my question is entirely different).

In the book I am probably just going to list the answers and let them speak for themselves, but by chance I think the question is an excellent window into how men view themselves and how they identify themselves through their penises. I think the majority of men either say something like "jeans and a T-shirt" or "nothing", with a healthy minority saying something about the question being stupid.

But quite a few go for their team colours and lots have it dressed up in 'fantasy' sexy clothes, like firemen outfits or soldier uniforms. Some even go for a mini-bondage style suit, which seems to be taking things too far.

It seems men dress their penis in a way that identifies how they perceive themselves and their sexuality. Some men identify themselves as humorous and think their penis would be too, and have it wearing a Monty Python T-shirt or a joke arrow through its head. Others feel bad about themselves and their penis's attire reflects this, such as a sad questionnaire from a man who thinks his penis would dress in the shabby clothes of a tramp. I liked the man who said his penis would dress up as Napoleon. A penis with a Napoleon complex. What a danger to the world that would be.

My favourite response, undoubtedly written for humour, but also saying so much about the man in question is: "It would probably like to get done up in Huggy Bear pimp gear, but I wouldn't let it leave the house like that!"

The man's needs and the penis's needs maybe not always the same. Or at least the public face of the man and the secret needs of his penis don't always match up!

Tuesday 17th December

I have been trying to lose weight this year. I basically started the day after Boxing Day last year as I felt sickened by my Christmas indulgence and was weighing in at a ridiculous fifteen-and-a-half stone.

I gave up chocolate and alcohol. I didn't drink until the end of February and have only consumed two tiny pieces of chocolate (one accidentally as it was in a toffee) since then.

I lost a stone in the first month and since then things have been tending downwards. The week before last I almost ducked under thirteen stone. But weighing myself this morning I was disappointed (though not entirely surprised) to see I had crept back up to thirteen-and-a-half stone. It's still a loss of two stone over the year, which is great, but is a reminder of how easily it can all pile back on, if you're not careful.

It is true that I have been partying and eating well, but I haven't really been starving myself all year. It is significant that I haven't done any exercise for a week or so. I was going swimming or running three or four times a week. But hangovers tend to stop you wanting to do that.

I think it's proof that all this stuff about metabolisms and big bones is largely if not entirely rubbish. All dieting boils down to is that you have to burn off all the calories you consume to maintain your weight, and slightly more if you lose weight. It's up to you. The power to achieve this is entirely in one's own head.

To be honest, losing the weight involved changing a couple of things in my life, but it's been pretty easy to get this far and provided you don't go crazy every single day you can still enjoy a big meal and some alcohol regularly.

I can't believe the multi-million pound industry that revolves around all these diets and exercise programmes. Because losing weight is simple mathematics. It's mind over fatty matter.

It is easy to get disheartened when you have been dieting and put on weight and start to stuff yourself again (I've certainly done that in the past), but I am determined not to get so fat again. I am going to enjoy Christmas, but I am not going back to those forty-inch jeans and I would really like to be twelve stone something by the end of January.

My changing weight would become a recurring theme of Warming Up *and it is dispiriting to see how many times I have tried to lose weight, sometimes succeeded, only to put it all back on again and more. If nothing else it confirms to me how little changes in our lives. The concerns of 2002 are not that different than the ones of 2008. We learn nothing!*

Wednesday 18th December

I had to write the biography section for my new website. Sat down to do this at around five o'clock, expecting it to take an hour, maybe an hour-and-a-half, but I didn't finish until around midnight and I worked fairly solidly (why can't I work like that on the film?). I had no idea that I had done so much.

I had also forgotten what a struggle those early years had been, how hard we worked for so little money, how much I hated writing for *Weekending*. I genuinely started losing it by the end. After a year of trying to look at the news from an 'amusing' angle, I couldn't take it any more and half-jokingly, half-seriously tried to hide myself away in two plastic crates and wouldn't come out.

I also realised how long it took me to get over the events of Edinburgh '88, for how long I assumed I would be hated for having gone to University. I had a chip on my shoulder about the chips on other people's shoulders, and as so often with shoulder chips, the chips I perceived in others were usually imagined or exaggerated. I was also scared of going it alone and not surprisingly, the roastings I got as a stand-up in the early 90s would terrify anyone.

To realise the extent to which you, personally, were a twat is quite an important step in life.

We were working so hard there was no time to step back from it all and work out how I really felt, or how other people really felt about me.

It's really only been in the last couple of years that I have relaxed about everything and started to gain any real confidence. Not coincidentally much of this is to do with having done some solo shows that have worked.

People often ask me how you make it as a comedian, and seem annoyed that they've done four open spots and no-one has realised how brilliant they are. The way Stew and me have got where we've got to (which really isn't all that far comparatively) is by working our arses off. We did an incredible amount of work. I can't believe it, looking back. We made it work by trying again and failing again, but failing better, to paraphrase Samuel Beckett. By being knocked down and then getting up again to paraphrase Chumbawumba. By occasionally trying to escape it all by hiding in plastic crates, before realising that you can't hide in plastic crates forever. That if you come out and complete the horrible thing that you don't want to do, then eventually you will get to do something you do want to do. Much as I hated *Weekending*, if I hadn't done it I wouldn't have what I have now and I wouldn't have learned some important things about writing.

I didn't like doing stand-up so I ran away from it. A big part of me wishes I had persevered (though it was good to give it another go when I actually had something to say). In stand-up terms I stayed in those plastic crates for a decade, and that was never going to work. Who'd pay to see a bloke crouched in a plastic box shouting, "Leave me alone!"?

Insert your own punch-line here.

Though at least in 2008 I am back doing stand-up and really enjoying it. So scratch what I just said. We learn a tiny amount.

Thursday 19th December

I have started drinking herbal tea to try and wean myself off of the diet fizzy drinks I constantly drink (can't be good for you – at least not in the quantities I consume them in).

I was drinking camomile tea yesterday afternoon and it struck me how much it looked like urine. To look at it you would think you were drinking urine, yet still you go ahead and drink it. I don't think it tastes like urine, but I couldn't say for sure as I have never drunk urine (and anyone who says that I have is lying).

Is it possible that the makers of camomile tea have somehow freeze-dried urine inside tea bags and are now selling it to people as a supposedly healthy and relaxing drink? Are they laughing up their sleeves at us, saying, "Ha! They think they are drinking a healthy alternative to caffeine or Nutrasweet based drinks, but in fact they are drinking my wee and the wee of my family and friends!"

For all I know it could be wee that they have siphoned off from public conveniences (it's possibly a bit too yellow, suggesting that it has been through some of those yellow disinfectant blocks you get in public urinals) or perhaps they have paid tramps to wee into bottles and I bet they are paying them an exploitative wage. Though it's not like the tramps can hold on to their wee for too long, in the hope of finding a higher bidder.

Some might argue that the palaver these evil herbal tea manufacturers would have to go to collecting this urine and then freeze-drying it from a liquid into a solid leaf-like substance, would make the whole process financially unviable. But maybe they aren't trying to make money out of it. Maybe they just like the idea of people drinking their wee (or wee that they have collected from elsewhere), maybe they hate the kind of people who drink herbal tea and are secretly teaching them a lesson.

The irony, of course, is that according to some people, drinking urine is good for you. So the joke's on you, camomile tea makers.

Think I'll go and make myself another cup.

> *Depressingly this is something that, as I go through this, I am again attempting – drinking herbal tea instead of diet coke. It is clearly doomed to failure – it certainly didn't take hold in 2002. It's probably best not to keep a record of your thoughts like this on balance. Please don't copy me. I am an idiot.*

Friday 20th December

What I love about my life is that after a very dull week, where I hardly stepped out of the house and could think of nothing to write about apart from a herbal tea that looks like wee, suddenly I get to do something extraordinary.

Tonight I was booked to do an extract from *Talking Cock* at the Theo Fennel Christmas Party. No, I'd never heard of him either, but it turns out he is a swanky jeweller with posh premises on the Fulham Road. Each year he throws a bash for a select group of customers. I knew Elton John was going to be there.

Now, I would usually have turned down a gig like this, because it was extremely unlikely to work – come on and do twenty to a group of people who are in the middle of dinner and have no idea who I am. It was really bound to fail. It was bound to be embarrassing.

But recently I have started to think I should say yes to stuff that I would usually turn down. Just for the experience. If nothing else it will give me something to write about in *Warming Up*[3]!

I have to say that I am delighted I agreed to do it, though, at the same time, all my expectations of failure were confirmed.

I arrived early for my sound check. My fear was that I would offend people with my cock talk, but Theo and his wife Louise (who proudly showed me her – I think fake[4] – diamond encrusted earrings. The one on her right lobe said "RICH" and the one on the left read "CUNT") both encouraged me to be as outrageous as possible. They'd had *Puppetry of the Penis* a couple of years ago. So I thought that maybe it would be OK.

That afternoon they had belatedly invited me to the actual party. I had considered going in what I was wearing (jeans and a crappy shirt), thankfully I dressed up a bit, because it was all very showy. I had been waiting upstairs for the party to start and when I came down nearly everyone was there. It was a fairly intimidating room of people to be in. The first person I saw was Posh Spice. Also there was Tim Rice, Lulu and Elaine Stritch. I had met Lulu before on the Steve Wright show, so tried to talk to her, but although she was polite enough it was clear she had better people to talk to. So for a while I was just standing alone on my own, not really knowing what to do. It was weird on a number of levels, mainly from a performance point of view, because you don't generally meet the audience before the gig, or have dinner with them. Elaine Stritch noticed me on my own and said I could chat to her and Janet Street-Porter and another woman.

Then one of the women from the shop grabbed me and said, "Have you met Lulu?" I could see Lulu's heart sink as she said, "Yes!" She was forced to talk to me again. Her and some other lady draped in jewels started discussing the trinkets in the cabinets. The other lady pointed out two earrings which were essentially just two enormous diamonds. She commented that they were different shapes, one slightly squarer, one more rectangular. I said, "So if I bought you those as a present you'd be annoyed by the shape differential?" She said she might be. I later found out the earrings cost £120,000 (more than it had cost me to buy my flat), plus they are bound to be different shapes and sizes – they're diamonds! They're not custom made in a factory. I was feeling more and more out of place, but it was all making me laugh to myself. It was such an alien experience. One week a Dr Who signing, the next hob-nobbing with the posh nobs. Tim Rice was nice enough to talk to me and introduced me to a bloke who said, "I'm Maurice… Saatchi." And so he was.

We got called over to dine. Luckily I was sitting next to Elaine Stritch who had already been friendly and Emma Freud, who I have met before. Also on my table were Elton and his partner David Furnish, Hugh Grant, Elizabeth Hurley (not together) and turning up a bit late Sarah Ferguson. I know this sounds like name-dropping, but really it wasn't something that greatly excited me, to be in the same room as these people. It was just surreal and frightening to think I would shortly be talking about men sucking their own cocks to them all. Plus there were only thirty people there, a very difficult number to perform to (especially in a well-lit room) as everyone is worried about being the only one laughing at the rude stuff.

Talking to Elaine Stritch was fantastic though. She is a very ballsy and eccentric lady, but I think she warmed to me (although she said she didn't like the sound of my show and that she was going to leave before I went on). She asked me what I thought had happened to Robin Williams, and we exchanged theories on comedy. She was very modest about her recent West End success and clearly vulnerable in the way that most comedians are.

Emma Freud was also extremely pleasant and somehow I was telling her about my whole life and past and present girlfriends within seconds of the conversation starting. But then I was nervous and had drunk champagne.

As pudding was being served, I waited to go on and talked to some of the staff. They asked me if I was nervous. I said I couldn't really lose, because even if all that happened was that I managed to appal Posh Spice then I had achieved something.

The gig, as predicted, went tits up. They weren't really up for it at all, got a few laughs early on, but it wasn't really working. I shuffled

---

[3] *I was thinking about doing this as a book, until I had a conversation with Dave Gorman who told me that Danny Wallace was doing the same thing. His book* The Yes Man *is now a film starring Jim Carrey. Bollocks.*

[4] *In hindsight I seriously doubt this. The diamonds were almost certainly real.*

around from foot to foot (never a good sign) and looked round the room at the slightly uncomfortable faces of some of our best-loved actors and musicians. After talking about erectile dysfunction I said "You're still standing aren't you Elton? Better than you ever did. Well that's Viagra for you." It didn't go down especially well. People made little appalled noises. It felt very like doing a speech at a wedding. In fact it felt like doing a speech at the wrong wedding, to a group of strangers... who were world famous. Elton started talking in the middle. That was the signal to everyone else that I had failed.

Afterwards the staff tried to comfort me, in the way that people do when a gig has gone badly, saying that it was funny and sorry that people didn't laugh much. It was embarrassing. One guy told me Elaine Stritch had hung around at the back and listened to some of it and had clearly been appalled. That was a shame. Richard Curtis came up and said some nice things to me, and when I went back to the table Emma Freud said it had been great. But she was just being nice. I sat there for a bit, feeling doubly out of place now, with a few nods and acknowledgments from the others, but mainly being ignored. I thought I'd better leave.

I was laughing to myself all the way home in the cab, feeling a mixture of humiliation and pride and also "What the hell was that all about?!" Posh Spice had stared at me blankly, yet astonished all the way through (which Emma Freud has noted as quite an achievement). And though I really had expected it to be like that and though I outwardly didn't care (it certainly didn't make me think that the material wasn't funny. After all, 500 people in the Bloomsbury had liked nearly exactly the same thing just last week), it is interesting that it still kind of got to me. Dying isn't very nice and being a comedian there's no way round it really. You're meant to make people laugh. If they don't, then you have failed. It was in a way like some of those early gigs I was talking about the other day. You go home, alone and have to deal with it. Which is one of the points that Elaine Stritch had been making.

I couldn't get to sleep.

It was fascinating though to see how the other half live and to meet the kind of people who will readily spend hundreds of thousands of pounds on some earrings. I felt very out of place. I didn't belong. It was probably the nearest I have come to being a jester in the Royal Court. And Elton John was the Queen.

> *Now that I have a lot more experience of stand-up I would*
> *almost relish another shot at this exact same gig. It would still*
> *have been a tough one and I doubt I would have got Elton*
> *laughing, but I didn't have the technical skills to get me through*
> *this experience unscathed. I am still very glad I did it. It is, if*
> *nothing else, a great story for dinner parties (where the other*
> *guests are proper, non-famous people).*

Saturday 21st December

Back to reality.

I have become obsessed with playing Scrabble on my Gameboy. I play four or five games a day, each game taking about half an hour (though it is possible to play while doing something else, as the computer takes a while to have its go – I am playing at the moment, as it happens!)

I like to kid myself that at least I am doing something intellectually stimulating, and that I am learning something about words. But it's just another form of procrastination

I have always loved Scrabble and generally annoy any human opponent I play because I have learnt all the acceptable two-letter words, but can't tell you what they mean. Of course any serious Scrabble player knows this is the minimum requirement of the serious player. Up till now I have always resisted trying to learn all the three-letter words, or worse all the allowable seven- and eight-letter words (those can really help you score big), but today I found myself attempting to start this task. Which is slightly worrying.

In the back of my mind is the notion that, if I put in a lot of study, then one day I might become the Scrabble World Champion. This is a ridiculous dream. I am simply not anal or autistic enough to beat the people who really love this game. There are thousands of Scrabble nerds out there who are a million times more committed than me. I think "goaters" is a word (of course it isn't) and I have to go to the anagram section of my OSL (Official Scrabble Lists) book to see that I hadn't even noticed "storage" as a possibility, let alone "toerags". And how could I have missed "orgeats"? What does that mean? It doesn't matter. That's why there is nothing educational about Scrabble. I have no interest in finding out the meaning of words. I just need to know if they are allowed or not. The Scrabble dictionary is just a list of words. No definitions. I don't care what "suq" means or "euoi" or "viold". All I need to know is that I can play them, and they are all very useful words to have up my sleeve.

All right, I had to find out. Orgeat is a syrup or drink made from almonds and sugar (formerly from barley). It comes from the Latin hordeum meaning barley. So has actually finding out the meaning of the word made my day any more worthwhile?

No.

If you are interested, I tend to win about 75% of my games against the Gameboy expert (who frankly isn't all that sharp a player, though he does know all the words that are allowed – plays like a twat a lot though). In recent games my highest score for one word was 140 for 'sledgers' (over two triple word scores) and my top score in a two-player game is 548.

Anyone think they can beat me? I've had a lot of practice.

As the Comic Store Guy says as he's about to be hit by a neutron bomb in the Simpsons, "I've wasted my life".

The Scrabble obsession continues into 2008. I have a new version for my Nintendo DS and play a lot of Scrabulous on Facebook, though I am currently writing a sitcom about Scrabble players, so manage to convince myself that I am now working while I do this!

Monday 23rd December

I have managed to wangle a pass to the British Library because of my research needs for the book version of *Talking Cock*. This is great for two reasons. One, I have access to every book ever written ever and two, because I can now use the British Library as a free office to work in.

The British Library has none of the distractions of home (like my bed) and I feel that having to "go to work" will really help me focus on getting stuff done. There are also other people around to look at when I get bored, which is much more interesting than my cramped office.

I got in reasonably early today and did some good work on my film. This is about a man who gets a mystery sexually transmitted disease[5] and as such I didn't really have to draw on the library all that much (though they must have some books on the subject). But it was kind of cool sitting in this austere library and writing rude jokes about sex and disease and male stupidity.

Not that it's as austere as the old British Library which I was also a member of in the early 90s (when I was working on the Macmillan Encyclopaedia of the Royal Family – which had the misfortune to come out about a month before the Royal Family started disintegrating, thus making most of the book redundant!)

Still it seemed oddly cool to be part of this scholarly elite, and best of all you can work on your laptop in there (there are even plugs). A place where, researching my book about cocks and my film about STDs, I am on an equal footing with the bloke next to me researching the poetry of some French-sounding bloke that I've never heard of.

My mother is embarrassed that my book is about cocks. She wishes I could be like my school friend who is writing a definitive biography of Shelley. Then she could show off to her friends. Last time I was home they quoted a friend of my grandfather, who heard one of my radio shows and said, "What a waste of a good education!"

Is it a waste to write about cocks?

Is it any more of a waste than writing about the poetry of a largely forgotten Frenchman?

I feel oddly proud that I am making a living out of something so base and stupid. And the British Library, God bless it, sees my research as being just as important as anything else in the building. I have earned my five-year pass.

---

[5] *The film, provisionally called I Know Who You Did Last Summer never got beyond the first few scenes. To discover why read the story at the start of February 2003*

I just hope no-one happens to look over my shoulder and see the terrible filth I have been writing.

> *I am currently editing this while sitting in the British Library café. I haven't come down here for a while, but have decided that I might be more productive if I get out of the house – it seems to be working. Though interestingly that entry has made me realise that my library card is now out of date, so it's a good job I didn't try to get into the Reading Room as planned.*

Wednesday 25th December

The Derek and Clive documentary that I was interviewed for was on tonight. It's taken a while to be aired, I did the interview in March. They used two bits from the hour-long interview, and not the bits that I would necessarily have chosen. I had found it very interesting to think about the filthy double act and think I'd actually come up with some quite interesting things to say. I usually wouldn't do those "I love rubbish old bits of nostalgia" shows and have in fact always turned them down, but I thought maybe I had something to say on this one. But, of course, the editing is up to other people and thus they are not really worth doing.

It is sad that Cook was in any way jealous of Moore's Hollywood career, a) because none of Moore's films were that good anyway and b) because Peter Cook was Peter Cook. You'd think that would be enough of an achievement for anyone. I know from experience that it can be competitive in a double act and much as you are happy for the other person's success, it can also inspire envy.

I am sure Peter Cook was generally pleased for Dud, but it is a pity if it made him unhappy. Cook was the greatest, funniest and most influential comedian of his generation. You'd think that would be enough.

Paul McCartney is another person who constantly flabbergasts me. You would think that being in the Beatles and writing all those songs would be enough for him, but he seems to constantly battle against the idea that Lennon was the cool and talented one. But Paul, you're Paul McCartney. You wrote some of the finest pop songs there have ever been. You know what you did, surely that is enough. It doesn't matter whose name comes first on the credits.

I think the Derek and Clive documentary overplayed Cook's nastiness to Moore. In the sketch about cancer of the arse, which Dud's dad had just succumbed to, you can clearly hear Dudley laughing. He's not upset. It isn't Cook having a go. They are laughing in the face of the horror. It reminds me of the relationship that Peter Baynham and I enjoy. We constantly try to shock each other with the most offensive phone messages. When we lived together in the mid-90s, I had just returned from my grandfather's funeral and was a little bit upset. I remember Pete seeing my grief and blankly commenting, "I am delighted that your granddad is dead". He made me laugh and cry at the same time. It was a beautiful moment of unacceptable humour between friends.

Friday 27th December

A year ago today I gave up eating chocolate.

This was a big deal for me. I ate a lot of chocolate, and as I've said before, it (amongst other things) was having a profound effect on my waistline and my health. I had been gorging over Christmas on both chocolate and booze and woke up on the morning of the 27th determined to give both up (at least for a while).

I lasted until the end of February on the booze (didn't even drink on New Year's Eve, which shows how sickened I had become with myself), but the chocolate thing has continued on. (I ate a tiny piece of white chocolate in a pudding at a wedding and ate a toffee that unexpectedly had a chocolate centre, but that's the extent of it and I was surprised at how little I enjoyed either occasion.)

I have given up chocolate before, and did so once for more than a year (the first time I ate it after that, it was literally like taking drugs; I was on the ceiling), but every time before I have craved it so badly, and then finally succumbed – the minute a chocolate has passed my lips I have stuffed myself again, even worse than before. I think this time I have really kicked it. Visiting a newsagent's is no longer a risk.

In fact I've got to the point where I can even look at the chocolate bars and not be interested. Even better (considering what I used to be like) I can see a new chocolate bar and not feel I "have to" try it, just to see what it's like. At a recent party I was able to have a big tub of Maltesers right beside me, I was able to put my face close to them and smell them, and I wasn't even tempted. In fact I thought they smelt a bit nasty!

I know chocolate is hardly heroin, but I am still quite proud of managing to kick it. I feel that I could now eat chocolate in moderation, that breaking the ban wouldn't result in the usual binging (as the couple of occasions that chocolate has passed my lips have shown), but I don't even want to eat it any more.

As a child chocolate is a reward and a consolation. I had continued to use it as such (and found spurious reasons for celebration or depression) and I think the fact that I no longer do that is a great success. Think I'll have a Toblerone to reward myself.

Chocolate equalling heroin is another theme that pops up throughout Warming Up. *I have succumbed a few times in the intervening years, and am currently experimenting with the drug again, hubristically convinced that this time I can control it, I have a bit of an addictive personality, though mainly for slightly rubbish, non-dangerous things. Thank God I was never interested in taking actual heroin or things would have been over a long time ago.*

Monday 30th December

God's omnipresence is a problem for me. Not that I mind him seeing everything I do, I just think the whole deal must be terribly dull and depressing for him. Having to sit through most of my own life is boring enough for me, but imagine having to experience the lives of everyone, simultaneously, every day, since the beginning of time. Having to watch people make the same mistakes over and over again, never learning from them, then their children making the exact same errors. Having to endure the teenage years of everyone, the ridiculous concerns and opinions and let's not even mention the horrible daily physical acts that you would have to witness.

Divine intervention has been documented, but it is very rare. How does God cope with having the power to put things right, but using it so rarely? Wouldn't you just want to scream at people, "Stop going out with him, he's clearly a wanker!" or "It isn't important which shirt you wear!" or "No, Buddhism is wrong mate, look here I am. The Catholics have it spot on!"?

Think of all those millions of years he had to endure being a spectator to the lives of the first amoebas and the millions of years of dinosaurs tearing each other apart (though of course to God that all just took six days, so I'm talking out my arse).

But the question that struck me today was, "Can God make himself not omnipresent if he wants?" He is all-powerful, so presumably he should be able to take time out if he wants, but if he did that, then he's not omnipresent any more. He must be able to stop, but he can't because that would diminish his omnipotence. But the fact that he can't absent himself from say, the middle of the Sahara desert at 3 in the morning when really nothing is happening, means that he isn't all-powerful after all. Of course the get-out clause for all religious people is that he wouldn't want to stop being omnipresent because (and these three words cover so much) He just is. It is not for us to question Him. Because the minute you start questioning it, it all falls to pieces. How can anyone be religious?

My concern for God remains. If he is so perfect how can he stand spending all eternity witnessing the lives of the clearly imperfect people (who he's somehow managed to create, despite being perfect himself)?

Who'd be God hey? Hardest job in the world!

Another religious question: can vegetarian Catholics take part in the Eucharist? If the bread is literally becoming Jesus' body then they are eating meat, and they're drinking blood too. Is it OK if it's bread when it passes your lips, if the transition takes place somewhere in your throat? Or are vegetarianism and Catholicism two things that have no intersection on the Venn diagram of life?

The New Year came, as it almost always does, with the resolution to give up drinking for a month. In fact I had, as usual, decided to not even drink after the new year had been welcomed in at midnight, making me a dull and slightly miserable guest at the party I had gone to. On the plus side I was able to drive S home afterwards, but on the negative I was uncomfortable amongst her friends and badgering her to leave before she was ready to. Perhaps things were starting to cool between us.

This month I started a tour of the stage version of Talking Cock which would lead on to a month in Australia in the spring. With S living out of town it was getting harder to find time to spend with her.

I put in my offer on my new house this month and with the inevitable tiny bit of haggling it was accepted, though I was having no luck selling my flat in Balham.

Thursday 2nd January

Balham pool has raised the price of a non-member swimming session from £3.05 to £3.17. What kind of madness is this? It's such a specific and inconvenient sum of money to pay. Why not just go the whole hog and make it £3.20? Have they found that some people get to the ticket desk and say "£3.20? I'm not paying that for a swim. I demand a three pence discount or I am taking my custom elsewhere."

Or couldn't they have just pegged it a £3.15? Does the extra 2p a person make such a difference? Let's say a hundred non-members use the pool a day (which I don't think for a moment they do, but I've set the figure deliberately high). Balham pool makes an extra two pounds a day. I can imagine the evil manager of the leisure complex sitting in his office, cavorting naked on his desk, covered with both those pound coins. Having said that it's a massive £728 a year. Over a ten-year period, presuming 100 non-members come swimming every day, the manager could afford to buy a fairly good second-hand car. Maybe he's not as stupid as I imagine him to look.

Or maybe he is. Because if he'd made the ticket price £3.19, he'd have that car in half the time. If he'd chosen a figure like £3.25, he could have had a brand new car within the next couple of years. But he didn't want to look greedy and went for £3.17. Of course, his plan has backfired because £3.17 is such an unusual and wrong amount to ask for, that it immediately raises suspicion. It doesn't take Sherlock Holmes to realise this is an elaborate long-term scheme to buy a reasonably reliable second-hand car. I just hope that it won't be long before the authorities catch on and the manager is imprisoned and prices can be brought down to the less irritating sum of £3.15.

I go swimming around three times a week, about 35 weeks of the year. So I would save £2.10 a year. Imagine how many years it's going to take me to get that car.

Friday 3rd January

Regular readers may have thought I was joking about attempting to complete the number plate game (1-999 in order) when I wrote about it last year. But I wasn't. I am still doing it, though mainly as a pedestrian as it is a bit distracting if you are driving.

I like to think I'm not taking it all that seriously, but today shows that I might like to think that, but I am prepared to go a certain way to achieve my ultimate goal.

It's been over a month since I started, so how far do you think I've got?

This morning I was up to 15. That's right, look impressed. Think how long this is going to take me. I have been looking for 16 for about a week, though I haven't been out all that much.

On the way back home tonight I saw a 17 parked in Sistova Road. This was really annoying, but of course this happens a lot in the "consecutive number plate spotting" hobby. (This would have made a great Simon Quinlank sketch. We came up with a few of those by copying and exaggerating things that we and our friends got up to!) It is very annoying. I almost considered waiting by the car, in the vain hope that a 16 might happen to pass. But Sistova Road is not all that busy. I may have had to wait for some days, even months. And it was cold.

Discouraged I walked on towards home, bags of heavy shopping in my hands. Yet within about six doors of my house, what did I see parked in my own street? A car with a 16 number plate. Now, this must have been parked by a visitor. I obviously have been keeping a look out in my own street and have never seen a 16 parked here before (not that I keep record – I'm not sad!). It was a beautiful bolt from the blue, the gods had seen my struggle and taken pity upon me. At last the elusive 16 had turned up, so close to home. It was perfect.

But it left me with a difficult decision. Should I go back to Sistova Road (it's about half a mile away, I guess) so I could also bag the 17 that very same evening? A sloppy CNPS player would doubtless think, well I've just seen it, I know it's there, so I'll just count it as seen anyway. NO! That is not how the game works. That way madness lies. You could start saying, well I saw an 18 three weeks ago, so I'll count that too. No, the whole point of the game is to see all the number plate numbers, one to nine hundred and ninety-nine, IN ORDER. So could I be arsed to jog back to Sistova Road, just so I could be one step further on in a task that, let's face it, I'm never going to complete? The choice was made even more difficult because I know that one of my girlfriend's neighbours also has a 17 (not that I'm keeping records, I just remember) and I am going to her place tomorrow. But what if I saw an 18 on the way? Could I live with myself?

I decided I had no choice. I put my bags in my hall and jogged back to the 17, hoping to God that it hadn't been driven away whilst I was dithering over whether to go back or not.

It was still there. I had taken two massive leaps forward in just 15 minutes. Such is life and CNPS.

It did strike me that it would be ironic if I had been run over or something on my way to look at the car that I had already seen. And how confused the police would have been. "He'd clearly been home. His bags are in the hall. So why did he go back out? And why did he head half way to Balham and then turn back again? I guess we'll never know."

Saturday 4th January

I went to dinner tonight with a couple who a) live in the same street as Alvin Stardust and b) even more impressively (if that's possible) have pretty much built their house from scratch. They bought a tiny, run down bungalow in the late nineties and have subsequently turned it into an impressive two storey house and it is now worth five times what it was before. I am totally in awe of anyone capable of doing such a thing.

I say this as a man who, if I manage to assemble a piece of IKEA furniture correctly, feels like I am Handy Andy's slightly more handy older brother, Simon, who resents the fact that his name doesn't happen to rhyme with handy – or anything, except pieman, which is of no use to a handyman – and so he never gets called Handy Simon, despite the fact that he is actually handier than Andy. You can understand his resentment. It is he who deserves the epithet, but he's not going through the indignity of a sex change and the expense of changing his name by deed-pole so he can be known as Handy Mandy. He has some pride. So no, he's not going to called Randy either, is he?

So to be meet a man who, in the sweat of his face, has built a new home for his partner and children is very humbling as well as being an affront to my own masculinity. How can I compete with such expertise? I considered driving back to Cheddar and seeing if my mum and dad still had the spice rack I made for them in 1979. To show me and him were cut from the same cloth. But I realised that by the time that the five-hour round trip was over, dinner might have got cold (and there was also the chance that mum and dad have perhaps misplaced the spice rack. I notice that they aren't using it anymore. But maybe they are keeping it somewhere for best. You know, if there's ever a very special occasion when some bottles of herbs and spices need to be held in place on a wall!)

I think being able to take raw, natural ingredients and hew and carve them into useful and functional items is one of the things that does still define masculinity. Imagine being a woman and having to choose between a bloke who can build you your dream house and a bloke whose toilet roll holder is currently on the floor because his attempts to fix it to the wall have all failed.

Not much of a competition.

I could counter: well could this builder man have made up a slightly amusing, improvised aside about a minor TV personality's almost certainly non-existent brother?

And yes, he probably could have. But is enough of a man to know that that would be both childish and a waste of his valuable time. Time he could have used to turn a local dilapidated stable into a school for deprived children.

So I think he wins again.

Incidentally, he also cooked a marvellous dinner.

The poof.

Sunday 5th January

What is it that makes joggers think that they should acknowledge other joggers? I have been jogging – or as I prefer to call it, running – quite irregularly[6] over the last year or so and I've noticed that about

---

[6] *I think I meant that in the sense that there was no definite schedule to my running jaunts, but it is also true of my actual jogging style, so two for the price of one!*

one in ten of the people who pass you running in the other direction either say "hello" or nod at you as if to say, "Yes, I am running too. I am one of you."

In fact it is always a jogger, never a runner, who does this. Runners are too serious and fit and generally going too fast to tip you a nod. (Maybe they do too and they are just going so fast that they are well past you before the greeting registers.) But joggers are usually short, overweight men in their late thirties who don't have any of the proper kit. Like I said, I'm a runner.

It happened today as I ran through the little Hampshire village where my girlfriend lives. As I was approaching the end of my circuit through the streets I passed a pasty-faced, chubby jogger (who had clearly decided just to take up jogging for new year, probably only on Sundays and for whom this was the last occasion he would be out in 2003). As I approached he gave me a cheery "hullo", and I grunted back out of politeness (not that it's polite to grunt, but I'd been running for 25 minutes and was too tired to articulate).

If we were walking past each other we probably wouldn't have said anything, so why does the fact that we were both going slightly above walking pace mean that we have to notice each other's existence? Are these blokes (always blokes, the women sometimes smile at you, though in a slightly wary, rather than flirtatious manner, but maybe that's just me) trying to make themselves feel as if they belong to some kind of club? Because there is no dignity in being a jogger. All you are saying about yourself by jogging is that you are out of shape and like eating food too much to stop. It's not something to be proud of. Maybe they understand this, maybe the "hullo" is more of a sardonic "you too, hey?" It's a shared expression of the unbearable shiteness of being overweight. We are suffering together.

But I don't want the jogger's greeting. I am not the same as them. I am not suffering. I am a runner. This isn't a new year's resolution. This is something I do. Three days a week, twenty-two weeks of the year. Unless I am too tired or not in the mood or hung over.

I've just had a horrible thought. Maybe the runners do acknowledge each other after all.

Monday 6th January

Rob Sedgebeer, the internet king, was coming round tonight to gather material for my new website and so I started looking through my big boxes of old material for flyers and scripts and photos.

I can't believe what a hoarder of stuff I have been. I found all kinds of rubbish, including a copy of the very first full length TV script me and Stew wrote called *CHT* about a TV celebrity called Coat Hanger Tim, who does a TV show involving coat hangers. This was based on a script that Stew had written for the Oxford Revue 1988 which was pretty funny, though I seem to remember that I did most of the work on the TV scripts, which was fairly lame. It involved a man somehow being sucked into his TV set and then being flipped between channels, which was hardly original even then.

I also found a script that I had totally forgotten writing for an On the Hour-style fly-on-the-wall documentary called *Corridor*. I don't know if we sent this to anyone, or what it was for. It was about a men's group meeting up on a hill somewhere, and we certainly did a version of it as a sketch in *the dum show*. (I'm pretty sure *Corridor* came first as I can vaguely remember giving a copy to Patrick Marber and him not giving it back, but there's certainly a very Steve Coogany character in it.) It's not all that bad, the bits that I read.

Both scripts were written on my old Amstrad Word Processor, so there's absolutely no chance of them existing in computer format anymore and I doubt Rob will want to scan every single page of them both, but I might try and put them up on here some time. Maybe someone will offer to re-type the whole thing into Word! Though I'm not sure I want to unleash *CHT* on the world anymore!

It was strange coming across something that we had slaved over and then forgotten and as this whole site has done, it brought back some memories and mixed emotions. I am glad I kept all this shit, although I still didn't bother with lots of things. The complete script of *the dum show* was never kept. I'm not even sure we had some of it written down, but the few bits I found were reasonably amusing. There was a great (and again forgotten) sketch that I'm guessing Stew wrote (but it may have been a collaboration between us all, as much of that script was) about an extreme stag night and the pranks that went on, funny mainly for the repeated use of the phrase "his trousers round his ankles", no matter how far the prank was going. I think Stew played the policeman who comes in to tell them that the groom has been found dead, lists all his many injuries and then adds that his trousers were round his ankles. It was all in the timing.

But I might be wrong. To be honest it might not even have made the final cut of the show. That's how little I remember.

It did strike me again what a missed opportunity that show had been. But then I am thankful in many ways that I didn't end doing a TV sketch show at that point and with those people (well with Marber anyway). The sketch show was then seen as very unfashionable, but it would have been an amazing group of people to try and make something of it. It was maybe a couple of years too early and the mix of personalities was wrong. And to be honest, so much of what makes a hit show is based on luck.

It's weird to be confronted with your past. The fact that you can now choose to put that past into a readily accessible public domain is even weirder. Or at least would be to the 1990 me, writing *CHT* in my bedroom in Acton.

Tuesday 7th January

Even at thirty-five you still get that same sense of childish excitement when you notice that it has been snowing overnight. It's especially great if it wasn't snowing when you went to bed and so it's all the more unexpected. It seems to me that it snows much less than it used to. Kids these days are missing out.

I went for my run this morning and enjoyed the sound of my trainers scrunching on the undisturbed snow. It brought back loads of happy memories of childhood wintery delight. I remembered having a massive snowball war in my back garden with all the kids in my street. At one point I fell over on open ground and all the other youngsters descended on me and threw snowballs into my face very hard from close range. It made me cry, though it was hard to distinguish my tears from the streams of slush that were also pouring down my face. My mum told the others they all had to go home now.

I remembered going for a walk on the Mendips on New Year's

Day when the snow drifts were about six feet deep and we got lost and eventually made our way home through the quarry. I was so cold by the time I got back that I had to be put into a hot bath, crying.

Yes, happy memories. Hold on. There must be some good ones. I went tobogganing with my sister and her friend, using those big industrial plastic sacks as sledges. That was great. Oh no, on the last go I followed her down too closely, spun round and collided with her and we had to go home 'cos she was hurt (at least in that one it's not me crying, though I probably did cry – I was that kind of child).

So snow is great in theory, but someone usually ends up getting hurt or cold or unhappy. Or all three.

This theory is borne out by something I witnessed on Tooting Common. I saw a mother and father with their child of about seven or eight years of age (the child was wrapped in layer upon layer of winter clothing, so I'm not sure, but I think it was a girl). The father had fashioned a snowball and was playfully chasing his child through the trees. The probable girl was squealing gleefully, really enjoying what was almost certainly her first conscious experience of the joys of snow. The father threw the snowball which found its target and the child immediately began screaming and sobbing – the wimp! At least I didn't cry until I had had the snowballs pounded over and over again into my face. This is why I have charitably determined the sex of the said child as female, in order to give it at least some excuse.

It was actually a beautifully comic scene, as the child had been enjoying the chase so much, but then the reality of being hit by a lump of frozen water shocked her enough to bring the fun to an abrupt end. The father pulled one of those faces you make when you have, through no real fault of your own, made a child cry. "That's right," he seemed to be thinking, "I have thrown something at my own child and made it cry. What a great father I am." I ran past and couldn't really contain my laughter. He smiled back, appreciating the universal comedy of the situation, whilst the mother (who had had nothing to do with the incident) comforted the surprised child. "It's just the shock," she said.

The snow teaches us all a lesson that we never seem to learn. Just because something looks fluffy and white and makes an endearing crunch when you step on it, it doesn't mean it isn't going to hurt you.

Friday 10th January

Given the relaxed nature of my self-employment I usually manage to avoid travelling on the tube at rush hour. But occasionally, like this evening, I still get caught up in it and it is an unpleasant and degrading experience. You all end up packed into the carriage like sardines who are trying to break some kind of world record for most sardines packed into a tube carriage. Or more accurately like some humans who are trying to break the human equivalent of that world record. Someone should tell the sardines and the humans that there is no such world record. Well definitely not the sardine one. Still if you're a sardine probably the achievement itself is reward enough, without the recognition from Norris McWhirter. (That's how stupid sardines are. They think Norris McWhirter is still in charge of the Guinness Book of Records.)

What surprises me, however, is the way that these (presumably) seasoned tube travellers always tend to cram themselves in to the first available train, when the electronic display shows there are another couple of tubes a minute or two behind it. Because if you wait, the second train is usually less crowded (still full-ish, but you don't end up with your face pressed against the glass) and the third one might even have enough room for you to stand without touching the person next to you. But still, people grapple their way on to the first train, as if that minute's wait is going to throw them hopelessly off schedule. Sure, a couple of them may really need to get somewhere, where sixty seconds makes all the difference, but is the time so precious to them all that it is worth enduring conditions that would be illegal if the humans were cows?

Maybe if you're on the way into work, you know you can't be late. But when you're going home? Surely it's worth waiting a couple of minutes.

I think people just like to give the other passengers the impression that their life is so important that they can't wait a single second more, even if that means making an unpleasant journey even worse.

But I'm speaking as someone who is usually still in bed at the time that rush hour finishes. And who has a job I like. And nothing to get home for. So what do I know?

Sunday 12th January

The girls who rent the flat downstairs are really annoying me. I have been waiting till after Christmas to get the fence at the front of the house fixed (the one broken when I had my bicycle nicked). For a while I left it in its normal fence position, but it was leaning over quite badly, so I took it down and laid it on the bit of earth that constitutes our front garden.

On Friday I came back home and the fence was leaning up against my front door. Now, I think that's rude. If they have a problem with where I've put the fence then they should talk to me (likewise if they think I'm being a bit slow getting it fixed). But by leaning it against my door they are saying "Please get this out of my garden".

Such a gesture isn't going to make me inclined to speed up the mending of the fence, or indeed put the fence parts elsewhere. Had they had a friendly word, explaining why this was a problem then I might have listened. But they didn't. So I put the broken bits back where they had been.

I find their behaviour especially rich because I own my flat and the girls are just renting. The renting issue isn't even all that important, but any mathematical appraisal of the situation says that I own half the house, and half the garden. The girls act as if they own the whole place.

A few months ago they rang my doorbell and said "We're having a party in the garden tonight. We just thought you should know."

"Riiiight," I said, and with that they left.

There wasn't the slightest whiff of an "Of course you're welcome to come along," which might have been polite (and they know I wouldn't have done). And what I should have said is, "Are you asking me, or telling me?" Because half the garden actually belongs to me.

I don't mind them having a party and to be honest with you I never go in the garden (so maybe they somehow think it totally belongs to their flat – which would make the steps leading down to it from my back door slightly redundant) but it's once again the rudeness involved. A few days' notice would have been nice. A note to check that I wasn't planning on using the garden that night would have sufficed. Whatever.

Anyway when I got back to the flat tonight the fence parts that I'd left (really unobtrusively, really doing no harm to anyone) in the front garden had vanished. I checked the back garden, but they weren't there either. Now it is possible that the thieves who stole the bike have come back, realising that the fence they broke is much more valuable than what they got, and made off with the broken stake of wood and the two iron poles. But it seems more likely, given the unusual shiftings of the material over the last few days, that the girls have moved it somewhere. Or worse, thrown it away. Which would be extremely annoying as I have a man coming to look at it tomorrow and I don't really want to have to pay for all new materials.

Jesus may have advised us to love our neighbours. But he might have re-assessed his opinion if he lived above these two (or from their perspective, below me).

Reading this back I sympathise more with the girls than the lazy idiot failing to repair the fence that got smashed thanks to his stupid recklessness. Not that I have got any more organised or competent in the intervening five years. It's funny how we can damn ourselves when trying to defend our actions (or lack of them). Still they could have invited me to the party – even though to them, I was no doubt the weird, unfriendly man who lived upstairs.

Monday 13th January

Ooooh get me. I hope my downstairs neighbours never read that. I was in a bit of stressed out funk yesterday. As the actor Kevin Eldon[7] would put it, I had shit in my pocket. Though it was actually very therapeutic to write it. It was like one of those e-mails that you compose when you're cross and then never send (which I also did yesterday), except that instead of not sending it, I've sent it to loads of random strangers. Hmmmmm.

I had left the girls a note and they returned the fence with a polite note saying they'd been storing it out the back (they must have hidden it). So I feel a bit guilty about slagging them off now. Though maybe they'd like to leave me a polite note next time they want to have a party, the silly cows!!!

Only kidding.

Luckily I am moving soon.

The site went live tonight, which brought home the fact that these words can be read by anyone (including my downstairs neighbours). Within about half an hour someone on the *notbbc* comedy forum claimed that using clues in previous entries they had pinpointed the location of my home to one square in their A-Z. I don't know if he got it right, he's got a different copy of the A-Z to me.

Luckily I am moving soon.

But I figure that there's no need to stalk me fellas, when you can just sit back in the comfort of your own home and read about my boring antics.

If you're really that interested I live at 123 Fake St.

It's quite nice for a fictional address. But the fence is broken.

Luckily I am moving soon.

I lived at 37a Cambray Rd if you are interested or wish to put together some kind of Richard Herring historical walk. I believe the false address I give in this entry comes from an episode of the Simpsons.

Tuesday 14th January

More tube tales.

I was on the Northern Line heading north (although despite its name it does travel in both directions). We got to Clapham Common

---

[7] *Kevin played Simon Quinlank and the false Rod Hull amongst many other characters, in our TV shows* Fist of Fun *and* This Morning With Richard Not Judy, *but is perhaps best known as Norm from the Twix adverts*

and there was a bit of a commotion further up the train.

It was some scrawny, rat-faced, screeching teenage girls (the only one I could see clearly looked like a slightly more sophisticated Tasha Slappa[8]) larking about. There was some kind of spree going on. And it became apparent that one of them had pulled the train alarm. There was an audible sign of resigned frustration from my fellow passengers. A sigh which clearly communicated the sarcastic rejoinder, "Oh ha ha, how amusing. That hilarious prank will result in an unnecessary four-minute delay to our journey. I am so glad you did that." The sigh does the same job, just better.

The girls kept screeching, but now one of their number was being mildly berated.

The rest of us sat, occasionally catching someone else's eye and exaggeratedly raising our eyebrows. Or maybe doing a little shake of our heads.

Except the bloke next to me who was engrossed in an Arsenal football programme.

The train had obviously stopped in the station because of the activation of the alarm, but it seemed like ages before anything happened. Thank God it wasn't a real emergency or we'd all have been dead before anyone arrived.

A long time into this ages, the man next to me, suddenly looked up and noticed we'd stopped moving. "What's going on?" he asked the middle-aged lady who was sitting directly opposite me. Why he talked to her, I'm not sure. He was addressing her so specifically that I wondered if they were together. But they can't have been.

"They've pulled the alarm," she replied.

The man seemed confused. "So why aren't we moving?" He had a Northern accent. He was clearly from out of town.

"They've pulled the alarm," offered the woman, raising her eyebrows and shaking her head at the same time. It was as if she was a bit annoyed that his ignorance had forced her to communicate with actual words. He carried on asking strange questions, which the lady attempted to answer, but the one that stuck in my mind was "Do these trains have drivers or do they operate automatically?"

Who doesn't know that tube trains have drivers? Who wouldn't

---

[8] *A character from the popular magazine* Viz.

realise that they run badly enough as it is without entrusting their operation to some kind of futuristic robot-driver or central computer? How could he even question that?

Had he been transported through time? Did he come from a past where such long, hollow, metal snakes that burrow underground would indeed appear to run by their own volition? Or possibly from a future where trains have independent thought and their own personalities (which would all be some shade of grumpy bastard)? Or did he come from Newcastle, where unbeknownst to me the Metro system is entirely automated?

What kind of a question was that for a grown man to ask? What does he know that I don't?

Eventually the driver ambled up to the carriage with a broad grin on his face, flirted a bit with the girls and then headed back to drive the train.

Or at least, that's what I'd always assumed that man at the front was doing.

But maybe he's just there to feed the hollow metal snake when he gets hungry.

*I think the trains on the Docklands Light Railway operate
without a driver, so it may be me, rather than the visitor to this
fine city who was the ignorant one here.*

Wednesday 15th January

I am playing York Opera House on Friday.

This is a big venue.

No really. A very big venue.

It has 1005 seats.

This time last week I had sold six tickets (which I felt was a shame as it would have been nice to have had over 1000 empty seats).

Today it had gone up to 116. Which would be a very good figure for any other venue, but still leaves an impressive 889 tickets to sell. Of course, unless you're Robbie Williams (who sells out within the first minute of the seats going on sale), most tickets do go in the couple of days before the gig. I would imagine there will be over 200 in. If I sell more than 150 in every venue then I will be very pleased. Of course most of the venues don't have over a thousand seats!

In an attempt to drum up some more punters I headed for Broadcasting House at midday, for a pre-recorded interview with Radio Leeds[9]. Through some kind of scientific magic (probably a telephone) it was possible for me to be interviewed by a man and a woman in Leeds, even though I was in a little cupboard-sized studio in London. Amazing! What will they think of next?

The couple were a bit nervous about interviewing me about my cock-based show, as they informed me most of their listeners were over sixty years old and they didn't want them having heart attacks. I wondered how effective this interview was going to be in increasing audience numbers. My guess was: not very.

I think they were worried that I might just shout out "COCK!" (I don't know why they were worried. It wasn't live and they could just edit it out, or not play the interview), but I told them that it would be fine and that I could talk about the subject in a delicate manner. There was some discussion as to whether we could say "Vagina Monologues" (I think it was the vagina bit they were worried about, but maybe the concept of talking to yourself is more frightening if you're a DJ on Radio Leeds!) or even penis. We decided that that would be OK.

It is frustrating, both as a person trying to publicise a show about cocks and as a grown-up human being, that there are subjects which have to be skirted around because a minority of people can't even hear the correct medical name for a part of the human body without getting offended. I made this point in the interview, saying that it is the fact that we won't talk openly about our genitalia which ultimately leads to all the shame, secrets and embarrassment. As one of the questionnaire respondents says in my show "I remember thinking if God created me with a penis, what was so dirty about it? Why must it be hidden from view?"

It is also a problem that I couldn't even mention the name of the show. In these circumstances I tell people we should call it "Talking

---

[9] *In fact Radio York – see 17th January*

Clock", and it's all about clocks. Men's big clocks.

In the end I think they were very happy with what we'd talked about. We had had a (mainly) adult chat about the problems men encounter with their genitalia and their identity. It was actually a pretty interesting discussion. I hope they don't cut it to bits (or Bobbitt it). And I hope the sixty-year old listeners of Radio Leeds will at least find it interesting, though I will be very surprised if any of them come to the gig.

Oh, and if you know anyone who lives in York, do give them a ring or e-mail them and tell them I'm on.

There, that message alone has probably sold me more tickets than Radio Leeds (ie more than none) and I didn't even have to leave the flat.

I think back in 2003 I was more upset by my lack of bums on seats appeal when touring, based on the false assumption that all the other touring comedians sold out everywhere they go. Now I realise that in fact my numbers have nearly always been more or less respectable and that only a very few of the big names sell out venues (certainly of this size). Having gigged more extensively over the last three years I am noticing a definite upwards movement in the average audience size on tour. Building a following is hard work, at least without television exposure, but somehow it is more gratifying when it starts to pay off.

Thursday 16th January

You know what it's like when you've been spending the last eight months thinking about cocks, reading about cocks, looking at pictures of cocks in various states of arousal or disease and reading thousands of responses to a long questionnaire that you've set up which is all about cocks?

Oh come on, surely everyone knows what that's like.

The thing is that after all that time (as you know) you start to think that you're probably not going to learn anything new about cocks. You've probably read about or heard about or at least imagined everything there is to know or imagine about them.

Then today something new.

I had ordered a book from Amazon called *Skin Flutes and Velvet Gloves* by Dr Terri Hamilton (there should be a law that people called Terri can't become doctors. I believe there may be such a law in the UK, but this Terri comes from America). It arrived today. It's about both the penis and the (let's face it) much less interesting vagina. I don't want to look at pictures of vaginas. It's cocks that I'm interested in. Or is it clocks? I get so confused.

It's packed with stuff, most of which I already knew at least something about. For example she claims that 1 in 100,000 men is born with two penises, a surprisingly high amount, but I knew that was possible. It's mentioned in the show.

But the thing that I had never even considered before, mainly because it seems beyond the realms of possibility was this surprising 'fact';

"Approximately 1 in 100 males is capable of self-penetration (inserting his penis in his own rectum)."

Well, bugger me!

Surely not. Surely that isn't possible, unless your penis is about twenty-five inches long and curves down and around like a jester's shoe or has a hinge in the middle. I mean how would it even work if you could get it all the way round and in? Surely you couldn't thrust backwards like that. Could it be anything approaching fun to do so?

And let's just suppose there is some freak in the world who can manage that, surely he is alone? Surely this isn't a 'gift' given to one per cent of the male population. Surely one per cent of the male population haven't even considered it as a possibility and tried it. If only I had asked that on the questionnaire (but I felt like I was pushing back the boundaries of imagination by asking if men had ever tried to suck their own cocks).

I have e-mailed Dr Hamilton in the hope that she will divulge her sources!

But later in the day, as tends to happen with these things, my doubts were cast aside. I read about a documented case of what I now learn is called auto-eroticism. You wait eight months for a story of self-buggery and then two come along at once. But the fact there's two of them doesn't stop them buggering themselves. Oh no.

I was reading *The Male Member* by Kit Schwarz who related the story of Dr Mikhail Stern, a Russian psychiatrist imprisoned in Kharkov in the late 1960s. One of his fellow prisoners was an auto-sexual, "a man whose penis was both flexible and rigid enough that he could insert it in his own anus, and by contracting his anal sphincter and his groin and buttock muscles could bring himself to orgasm." Dr Stern commented that the auto-sexual was "virtually autistic; he says very little or nothing at all, and he rarely seeks out the company of his fellow inmates. He lives in absolute solitude but never seems affected by his loneliness."

Well I guess if you had that as your party trick you wouldn't have much call for friends. And quite possibly they wouldn't really want to hang around with you. "Oh yes, that's my mate. Yes, the bloke sitting on his own penis and rocking back and forth. He's great."

I fear what unimagined things I will be forced to confront in the coming months. What Hell I have created for myself.

As with a few of the penis-based entries from the blog this exchange found its way into the book Talking Cock, *but given that so few people ever bought that I have little hesitation in repeating the stuff here. It's a really good book if you can find it though. At the time of writing there are six second-hand ones available on Amazon and five of the American version of the tome, which are the same except it replaces the word "jelly" with the word, "Jello™". You might not be able to cope with such sacrilege.*

Friday 17th January

I was woken up in the early hours of the morning by a female voice bellowing (really bellowing, as the sound was coming from some way up the street), "It's five o'clock in the morning!"

In that strange place between sleep and waking I wondered if

Balham Council had re-introduced Town Criers and no-one had told me. If so, I reasoned, it was probably as well for them to lay off telling us the time after about 10pm. And she'd missed off the "And all's well" bit. Unless of course, all wasn't well. What did Town Criers do in such circumstances? "It's five of the clock and I've got a bit of a headache! Do you mind if I don't ring my bell?"

But a quick glance at my alarm clock showed that it was in fact 5.22am. No Town Crier worth his salt would be twenty-two minutes out with the time. He'd have to hand in his bell. And as I became more awake I realised that there had been no bell and that the voice had been female (and Town Criers have to be male and fat and have big bugger-grips into the bargain). And as I became more awake I realised that this was just one of those stupid things you think when you're not quite awake.

The voice then aggressively, derisively added, "Every morning!"

Clearly the woman up the street had been woken by someone else. Someone who was doing something every morning at approximately five o'clock (though more correctly approximately 5.30 in this case). But someone who was doing something that hadn't ever woken me up and so was considerably quieter than this woman's foghorn, forlorn voice.

If I'd been up to it I could have joined in the conversation (and woken up even more confused people further up the road) and shouted, 'Your protestation against someone else's noise, has ironically woken up several people who didn't hear that original sound. In future perhaps you'd like to just drop a note to the miscreant asking him or her to be quieter from now on. Of course dropping you a note is something I should have considered before joining in with the cacophony, but I was half asleep and that thought has only just struck me. Incidentally if you are going to shout out the time very loudly in the middle of the night, could you make sure you get it right – you know, to the nearest half an hour at least. You don't have to ring up the speaking clock or anything. Sorry, I should have put that in a note too. Could you just shout me your address and then we'll say not more about it? Back to sleep everyone!"

But instead I fell back asleep.

(Incidentally the York gig went very well and there were over 200 people in. The place looked quite full! The couple who interviewed me on Wednesday, Jules and Julia, were also in. They seemed to have enjoyed the show and they were really great. So I'd like to apologise for insulting them in my earlier entry. They are actually on Radio York, not Radio Leeds.)

Saturday 18th January

Dr Terri Hamilton has replied to my email (see entry from Thursday 16th) in quite glorious detail!

This is what she has to say on the issue:

"As to the reference for the self penetration figure – BTW, the practice is technically referred to as 'autopederasty', which involves pushing aside the testicles and stuffing a well lubricated semi erect glans into a well lubricated anus – my first citation of the figure dates back some twenty-five years to a workshop with William Hartman, PhD, a noted sex researcher in Southern California (I did my first round of sex therapy training with Dr. Hartman and his partner, Marilyn Fithian). It was an entry among other notes involving various unusual physiological 'acts and antics', including fisting, self-fellation, etc. Hartman and Fithian did quite a lot of research in their own lab, and also had associations with Kinsey, Pomeroy, and other pioneers of the time, so I'm not sure if it was based on their own work or derived from other existing data. The figure has also been cited by 'penis researcher' Gary Griffin in his books (*Penis Size and Enlargement*, etc.).

"The citation mentioned in the Schwartz book actually refers to a very rare type of autopederasty...a man who not only could get his penis in his anus, but could also bring himself to orgasm. Be aware that men who can do the former (more than a few) generally cannot do the latter (hardly anyone!)"

What a fantastic woman she is.

Don't you just love the internet? Ten years ago, I would have had to write a letter to her agent or publisher and then maybe got a reply in a couple of months (if she'd ever got the letter and could be bothered to buy a stamp), now I get an answer within foty-eight hours.

Admittedly the sense of wonder is slightly soiled by the fact that the information being passed is about men putting their penises in their own rectums, but even so!

Sunday 19th January

A couple of weeks ago my girlfriend's baby, P started playing with the clip in his mother's hair. It was one of those big hair-clips, which resemble if anything the skeletal jaw of an animal with lots of long, thin, pointed teeth. So naturally I took the hair-clip, held it up, opened its jaws and made a scary growling sound. "Grrrrrrr!" Yes, that scary.

P wasn't sure how to take this. There was a part of him that was certainly immediately frightened by this speaking, disembodied jaw, but he was also quite fascinated. He wanted me to do it again, but each time I did, he looked at me or his mother with wide and vulnerable eyes, as if he was thinking about crying. Then he'd look back at the strange jaw beast as if he wanted to see it speak again, if only to confirm that it was scary. He made his own tentative growling sound in response. So I played along and did it back.

It was only when I put the hair-clip in front of my own mouth and made it roar that P became more scared than curious and began to cry. Understandably S was a bit annoyed with me, but I felt I had just been giving the audience what it wanted, even if in the end what I had achieved was to make a one-year-old child cry. If nothing else it had been an interesting indication of how human beings have a fundamental desire to be frightened. Again, I'm not sure it was worth making a one-year-old baby cry to find this out.

In my defence he was egging me on.

S has told me that P has seen the clip a couple of times subsequently, lying on the bed or whatever, and has been a bit spooked. He's looked at her, with timid eyes, afraid to touch it in case it comes to life again, but has often made the growling sound he now associates with the object.

But time has made him bolder and whenever he sees me now he does a big growl. To be honest with you it's not as scary as mine, and even if it were the effect would be somewhat diminished as it is being emitted by a tiny, chubby baby, but he's doing his best. I will come back at him with yet more scary growls. Occasionally he looks a bit shaken, but even when he has registered surprise, he will consider for a second before letting out a bigger and better noise. And then he will laugh.

It is wonderful to converse with this tiny human being in however ridiculous a fashion. He's at a frustrating age where he understands words, but cannot articulate his thoughts. We are communicating and understanding one another. And we're laughing in the face of fear. If only all he had to fear in life was a hair-clip.

But it's a start. Once we've overcome the dread of hair-clips and other hair-based accessories, we can move on to conquering other demons.

And what is Osama Bin Laden, if not a giant, sophisticated, well-armed, growling hair-clip?

Tuesday 21st January

This morning I had a meeting at my bank with Alan Goodman, who is my Premium Manager. I don't know what that means exactly. Whether it's that he's better than the other managers, or I'm better than the other customers. And whether, if I was better than other customers, this had been judged on financial or personality issues. I hope it was the latter. It would be nice if banks gave you a pat on the back for being a good bloke. It's not all money, money, money.

Anyway, I hadn't been very clear about why I'd been invited in.

It became apparent that essentially under the guise of checking through my details, Alan Goodman was trying to sell me stuff.

Alan Goodman seemed a very pleasant man. He was mild-mannered and polite, attempting light humour to put me at my ease. I liked him even though we are very different people. He's been working in banking for seventeen years and oversees the accounts of 700 people. I write about cocks.

He is a bald man in a suit, I am a hairy man in jeans. He'd probably had a shower this morning, I hadn't had time. And the office was small and hot. Sorry Alan.

There could be no two more opposite men on the face of the earth.

I felt very quickly that I was not his typical customer.

He had filled in the details he already knew on his form. When he got to occupation he said "I've put this in pencil 'Writer and comedian'. Is that still what you do?"

As if being a writer and comedian was a fantasy job that no one could ever make any money at. Something that I had claimed to be, whilst unemployed, but had now accepted that would never happen.

Not that I think he was being unreasonable. He's worked hard to get to the position where he's the Premium Manager for 700 (premium?) people over a period of many years. I write about cocks. You know maybe if he'd realised that you could make a living out of doing that seventeen years ago he might never have got into banking.

Even so, it was still quite a kick to say, "Yeah, I'm still doing that. You can probably put that in pen." He said he'd do it later. It would be neater. He was going to rub out the pencil and write it in again in ink. That was the kind of man Alan Goodman was. A good man. Like he'd been named by the uninventive mind of William Thackeray.

He inevitably asked me what I'd been working on recently. I told him about *Time Gentlemen Please*. Like most of the population, he had never heard of it. And although he didn't ask, I couldn't resist telling him that I was currently working on a show called *Talking Cock*.

He literally spluttered and said something like "Is that what it sounds like?" He attempted to write it in his notes, but his hand resisted him. When he came to write "Cock", he stumbled and got the letters all mixed up. He laughed at this. "I can't even write it!" he said.

Two worlds colliding; worlds that were never meant to meet.

I hope it goes in his final report.

I was going to ask him at the end if I'd been called in because I had some money in the bank or because he'd heard I was a good bloke. But then he tried to persuade me to sign up for NatWest Premier banking, where you pay £150 a year in order to look like a swanky tosser (as far as I can tell from reading the bumph).

So he sort of answered my question.

Wednesday 22nd January

If you're going to kill a tree for Christmas then I think it is at least polite to dispose of it properly when the Yuletide season is over. I'm not saying you need to organise a special funeral for it or anything, but it's not all that tricky to mulch it up, or have a bonfire or take it to the dump.

It's best not to do what the people at the end of my road have done, which is just dump it on the pavement and hope it goes away on its own, like some kind of friendly festive Triffid.

It's not a tiny tree either. It almost completely blocks the pavement and you practically have to step into the road to get round it. And it's been there for over two weeks. Yes, eventually it will rot away, or be made into nests by voles and other small creatures, but I'm not sure I should be made to wait that long. The stupidest thing is that it presumably also inconveniences the people who put it there as it blocks the pavement outside their house – unless someone from a different street crept over to ours in the dead of night and dumped it. Surely more hassle than just disposing of it normally. But possible. It would be typical of those idiots who live in Sistova Road. I'm guessing it belongs to the house which it is directly outside. And I'm no Miss Marple (and anyone who says I am is lying), but a tell-tale trail of pine needles up their path would suggest I might be right. Again I wouldn't put it past the Sistova Road Cissies – as we call them in my road – to counterfeit this evidence. That's the kind of sad people they are. All of them.

Dumping your tree outside your own house is rude and it's lazy. Admittedly my fence is still broken, but that's only because the bloke I got to come and give me an estimate for it seems to have disappeared off the face of the earth.

But last night on my way home in the cold drizzle, I passed the decaying tree, and the smell of the damp pine needles hit my nostrils. In a remembrance of things past, I was transported back to happy family Christmases. More specifically to when we took the tree down. It was the one time of year that I volunteered to do the Hoovering, so that I could vacuum up the carpet of brown pine needles from behind where the tree had stood. I'd love to hear them crackle as they were sucked through the rollers and into the Hoover bag. I'd forgotten about that, but thanks to the wonder of olfactory memory, it all came back in an instant and made me smile.

But I don't believe that the people who dumped the tree did it to spread such fleeting happiness. It'll be interesting to see how long the tree stays there. If it last till next Christmas I might nick it and put it up in my house. It would frighten off burglars.

Thursday 23rd January

My gig in High Wycombe turned out to be a battle of the (sort of) West Country based comedians. In the main venue at the Swan Theatre was Cornish (in the real, rather than *Fist of Fun* sense, though most Cornish people are a bit cornish[10]) mainstream comic Jethro. In the smaller Town Hall was pretend Somerset[11] cult (ie unpopular) comedian, Richard Herring.

The battle was one-sided. Jethro comfortably won. For starters he had a support act and two (count 'em) tour vans. I accidentally went into his venue when I arrived and there were a dozen or so technicians milling around.

I had turned up in my Automatic VW Golf and my team consisted of Simon Streeting[12], who does all the organisational stuff pre-gig, sets up my equipment and operates the show. And no-one else.

But as Jethro would learn if he came to see me, it's not size that's important. It's how much happiness you bring to how many people.

Oh dear.

Jethro was a massive sell-out (I'm guessing 500 seats). I had my average crowd of around 150.

But who was funnier? Jethro started half an hour before me and I listened to a bit of his show on the intercom backstage. There was a good thirty seconds with no audience response at all. Ha ha. I was going to win. But then he got to the swearing punch-line of his

---

[10] On Fist of Fun, *for some reason, Stew and I used* cornish *as an adjective to describe someone pulling a disdainful and curmudgeonly face.*

[11] *I was actually born near York, which is why I support the soon to be extinct football team, York City*

story and the roar of the audience was practically enough to knock me over, even coming from a tinny speaker.

My gig went fine though. I think we had fun and on a couple of occasions when I did one of the naffer jokes and the audience groaned I chided them and said "Well you should have gone to see Jethro!" Disappointingly no-one was sharp or brave enough to come back with "We tried to, but HE was sold out!"

There was an elderly couple near the front, looking slightly uncomfortable during some of the filthier bits of the show. Maybe they'd been turned away from Jethro and sought solace with me. Or perhaps they'd just wandered into the wrong venue. I wonder if they noticed the difference.

After I'd done the gig and signed some programmes I headed back to the car park. Jethro had just finished as well (he even does longer than me, will I never win?!). His audience were returning to their cars.

I had to sit in my car for fifteen minutes as I waited for a queue of seemingly hundreds of cars to get out. That's not a problem you'll have if you drive to my gigs. You'll be straight out the car park (unless Jethro's on nearby).

So at least in one respect I was victorious.

Friday 24th January

At around 3.15 Simon Streeting (who was driving ahead to the Canterbury gig in a hire car) rang to tell me that the traffic on the A2 was terrible and that I might like to head off earlier than I had intended.

So I finished off the work I was doing and jumped straight in the car. The only problem was that I had just drunk a pint of Ribena and a big cup of tea.

The South Circular was moving incredibly slowly. I began to panic a bit, because if this carried on right up the A2 I might be in

---

[12] *This is the first mention of my "arrogant" tour manager, who attained an odd degree of micro-celebrity thanks to this blog amongst the select band of regular readers who would bring him gifts to gigs, wrongly perceiving that I was bullying him. All I can say is that they did not have to put up with his overbearing self-obsession.*

trouble. I was also aware of a desire to urinate. But I didn't want to stop off at a pub or garage until I was sure I was well on my way.

Half an hour later and still crawling along things were a bit more desperate. I wished I had stopped at the last petrol station I'd passed. I could have parked up and found a café or bar, but didn't fancy trying to get back into this awful queue of cars.

Nonetheless it was bad enough for me to decide I would definitely stop at the next garage. But no garage was in view. I was considering urinating in a bottle, but it was still daylight and also I thought from this seated position there was quite some danger of spillage.

Eventually a welcome Texaco sign loomed ahead and relief was soon in hand. On occasions weeing is the most pleasurable thing you can do with your penis.

Got to the gig on time. It went really well (about 180 today, it's creeping up). I've really been enjoying the show this time round and that really helps. I found myself thinking, "This is my job!" at one point. It's great that after all this time I am still finding new things in the show, but also that I am constantly learning more about performing.

The drive back to my girlfriend's was much more fun. I love the motorways at night because they are relatively clear and you can go nice and fast. In fact, as I was cruising at ninety on the M25, I spotted (too late) a police Land Rover passing me in the fast lane. Luckily tonight he had better things to do than stop me. Thank God for serious law breakers!

I have clearly learned nothing in the last few years as this lack of urinary planning is something that I am regularly forced to confront, especially when having to cross London to get to a gig. I keep meaning to knock up some kind of portable urinal for such occasions, but that would be too much work. Maybe I should take a leaf out of the book out of that mentallist astronaut woman and wear a special space nappy on all my long drives.

Saturday 25th January

S, P and me had a late lunch at Ask Pizza in Petersfield. Even though it was past two by the time we got there, the place was rammed full (we'd already been to Pizza Express and been put off by the long queue; pizza is very popular in Petersfield). Even at Ask we were told it'd be fifteen minutes before a table was ready, so we took a seat on some sofas by the bar and waited.

As we settled down, a sullen-faced middle-aged man approached the bar. "Any time you are ready with those coffees," he huffed sarcastically. His cheeks were flushed (whether through anger or through thirty-five years of drinking, I'm not sure) and he was reacting as if the late arrival of his post-lunch beverage was on a par with the worst excesses of Nazi Germany. Admittedly I hadn't seen how he'd been treated in the restaurant, but I felt whatever had happened to him, it couldn't have been so bad as to elicit such exasperation.

There was something unpleasant and arrogant and a bit shifty in his appearance. He had that sort of Jeremy Clarkson sneering face that you immediately just want to punch[13]. In fact, thinking about it, he looked quite like a Jeremy Clarkson who had been severely facially beaten. Surely it was too much to hope that this was actually the case.

He had a face that was very much the shape of a potato. Of course, potatoes come in all shapes. This potato was in the shape of the face of a pompous man with eyes that had become perpetually small and slitty due to his continual diffidence towards the world and its general refusal to treat him as if he was the most important thing in it.

He was clearly complaining in a loud and self-important voice to let everyone else in the restaurant know how aggrieved he was at this outrageous treatment. Certainly at least one of his uninvited audience was thinking "Twattish tosser", but I can only speak for myself. Maybe the others thought he was really cool. Or maybe not.

The restaurant was clearly busy and the staff seemed to be

---

[13] *Or what might be called a 'cornish' face.*

working as hard as they could. But perhaps time would show us that the man was right to be so pissed off.

A few minutes later and we were still waiting for our table, the man trounced back up to the bar, theatrically and wearily sighing, "Can I have the bill?"

The teenage waiter who had been serving him, possibly foolishly or possibly for the craic, politely said, "Did you enjoy your meal, sir?"

"No!" came the blunt and sing-song response.

Once again we were forced to be unwilling witnesses to the tragedy of the potato-faced man's life, and despite ourselves we couldn't help paying attention.

"Well let's just say I didn't enjoy the service," he continued.

"I'm sorry to hear that sir. What was the problem?"

"Well for a start, you forgot to bring us our desserts!" (So presumably everything had been OK up to then. Not as bad as I had been anticipating.)

"I didn't forget," said the lad, a little too abruptly, finally losing the veneer of politeness.

"Yes you did," insisted the curmudgeon, "and you certainly forgot the coffees."

Was that it? Was that all that had happened to cause this discontent? Surely the chef had also accidentally flambéed his baby?

The rude man signed his credit card receipt with a self-regarding flourish (I'm guessing there wasn't a tip) and left the restaurant mumbling his disapproval. And behind him trailed his dining companion, who I had not seen up until now. It was a small, sad-eyed eight-year-old girl. She looked as if she was so used to this behaviour that was beyond embarrassment. She followed him dutifully, but her presence just made the outburst seem even more inappropriate. If this had been a high-powered business lunch and there was an important meeting to get to, then maybe snideness and rudeness would be called for. But a Saturday lunch with your small daughter? Surely you could relax a bit. You might want to not act like a pillock, just to give your child the impression that you weren't one.

When he'd left the mood in the room noticeably lifted and there was an audible chuckle from the diners and staff.

> *What I enjoy about the blog is that, as often as not, I am*
> *the angry, unpleasant man in these circumstances, rather than*
> *just the observer. It's more fun to be watching this kind of thing*
> *than to be participating, but I guess all of us have the propensity*
> *to lose our rag and make ourselves look like a dick.*

Sunday 26th January

I last visited the Hull Truck Theatre on the 17th April 1998 on the TMWRNJ tour. I know this because I kept a diary of that tour[14].

As I arrived tonight I was greeted by an oddly familiar face. It was Dave, the same technician who'd been there almost five years ago. In my previous diary I described him as a "smiley cross between Charlie Chuck and Rod Hull". This description is still fairly accurate, though he's had his hair cut. It is quite rare for a theatre technician to stick in your mind (touring is such a whirlwind of venues and faces that I often can't even remember if I've played a theatre before), but although I hadn't thought about Dave in the interim, he had stuck in my mind. The reason being he is an extremely friendly, helpful and competent man. This makes a big difference. I was happy to see him again and was made to feel welcome. Immediately the night was off to a good start. Funny how these things can help a performance (and it's true in any job – people forget the value of being a decent human being).

I was interviewed before the gig by a journalist from the *Big Issue*. He is aware of this website and had read my previous entries. So he will probably read this. Hello.

I blathered away to him about myself and cocks (my two favourite subjects). My computer was on in the dressing room and reverted to its screen saver thing. In Edinburgh last year Dan Antopolski or Chris Addison (or maybe both) had changed my screen-saver to a floating and cascading sentence saying, "Herring is a gay". This was

---

[14] You can still read this at www.leeandherring.com

a kind of funny joke.

I noticed the journalist looking at this and then clumsily tried to explain why it was there. I didn't do a very good job. It looked like I was trying to say that I wasn't really gay despite what my own computer was claiming. I suspect he thinks I'm insane (actually he's read this diary, so he probably thought that already).

The show itself was good and as with 1998 (I notice from that diary) there were around 200 people in (but no Steve Coogan performing in town tonight to steal away the audience – Maybe Jethro was on somewhere in Hull!). A woman was eating crisps in the front row for the first five or ten minutes. This was very distracting, though I resisted the temptation to tell her to shut up or wait until later to eat crisps. There's always the danger that telling off an audience member in the first couple of minutes will make you look like a sour and potato-faced curmudgeon.

It was worse because she was making a cursory effort to eat them quietly, but I could hear the way she was trying to deaden the crisp crunch against her palate. So that was worse and prolonged the noise. It was as if I was actually inside her mouth in some kind of Fantastic Voyage fantasy. The sound reverberating round my microscopic ear drums. Huge bits of crisp and gushing drops of saliva falling around me from her slavering gums, Raquel Welch covered in anti-bodies and me having to rip them off from around her throat and breasts to keep her alive.

Don't eat crisps in the theatre. That's the lesson for today. Though it was nice to be reminded of Raquel Welch covered in bodily fluids.

Dave cheerfully helped us pack away after and told me he'd enjoyed the show. He sent us on our way with a smile and a joke. What a top bloke.

I hope I don't have to wait five years to see his funny face again!

Dave left Hull Truck two or three years later, though I was pleased that I was asked to comment on his departure by a local newspaper. Good luck Dave, wherever you ended up!

Monday 27th January

I haven't had a drink since New Year's Eve.

Of alcohol, obviously; I'm not a camel.

I usually go on the wagon for January as I am sick of booze after the excesses of December and generally I am starting work on something and it's good not to be hampered by the hangovers.

For the first two or three weeks I am an evangelical teetotaller. It's great to feel healthy and clear-headed and to not do or say any of the stupid things you do or say when you're pissed.

But around about now I start to feel very boring and restricted and in real need of going out and getting bladdered and saying and doing stupid things, with the valid get-out clause of being blotto. 'Cos it's a great excuse: "Sorry, about last night. I was drunk." As if when you started drinking red wine like it was cherryade you hadn't realised what the effects would be. "My goodness, I behaved like an arse. I have no idea what could have caused it. Wait a moment, you don't think it was this red stuff do you? Yes thinking about it, I did start to feel a little queer after the third bottle."

I was thinking of giving up for two months (I did last year) but I have a feeling that I may be persuaded to have a vodka or two after the gigs this weekend.

The devil on my shoulder is starting to drown out the angel. In fact the imp has just made the excellent point that Jesus himself was very fond of a drink (his enemies called him a winebibber, remember). The cherub is now blustering. He's flustered. It's not looking good. To criticise booze-hounds would be to have a go at his boss's son. Let's face it, the kid will be in charge one day, the old man can't hang around forever. The angel is saying, "That's hardly the point. If Jesus told you to go and jump in a lake, would you do it?"

"I'd have to wouldn't I? That's the whole point. If I had enough faith I'd be able to walk on the water with him."

"Oh shit, yeah. Ummmm…"

Throughout all history the people in charge have told us to do one thing, whilst wilfully doing the opposite themselves.

And the pantomime demon is laughing away. He's telling me there's some vodka in the freezer right now. I don't have to do any work today. I'm self-employed.

"Go on, Rich. Drink it! DRINK it. If you drink alone in the daytime then you don't have to worry about embarrassing yourself in front of other people. So you'll keep your self-respect."

"But I need to write my book about cocks."

"Write it drunk. You're much funnier when you're drunk anyway. Everyone says so."

"It's a very persuasive argument. I do FEEL funnier when I'm pissed. No wait, you're trying to trick me too, Satan. How unlike you. I'm very disappointed in you." The devil is looking a little shame-faced, but he's got a bit of a grin on his face too. He's such a loveable rogue. You can't stay mad at him for long.

"I knew you'd see sense," says the angel sanctimoniously, "That's right. Don't drink, work hard on your book about cocks. Oh hold on. I'm not sure how the big guy would feel about that. Why not write a book about parsimony instead?"

"Parsimony?"

"Yeah, I don't really know what it is either. It was the first thing that came into my head and it sounds really holy."

"You can both shut up. The problem with you shoulder angels and devils is that you are both so extreme."

Why can't I have a couple of shoulder normal blokes? You know who can give me two balanced and less fanatical opinions. One might say, "Look there's nothing wrong with drinking in moderation, why not limit yourself to a couple of glasses of wine a night. Then you won't feel left out, but you won't embarrass yourself or get a hangover." The other might then interject "Yeah, Simon, that's not a bad idea. But I think Rich is one of those guys who likes to drink to get drunk, so whilst not knocking your good idea, I would suggest that Rich maybe just drinks on Friday and Saturday nights, you know, when he probably won't have to work in the morning."

"That's a good plan too, Pete. But you know, if he feels like having a small drink on a Wednesday he shouldn't beat himself up about it."

"Absolutely not. But you know Rich, you don't have to listen to us imaginary, shoulder, normal blokes. You're thirty-five, you're old enough to make these decisions for yourself."

But your imagination wouldn't employ the shoulder normal

blokes. Like a daytime TV producer your imagination will only employ people with the most zealous opinions. And if they are prepared to dress up in a ridiculous costume, all the better.

Which is a shame, 'cos Pete and Simon were talking a lot of sense.

I might ask them if they fancy coming out for a drink with me tonight.

This is one of those entries that has particular resonance five years later. It is currently the middle of January 2008 and I haven't had a drink this year and am feeling healthy and evangelical, like I can keep it up forever. Then I read this, see that in a week or so my resolve might be slipping and am also slightly depressed by the cyclical and repetitive nature of my life.

And now it's the end of April and I am working on the second draft, so I can tell you I made it to 100 alcohol free days in 2008, and since then have only drunk occasionally in moderation. Maybe I have turned a corner!

Tuesday 28th January

Streatham Megabowl! Tuesday night doesn't get any better than this.

Ten-pin bowling is the great leveller. From dustman to queen, there's no telling who will be bowling in the lane next to you (though the Queen is unlikely to be there at the moment, what with her dodgy leg and all). Families can take part, courting couples, a gang of small girls or a group of fat, middle-aged men. Each as likely to win as the next. This is what a sport should be.

In my lane, three Oxford graduates in their mid-thirties whose bowling skills are severely limited. Next to us a sprawling family of almost indeterminate number, with the youngest being under two. This youngster wasn't bowling, thankfully, but instead chose to spend a fair amount of time running into our lane as one of us was about to bowl. He was in danger of being bundled over, or even caught up in the swing and being sent careering down the lane towards the pins. What a strike that would be. But as Oakesy said, the family next to us were possibly the kind of people who would take offence if you suggested their child might be in danger and they might want to keep an eye on him.

We were right up one end of the alley, next to the video games. An eight-year-old girl was playing on a machine where she had to dance along to the music of Steps. That had the potential to get quite annoying.

Also hanging around the video games was a group of four youths. Young lads of about fifteen or so, dressed up in their posiest clothes, and ultimately doing nothing. They clearly had no money and so were forced to spend their Tuesdays (and maybe other week days) hanging around in the Megabowl, watching the world go by, ruefully hoping that they might meet some teenage girls. Two of them spent about half an hour, leaning over the barrier at the end and watching us bowling. This was a bit intimidating because we were rubbish enough already, without having an audience. But also a bit sad. Ten-pin bowling isn't the greatest spectator sport, even if you know the people involved. But me, Mackay and Oakesy are, at best, inconsistent players. Not that the boys were really interested. We were just something to look at, to pass the time; they were bored and restless. It's no wonder that kids turn to vandalism if this is the best they can hope for from their weekday night. Eventually they wandered off into the night.

The Megabowl seems bright and noisy and exciting (just look at the name – it's not a normal bowl, it's mega), but there is a depressing undercurrent. A gathering place for the dispossessed. With warmth and a kind of company and stuff to look at. A sad eyed old woman was sitting on a bench behind our lane. By the toilets a man in his thirties, still in his coat, with a grubby rucksack on his back, was staring intently at a shooting video game. No-one was playing it, he was just looking at the guns. When I came out of the toilet he was still there, still blocking the way. Still staring.

All the lonely people, where do they all come from? I can't answer that one. But I think they probably all end up at Streatham Megabowl at some point in their journey.

Wednesday 29th January

The Battersea Arts Centre audience looked like they were going to be difficult. For the first couple of minutes they seemed reluctant to laugh, unsure of what they were going to get. I felt maybe some of the crowd had prejudged the show, had almost come to have their expectations confirmed. It's going to be laddish and misogynist. Of course I can't be sure they were thinking that, I'm not a mind reader. Maybe they were just cold. But that's how it felt.

My early "lazy lesbians" joke got a big laugh, but also a couple of loud tuts, which seemed to confirm my fears –

"I have to apologise, the show's changing every day, so I will be reading some of the stuff off these bits of card. But I went to see the *Vagina Monologues* the other day and they're still reading it off bits of card after seven years! Lazy Lesbians."

When I wrote the show I had initially feared that people might be offended by that line. I hadn't intended to do it in the proper show, it was just a way of excusing the fact that I still hadn't learnt some bits, but people really liked it and I think also understood where the joke was coming from, so I kept it in.

Things warmed up very quickly, but I feel some people were still a bit unsure about which way the show was going. In the penis envy bit, where I ask the men in the audience who is to blame for the penis's bad reputation (given that it was once so loved) and start to imply that maybe women are responsible. Tonight the voice of a female European (I think she was French) said "Zat's right. Ze women are always to blame." I did an impression of her accent and said "Yep, either women or foreigners, one of the two." But again, the audience were suspicious of my motives.

What's nice about that bit of the show is that I turn that implication on its head and then clearly state that penis envy is a ridiculous concept and that the way men feel about themselves and their penises has nothing to do with women.

From then on in I felt the resistance was gone. The worried members of the audience relaxed as they realised I wasn't out for a war between the sexes or their genitals and it was a really good gig.

I'm on there again next week. Do come along and tut if you want!

Again I suspect I might have handled this situation better now than I did then. I think my natural inclination then was to see any heckle as an attack that needed to be aggressively counter-attacked and was thus too defensive and too easily rattled. But it's funny how sometimes an Arts Centre audience will be overly suspicious of possible political incorrectness and how you have to prove your credentials to them. But in some ways this is my favourite sort of audience, because comedy should be challenging people and making them question why they think certain things, even if ultimately they conclude they are correct to do so. Talking Cock was a good show for this because a lot of people came with preconceptions and I think I did a good job of confounding them.

Thursday 30th January

Living in London can sometimes be a degrading experience.

I left the British Library at 6.30 to head into town as I was going to see a film with my friend Andrew.

It was snowing and the pavements were damp with slush and ice and the air was freezing cold. The people walking to the station were miserable and barging past each other. Conditions get slightly uncomfortable and all politeness flies out the window. I was as guilty of this as anyone.

When I got to Kings Cross people were pouring up the stairs and an alarm (not an impressive one, it was like a car alarm or one of those coach reversing warnings) was sounding and a sign was flashing telling me not to enter. I immediately thought there had been a fire or an Al Qaeda attack, but of course I know now it was just to do with the weather and the fact that the Underground trains are falling to bits. Forget dirty bombs, Bin Laden just has to send over a few ice cubes and wait for the engines to fall off our trains and the capital just grinds to a halt.

I walked up to Euston. The buses were crammed as people desperately tried to get anywhere other than where they were. But it seemed to be the same story at Euston. The escalators were packed and the queue spread out on to the station forecourt.

Fuck that.

I decided to walk. Andrew had rung and was having similar problems in Holborn. So at least we were both late.

A woman beggar asked for some change, I thought, "Fuck you, I've got problems of my own here. The tubes aren't working and I've got to walk to Leicester Square in the cold." I was a few paces on before I even considered my selfishness and lack of empathy. A bit of cold and all human decency is lost. I just hope the other tramps made it to the warmth of the Streatham Megabowl before the bad weather set in.

When I walk in central London I am always surprised about how small it really is. Because I generally use the tube (or get stuck in cabs in traffic) I picture Euston being way up in the North of our capital, but it's just a spit away from Tottenham Court Road. If I had just set off walking at 6.30 I'd have been at Leicester Square by seven and on time.

The conditions weren't ideal and I was carrying a rucksack with a very heavy laptop and several thick books about the penis (the books were about the penis – I hadn't strapped several thick books about my penis, and anyone who says I had is lying), but it was certainly quicker and more comfortable than being on public transport at that moment.

Finally my trek was nearly over. We'd decided to change our meeting place to Starbucks so we could have a warming coffee, but as I got to Leicester Square I was blocked by crowds of teenage girls waiting to see Hugh Grant and Sandra Bullock going into the premiere of their rubbish looking new film. Was I to be thwarted at every hurdle? I considered hanging around and shouting out to Hugh "Hey, it's me remember, the cock bloke from that party," but I needed over-priced milky coffee.

So thirty minutes of feeling a bit degraded and being forced to walk a couple of miles in the slush. My plans for the evening were mildly inconvenienced. Can there be anyone on this earth who has a worse life than me?

Friday 31st January

We braved the extreme weather to bring my unique blend of cock-based humour to the mustard eating people of Norwich.

There was some debate as to whether we would even make it through. The M11 had ground to a standstill overnight and people had been trapped in their cars for up to twenty-two hours. Using our skill and judgement we decided to avoid the M11 and go via the A1(M).

Conditions were far from perfect and the outside lane was generally still partially covered in thick slush, but we progressed at a reasonable pace. Simon was particularly enjoying the way that chunks of snow would randomly fly off the roofs of the cars in front and explode on to the road. He is a simple man in many ways. He had prepared well in case of the disaster that we too became trapped in traffic or snow, bringing a bottle of water and two king-sized Snickers. But he had eaten one of these within the first fifty miles. He was also going to bring his sleeping bag, but had concluded (rightly) that in the event of emergency I would have nicked it off him, so he'd left it at home. How long could we survive on one (admittedly large) Snickers bar and holding on to one another to keep warm (was that his perverted plan all along)? It could very quickly descend into an *Alive*-style scenario, and there's not much meat on Simon, so after I had dispatched him and cooked him on the car radiator, I would be forced to consume my own (also admittedly small) legs.

It struck me that Simon must be thinking the same thing and I considered making a pre-emptive strike right there and then (despite our reasonable progress). That Snickers bar in his stomach would not even yet be digested, adding to his meagre calorific value.

Fortunately for Simon I remembered that I am not eating chocolate any more. I would have to wait until it was out of his system. He was lucky this time; I only had to be lucky once[15].

It was quite exciting, waiting for the moment when we wouldn't

---

[15] *Here as I am wont to do I am paraphrasing what the IRA said after Margaret Thatcher survived the Brighton bombing. It will always be one of the coolest things a terrorist has ever said and I am glad that Irish Republicans are now letting their mouths do the talking rather than their bombs.*

be able to go any further, pondering on whether we would be able to walk the last thirty miles with our equipment on our backs. We had to get through. We HAD to. But although we saw a few cars that had been abandoned or had veered off the roads I don't think we even got to a point where we were stationary in traffic. All the worries and the Snickers had been for nothing. I looked at Simon and thought how stupid I had been to have considered devouring him. A drive through a small amount of snow to Norwich can do strange things to a man.

Unfortunately even though I had risked my life and travelled hundreds of miles to get to the gig, the inhabitants of East Anglia were not so brave and I played to the smallest audience of the tour so far.

Apparently the next day they had some explorer coming to do a show at the theatre. He had crossed the icy plains of Siberia on his own. That afternoon he had rung up the theatre and asked what the conditions on the local roads were like. He was worried he wasn't going to be able to get through and should he cancel? He'd crossed Siberia and was worried about getting down the A505.

No amount of snow would stop me from getting to a gig. But next time I'm going to employ a fatter tour manager.

 The Talking Cock tour continued, to moderate success, but my writing commitments were not faring quite so well. I was still struggling to get my Talking Cock book into shape and progress on the film script I Know Who You Did Last Summer was even more sluggish. In fact more like a slug that was dead and had been nailed to the floor and the floor was made of salt. I think part of the problem was penis overload and not in any exciting way. The book was clearly all about spam javelins, but coincidentally so was the film. It was based on a routine by the brilliant Canadian comedian Glenn Wool, in which he recounted a true tale of genital misfortune. To summarise: one day, whilst bathing Glenn had noticed a strange spot on the end of his little fella. Eventually he went to his local clinic, where he was treated to the usual prodding and poking and insertion of plastic scrapers into places that really shouldn't have things inserted into them and then certainly shouldn't be scraped. But after all this discomfort and indignity Glenn was told by the doctor that he did not know what this mysterious condition was and that in order to find out he was going to have to perform a biopsy – that is, the offending abnormality would have to be sliced off Glenn's acorn and sent away for examination in the lab. As you can imagine, Glenn was not too happy about having a scalpel taken to his pride and joy, nor when he heard that the resulting wound would require stitches.

But what could he do?

The procedure went ahead and Glenn was told to abstain from using his penis for anything other than its urinary function so as not to risk bursting the stitches. But predictably after a frustrating week and a half, the randy Canadian decided to take the chance, had a wank and the inevitable occurred and he found himself being rushed to hospital with blood gushing from his private parts. And remember an erection is all to do with blood, so there was a lot of it.

We felt that this could form an amusing set piece in a film about promiscuity and its consequences, but I just didn't seem to be able to get anywhere at all with it. I had the first scene written, but beyond that could not apply myself and was getting into trouble as deadlines passed by. In the past I had been pretty reliable, but both my cock book and my diseased cock film were way behind and nothing was inspiring me. Warming Up, started with the hope that it might get creative juices flowing, was not helping. If anything, as often as not, it was the only thing I wrote all day.

I genuinely think I was being driven slightly mad by the cock-based nature of all my work. I had spent months thinking about cocks, reading about cocks, talking to men about their cocks. I was beginning to wish I had written a show about really big tits instead. But around this time things took a really strange and slightly spooky turn and this was something that, not surprisingly, I chose not to write about in the blog (though I did consider it, aware that it was funny even if it was intensely embarrassing and personal). Just before Christmas I was having a bath, when I noticed something strange on my own purple policeman's helmet. To begin with I thought it must be a trick of the light or just some residue from my bubble bath (I am in touch with my feminine side and enjoy long soaks in those girly Lush products), but the more I looked, the more I was sure. Like the character in the film I was writing, in the same circumstance, I was seeing the same thing. Was this psychosomatic? Was I just going mad? The fact that this phenomenon coincided with me being in a serious monogamous relationship for the first time in a couple of years made it more baffling?

I tried to ignore it for a while – the spots were small and I probably wouldn't have noticed them at all were I not obsessed with this subject at the moment – but after a week or so I decided I *should go and get it checked out. If nothing else it would be good research for the script. I didn't realise quite how good research. I got to the clinic, and after a couple of hours in the waiting room, hoping I wouldn't get recognised (but then anyone admitting to spotting me there would have to acknowledge that they were there too, so maybe I'd be safe), I was shown into the doctor, who did all his pokey, scratchy stuff and then looked at the spots and unbelievably was bamboozled. Just like the doctor in the film. He didn't, as in the half-written scene I had come up with, then call in everyone else in the hospital to see if they could identify the mystery illness, but he did say that the only course of action was to perform a biopsy. I mean, what are the chances? This was unbelievably weird. I wrote it – it came true. I was like Richard Burton in the porn version of* The Medusa Touch, *except that in my current condition no one was going to want to have sex with me. Though my Franken-cock would turn anyone who saw it to stone.*

So just like the fucking film and with a sense that I was participating in a dream that someone else was dreaming, I went through the exact procedure that I was supposed to be writing about: was this punishment for my laziness? Part of my Honourable Member for Fuckinghamshire was cut off in front of my incredulous eyes (though I had to look away) and I have to tell you I don't have enough down there to justify losing some. Then, feeling distinctly nauseous, I allowed a man to take a needle and thread to my purple-headed womb broom.

He told me not to use it for a fortnight – not that I needed to be told that – and said the stitches would then drop out of their own accord. I had told my girlfriend nothing about this, partly out of shame, partly out of a fear that she would wrongly jump to the conclusion that I had been playing away (or would be forced to admit that she had been playing away), but now there was no way of hiding the truth, unless I literally hid the truth for the next fortnight (actually the way things were going that might have been possible). She took it well, given that there was every chance I might have passed this new undiscovered disease on to her. It was all very embarrassing and unfortunate, but also made me less inclined to write more of this film, for fear that it all might come true.

Within a week the results were in and thankfully, like the occasional lie detector guest on the loathsome Jeremy Kyle Show, I was vindicated as the condition was a perfectly harmless, non-sexually transmitted skin condition, just as it was in the film – I should have realised, though not exactly the same one. Just in case you thought I'd got it off Glenn. It wasn't like that with us. But after two weeks the stitches hadn't fallen out. And after three weeks I was getting to a very unhappy place. I had never been so long without an orgasm in my post-puberty life. In fact, I had probably broken my existing record after thirty-six hours.

And after three weeks, with the stitches still in I could hold off no longer and despite the precedent of the script I took the chance and made my own amusement. I have to tell you, self-abuse fans, that there is nothing quite as amazing as the orgasm that comes after almost a month of abstinence, though alas it was slightly spoiled for me by the fact that I assumed that the exploding geyser that I had unleashed was inevitably shooting blood all over the room. Luckily for me, the doctor's sewing held. In fact, it turned out, he had used the wrong thread and it was never going to fall out naturally, which meant the additional indignity of having to return to the clinic for another long wait before the doctor cut the thread for me. Thank God he had a steady hand.

Not surprisingly this strange madness completely put me off writing the script and I wrote an email to the person who had commissioned me, making some attempt to explain my reasons for not continuing. I think I must have scared him, because he never replied, but he did ask my manager if I was all right (the implication being that he thought I might have cracked up and maybe I had). I later told Glenn why I had binned the script and he took it very well, given that this meant the whole thing never happened. He did remark that I was doubly screwed as the fact that he'd already done the routine meant that I couldn't even get some stand up out of it. Which is true. Though finally the whole awful story has been told (and I'm not sure that's for the best) but it's some interesting background for you. I don't know if it will make you look at what I did write in a different way. Sharing isn't always a good thing.

Saturday 1st February

On the long drive from snowy East Anglia to a sunny Devon I had plenty of time to contemplate how easy it must be for the person booking the dates on my tour to put me in two towns so far away from each other on consecutive nights.

You can imagine the logic -

"Exeter and Norwich are both in southern England, obviously, so it can't take that long to get from one to the other. And it's not like there's any danger of adverse weather conditions at this time of year. Yeah, great, let's put him in Norwich, then Exeter and I reckon we could get him into Wolverhampton the next day. I mean I tried for Ayr, which would have been better, but Jethro is on there on Sunday. That bastard managed Aberdeen followed by Penzance followed by Ayr. That's what I call tour booking."

Until I did the trip I wouldn't have imagined that the journey from Norwich to Exeter would be equivalent of going to Scotland. But Britain is a surprisingly large place. Luckily I wasn't driving, and thank God for CNPS (41-45 all spotted without even trying all that hard!)

When you live in London it is nice to be able to get out and seeing the beautiful landscapes of England. Passing through all those pastoral idylls made me understand better the odd people who come to my town every now and again in support of countryside.

Now, I am a big believer in countryside too. You understand what I mean, don't you? Like regicide is the murder of your king and fratricide is the murder of your brother, countryside is the murder of those 'idiots' who take part in fox hunting. Don't know why they spell it 'countryside' in this instance, but if their marches result in the death of just one member of the landed gentry then the formation of the Countryside Alliance has been more than justified.

(I was very proud of myself for making that joke up. But I find it hard to believe that no-one else has ever thought of it.)

The Exeter gig was fun, if a little unpredictable (and it was sold out. They even brought in extra seats!). They particularly enjoyed my joke that the smell in Bridgwater is due to the unwashed genitalia of the male populace there. God bless Bridgwater, the whipping boy of the M5.

But towards the end of the show, one man took issue with my metaphorical assertion that men and women, like the European Community, could do with a common currency. I berated him, quite severely.

Apparently I could have been lynched for my pro-European sentiments. The Devon community are generally opposed to European Union.

Sometimes I think that countryside is too good for these people.

> *It turns out that the cuntricide joke has been made before. But how could it not have been? I am still proud to have re-thought of it!*

Sunday 2nd February

I had forgotten how depressing touring can get. It sounds like it should be exciting, but there's a lot of travelling, a lot of waiting around. You hope you will get whisked away on some exciting night of adventure after each gig, but instead you generally find yourself sitting in an empty hotel bar with the person you've just spent all day sat in a car with.

We got to a cold Wolverhampton about six hours before the gig was to start, already aware that the ticket sales were poor (even by the medium standards of this tour). I was going to be performing on a very high stage, in a large echoey hall, without any real prospect of the bodies of the audience deadening the sound. It didn't augur well.

Simon Streeting wasn't in the best of moods either, but I was irritable and low (I had had a couple of drinks on both Friday and Saturday and wondered if that had had some kind of depressant effect). I decided to head off and look at what shops Wolverhampton had to offer on a Sunday afternoon.

I bought a book about the Yorkshire Ripper investigation, which was my cheery pre-show reading material. Probably didn't help to lift my mood. Nor did the news that we had sold only sixty-three tickets, which Simon cheerfully made worse by telling me how many thousands of seats Dave Gorman had sold in the bigger theatre next door just two nights before.

But the gig was actually pretty good. They were up for it right from the start, which is always great, so I had fun. Though it was weird looking down on so few people from a stage that was about ten feet above them. It felt like a very unsuccessful Nazi rally (you know, except about cocks, not racial hatred). Rather than the scale of the stage making me look powerful or important, it made me feel a bit pathetic. Especially given I was looking at a massive room, a quarter-full of chairs which were themselves about a tenth full.

It's like putting the statue of Nelson on a massive column, rather than a regular plinth, is so grandiose, that it begins to look sarcastic. "Oooooh, look at me. I'm Nelson. I'm so important I have to have my statue on a stand that is so big that you can't even see me." That's not a statue, it's a bird-perch.

One day I will return to Wolverhampton, and that auditorium will be full. Either that or I'll just invite the audience down to the dressing room and do the show there, standing on a milk crate.

Monday 3rd February

Poor old Michael Jackson. So out of touch.

You'd think if he was going to do a big TV interview to show that the pre-conceptions and rumours were wrong that he'd have a big team of advisers telling him the kind of stuff to say, and the stuff not to say. If he has then they are doing a truly appalling job.

"I know Mike, why don't we scotch those kiddie-fiddling allegations by having you sitting with a twelve-year-old boy and holding his hand, whilst you admit that you let him sleep in your room. Then everyone's going to love you."

Was there no one there to say, "Let's not do that, it's a bit noncy"? And if there was did Jackson just over-rule him?

In a sense you can almost see that it's a good plan. "I will be totally honest, I've got nothing to hide. I don't see anything wrong in what I'm doing, so why lie?" You do start to think that, yeah, Jackson has an unusual take on life, but quite possibly his friendship with kids is extraordinarily innocent. He's had a lot of bad stuff happen to him, he's lived his life in the most bizarre of circumstances and psychologically he has remained as a child and so feels comfortable in the company of other kids. It is ignorant and judgemental for other people to read ulterior motives.

Yeah, OK. I almost buy that. Because it's the only thing that makes sense of the devastating and unnecessary honesty.

Oh, but wait, Jackson also says he has only had plastic surgery twice, on his nose and nowhere else. He claims to be being completely truthful, despite the interviewer's disbelief and the fact that his face has changed in strange and unnatural ways.

So if that's honesty, it kind of puts his earlier 'honesty' in a different light. Maybe he has fooled himself into believing his face has changed on its own, which also unfortunately means that he could also have fooled himself into believing that his relationship with children has not crossed a particular boundary.

In the course of my research for my book I found a series of letters from Lewis Carroll to the parents of some pre-pubescent girls he wanted to photograph. His attempts to make his motives appear innocent and to give excuses as to why the parents should not be present at the sessions is amusing until you think about the dark side of what's going on. Eventually he gets affronted that there has been the implication that a chaperone is necessary and says he doesn't want to do the photos now and how sad the world is for thinking his interest is in any way suspect.

But I still feel sorry for Jackson. His life has been so abnormal it is no surprise that he has such unusual views. I think he's fooling himself, but that doesn't necessarily mean that he has abused these kids, even though practically anyone else would see why having unrelated kids sleeping in your bedroom is a bad idea, whoever you were and whatever had been said about you before.

He must have PR people and they must be aware of how all this stuff makes him look. Is it possible that the PR people are happy for him to appear this way, because it gets him massive exposure and that makes them money? Or is Jackson so in charge of his life that he can tell all his minions that he knows what he's doing and not to interfere?

Maybe it's the latter. I liked the incredulity he displayed when Bashir suggested that the stuff he was buying in Vegas might be 'tacky'. He couldn't even countenance it. Anyone who challenges him is ignorant or silly.

Poor old Michael.

Tuesday 4th February

My girlfriend is a bit concerned. She thinks I'm obsessed with serial killers. A couple of months ago I read Patricia Cornwell's awful book about Jack the Ripper and now I'm reading a better book by Michael Bilton about the police investigation into the Yorkshire Ripper.

I've tried to explain to her that I'm not unnaturally interested in murder. I just like books about ripping. It can be paper that's being ripped, or cloth, or the fabric of the space-time continuum or it can be the flesh of young women. I don't care, as long as there is ripping in it.

She argues that so far in her experience the ripping has all been from the latter category and I have to admit it looks a bit suspect to a casual observer. But the problem is, with my interest, that there just aren't that many books about other kinds of ripping about. It's an area that is woefully unrepresented in literature. It's not enough for me that there is just a bit of ripping in the book, you see, because plenty of books might feature someone ripping up a letter, or some clothes. For me the book has to be mainly about ripping and preferably have the word "ripping" or "ripper" on the cover.

That doesn't mean that I would enjoy a book from the fifties called *Ripping Adventures for Young Boys* or a book of scripts of the TV show *Ripping Yarns*. Because, although these tomes have ripping in the title, there would be little to no ripping inside them. It has to be both.

For example I particularly enjoyed the recent *Diary of Jack the Ripper* as not only was that about (and supposedly by) a bloke who enjoyed ripping, the actual original manuscript was found in a book that had several pages ripped out of the front. I think James Maybrick must have been the Jack the Ripper. He clearly liked ripping things and it just got out of hand.

My interest in ripping is purely academic and anyone who

suggests there is anything prurient about it, or that I am about to begin a campaign of serial killing/ripping carnage, is ignorant. Just silly and ignorant.

Today's entry has been a practice run for my forthcoming interview with Martin Bashir.

Wednesday 5th February

Today I wrote to Nestlé, the maker of Polo mints, with an enquiry for my book. Here's what I said:

"Dear Sir or Madam,

I am a writer and am currently working on a textbook about the anatomy of the penis for the good people at Ebury Press. I know this might not seem in any way relevant to your good selves at Nestlé, but please bear with me and I'll think you'll see that it is.

This textbook aims to revolutionise the study of biology in schools and I am working along with examination boards to totally re-define the dull terminology which is currently employed in biology text books. I am sure you remember from school how confusing and off-putting all those Latin terms for body parts could be. We have realised that if children are going to learn about and more importantly understand how their bodies work we have to re-invent the language of biology, to make it hip and "down with the kids" so to speak.

Still don't see how this would involve Nestlé? Stick with me, I'm getting to that!

You must also be aware that education is currently in financial crisis. We are constantly searching for ways to pay for all the books and equipment that schools need. Sponsorship is obviously a great thing for both the schools and the companies who give them money. The kids are your target market for so many of your products, so obviously if they see your brand names in their lessons, they are more likely to buy your wares. Surely that kind of publicity (as well as the good publicity of helping the cause of education – and I don't need to tell you that Nestlé could do with being seen as the good guy at the moment) is almost priceless to you.

So, how can we make this come about? Simple. One of the essential components of the penis is a body known as the CORPUS SPONGIOSUM. I know. Dull, dull, confusing name. But it strikes me that what this body most resembles is a tube of spongy Polo mints. My idea is to re-name this structure "The tube of spongy Polos", and I think kids will respond to the power of the imagery, as well as the humour. We will be bringing science and the penis to life for them. Of course, I wouldn't want to give such advertising away for free.

Clearly if Nestlé were to sponsor this book and the new terminology, then we could tie in some promotional idea. Perhaps the guys at Polo could even bring out a special edition pack of spongy Polos as a new line! Think about it. The opportunities are endless.

I'm hoping we can come to some arrangement and I am in negotiations with other firms about other possible tie-ins so would appreciate a swift response.

I hope we can work something out on this one, for the good of education and of Nestlé.

Yours faithfully
Richard Herring"

Don't worry, I won't accept their dirty money if for some insane reason they agree to go along with it.

But I will let you know if they get back to me.

And for those many, many people concerned about my fence, Simon Streeting came round and fixed it for me today. So all is back to normal. The nightmare is over.

Nestlé never replied to this letter. I am actually surprised as you'd think they would at least send an acknowledgment, but then they are very busy selling powdered milk to the Third World, so maybe they didn't have time. I would support the

boycott of Nestlé that many non-Perrier nominated comedians
have called for, but I really like their Fruit Pastille lollies.

Thursday 6th February

At Baker St tube station I saw a lady in her late middle age struggling up some stairs to the Metropolitan Line with a heavy suitcase. I offered to help her and she reacted as if I was Jesus Christ returned to earth (which as you know if you've seen *Christ on a Bike* I might very well be). But to be honest, I am not always so helpful. Sometimes I behave like the other commuters who were passing her. I look straight ahead, walking swiftly, as if I have somewhere very important to be. As we know commuters can't afford to waste a single minute of their day, even if it means that a little old lady has to die of a heart attack.

This time my conscience got the better of me and I helped.

I have to say the suitcase was phenomenally heavy, I have no idea how she would have got it up the steps on her own. She walked ahead of me, thanking me profusely. I had done something useful with my day and I also felt better about myself. It takes so little to be polite and yet the rewards are so great. I was thinking that if everyone in London did things like this maybe it would be a less miserable place to live.

She was a bit lost and asked me, "Where's platform five? I need to get to platform five." I looked around. We were on platforms three and four, across the tracks I could see platforms one and two. We wandered up the platform – I was heading up more stairs to the Hammersmith and Shitty line (where incidentally I had to wait eight minutes for a train. What a surprise!).

Now I had invested time in this woman, I was duty-bound to help a bit more. But I was a bit flummoxed. There was no platform five. "I'm sure it is platform five. Bakerloo line, platform five." The Bakerloo line was miles away. I had just come up from there. It was down the stairs we'd come up and then down an escalator and still a bit of a walk. I had carried this old cow's bag of concrete up all those steps for nothing. And yet if I'd hit her, it would have been me that was in the wrong.

"Oh, that's back down there," I said, not wishing to commit myself to a return journey.

By now we were well up the platform and she thanked me for my help and turned back. I could have offered to carry the bag down for her again, but there was a danger I may have got trapped into a never-ending cycle of good deeds. I suspect this is how slavery initially began. Someone was helpful, then the person they had helped wanted just one more thing, before the helper knew it, he'd built the Pyramids.

She didn't expect any more assistance, but as I waited for eight minutes on a platform, I felt slightly ashamed that I hadn't just got her bag back down those stairs. It was on wheels and the escalator was working, so it would just have been nice to get her on her way. I vowed always to help people wherever I could.

On my way home that night I was tired and was experiencing my first proper hangover of the year. I was lucky enough to have a seat, but an elderly Japanese couple got on and were forced to stand. I was so tired and grouchy I just couldn't be bothered. I buried my head in my paper.

Friday 7th February

Wellingborough tonight and the most difficult gig of the tour so far. Not the worst attended, but the good people of Wellingborough seemed to react in a unique way to the show. Some laughed uproariously at the more serious bits and many of the banker jokes got a somewhat muted response. Perhaps I have just been spoiled by the good shows so far (and the particularly great one on Wednesday), but it seemed I had to work hard to get a response.

I think at some theatres maybe there are people who just come to see whatever is on and there seemed to be a lot of real (or mock) shocked responses to some of the (admittedly) rude stuff.

Not to say there weren't some people enjoying it. The people in the front row were priceless and really getting into it. Thank God for them.

They were also the first audience in which the women expressed the opinion that it was impossible for a man to fake an orgasm.

Usually when I ask, "What do you think girls, can a man fake an orgasm?" I get a few mumbles, an odd bit of dissent, but usually a very loud "Yes" from someone. So much so that I can say, "Oh, yes! They have to with me. I'm useless at it."

This surprises me, not because I don't think men fake orgasms (I am sure they do), but because the generally accepted stereotype of men is that we always come much too quickly. So I would have thought women would vehemently protest that men don't fake and that it would be impossible in any case.

And in Wellingborough (the contrary town) that is what happened. Particularly the woman in the front row. "No!" she shouted, derisorily. "Of course they can't!"

So the expectations of the crowd were confounded when I revealed that one in three men claim they have, and when I went on to recount the story of the man who was having sex with his girlfriend from behind, knew he wasn't going to come, so he withdrew and then to simulate orgasm, he spat on her back. This usually gets a groan or a laugh or a groaning laugh or a laughing groan (didn't David Bowie write a song about that?).

But in Wellingborough the priceless, good value lady in the front row shouted "No. It wouldn't be warm enough!"

She would see through the ruse, because of her ability to differentiate the temperature of various bodily fluids. I will allow your own imaginations to ascertain how she became such an expert on the thermal dynamics of spit and sperm, as I think it would be ungentlemanly to commit the scenario that I am imagining to paper.

On the night I found this very amusing and accused her boyfriend of having particularly hot sperm.

I didn't really have time for an in-depth discussion, but I would have thought that, if anything, spit would be warmer than sperm. The reason that the testicles are outside the body is so that sperm can be kept cooler than body temperature. From my own experience of sperm (so far always my own) I would say it's usually quite cool (compared to spit anyway – or am I abnormal in some way?) But I'm only working from memory and it's not something I really want to do an experiment with here at my desk. And seeing as I've just found out that my mum reads this diary, I think I'll have to leave it there.

But if any scientist reading this can let me know which bodily fluid is the warmest then it would put my mind at rest. Only scientists please. I now have an unpleasant mental image of everyone reading this doing some nasty experiments. I need laboratory-tested statistics only, please.

Saturday 8th February

Avril Lavigne is heading for a fall. I have many problems with her catchy but self-satisfied hit record *Sk8er boi*.

I know I am thirty-five and should have better things to do than de-construct the lyrics of a song written by a petulant teenager, but I don't. I also hope that if I do this then Avril may look herself up in a search engine (oh, she does it, believe me, don't you Avril?), find this page and realise the folly of her youth and change her ways.

OK, I'm working from memory. The song begins,

"He was a boy, she was a girl, can I make it any more obvious?"

Let's skirt over the fact that just because two people are of opposing gender that doesn't necessarily make it obvious that they want to shag each other. I am a boy and Jeanette Krankie is a girl (admittedly one who dresses like a boy. Could I have chosen a more confusing example?) and... well maybe I'm wrong on that point.

"He was a punk, she did ballet. What more can I say?"

I would like a bit more information to be honest. Avril seems to be labelling the girl by what she does. The rest of the song argues that such labelling is a bad thing, but Avril does not notice the hypocrisy of her statement.

"He wanted her. She'd never tell, secretly she wanted him as well."

Here we start to see a recurring problem in the song. She would never tell. How do we know about this secret love? At the moment we possibly presume that the girl is Avril herself.

It transpires that they can't get it together because the girl's friends have a problem with the punk's baggy clothes. Clearly these people are at school. They are all quite superficial. Even had the boy and girl got it together I think it is statistically unlikely that the couple would be together in five years.

The chorus tells us that the snotty girl tells the boy (who also likes skating apparently, though it isn't made clear if this is roller or ice) to sling his hook, because he isn't good enough for her. What a nasty attitude. I would imagine the bloke would probably think "Cow!" and forget her.

But the second verse sees an almighty and unexpected twist. It's "five years from now" (What does that mean? Was the first verse set in the present and the rest happens in the future? Does she mean "five years from then"?) and the snobby girl is in desperate circumstances. She's landed herself as a single mother and is looking after a kid, all alone (presumably at some point in the last five years, she let her high standards slip a bit). She turns on MTV and sees the sk8er boi rocking (again whether this is on a horse or simply back and forth is not clarified). She calls up her friends who already know and have tickets to see his show (though at no point have any of these "friends" said to her, "Hey remember that bloke we were at school with? He's a big rock star now. I wish we hadn't had such a problem with his baggy clothes, we might have been able to get free tickets.")

She goes along to the show and looks up at the sk8er boi, slamming on his guitar (he doesn't even know how to play it). He is the boy she turned down.

Yeah, the boy she turned down for a date at school. Like I say, it seems unlikely that they would still be going out now if she'd said yes. Avril seems to be implying that the single mother life-style she is now suffering is a direct result of her snobbishness. Rather than feeling sympathy for the woman in her early twenties who has been let down by some man and left with a child, she is crowing at her, saying, "Does your pretty face see what he's worth?" OK, this girl judged the sk8er boi because of his baggy clothes (in the same way that Avril judged her for liking ballet), but surely she doesn't deserve to be punished for turning him down, even if she did secretly fancy him.

And how do we know about that secret fancying? Surely the rest of the song will tell us. Perhaps she will go back stage and meet the sk8er boi and apologise and say, "Actually the irony is, that I did fancy you all along. Now I'm no longer a teenager I appreciate that it was shallow of me to judge you by your clothing and I would like to apologise, but you're doing really well now, so I'm sure it can't bother you that much."

But no, that doesn't happen. The girl and the boy never meet again. Instead Avril starts bragging about the fact that she has got the sk8er boi now, how they are in love and how they rock each other's world. He's a superstar. You fucked up and I'm more than just good friends with him. Oh yeah, I'm doing him and everything.

So how does Avril know about this girl? There is no connection between them. The ballet girl never told anyone that she secretly fancied the sk8er boi. Presumably they are no longer in touch, so how does the sk8er boi or Avril know that the girl came to the gig? Clearly the only way Avril could know about this girl is because her fantastic boyfriend has been going on about her. It was obviously of great importance to him. And Avril, overly pleased with herself for having landed a cool rock-star boyfriend (not that she judges by appearances and would presumably still love him if he was an out-of-work ballet dancer), is fuming with jealousy that her boyfriend had this (apparently) unrequited love at school. So much so that she has invented this scenario where the pretty-faced girl has had her life fall to pieces.

Or possibly she is so in love that she hasn't noticed that her boyfriend's story just doesn't hold together. Perhaps the two actually did get it together and he fathered the baby, but didn't want to know. Now he's invented this story that she is a mad girl from school who is stalking him and coming to his concerts. He makes himself appear the victim by saying that he was in love with her, but she never gave him the time of day.

Whatever the truth of this twisted story I think Avril is being short-sighted, both in terms of the relationship and her boyfriend's career. It is very easy to be smug about how well things are going, but I want Avril to think about how things will be five years from now (or ten years from now, if the concert and everything is actually happening five years from now).

Most rock stars' careers have a very short shelf-life. Certainly something as ephemeral as sk8er-based rock is unlikely to be around for that long. Perhaps the sk8er boi will re-invent himself, but more likely I think that he will have fleeting fame and then have to cope with the after-effects. In the meantime the ballet girl will have a growing child and probably have found a lasting relationship with someone mature enough to take her and the child on. She'll probably be finding her feet. She'll look at MTV and see the sk8er boi is having troubles with drugs and money. Her aging-but-still-pretty face will see what he's worth now, and in any case realise that there are more important things than material wealth and fame. Maybe when she was struggling with a toddler, the glamour of the rock star seemed exciting, but the reality is that it could never have worked out. She is aware that if she did fancy him a bit at school that wouldn't have been enough to base a life-long relationship on. Sure, she was a bit shallow back then, but through the trials of her life has realised what is important.

Avril Lavigne on the other hand will have had time to see that her sk8er boi boyfriend is not all he was cracked up to be. They may have rocked each other's world to begin with, but things quickly soured. Especially when she started getting much more successful than her boyfriend (largely due to a song she had written about his life, which must have been annoying). She has realised that having a famous boyfriend isn't as important as being with someone who cares about you.

Another five years from then, something else could happen. My point is that it's short-sighted to brag about how brilliant your life is. Especially when you are essentially kicking a woman who is down enough already.

I am spending too much time, driving around in cars, listening to the radio and thinking about lyrics that were not made to be thought about.

This was one of the breakthrough Warming Up *entries, causing thousands of new hits to the site as people linked to it on their own sites or emailed their friends to have a look at this timely deconstruction of Lavigne. I don't know how many of those readers came back again, but it all gave me some idea of the way the internet can disseminate an idea. Had I been doing stand up at the time I think this would have made a good routine, but it would seem a bit old to do it now.*

Sunday 9th February

Five years ago I refused to have a mobile phone, thinking they were an unnecessary affectation. Now I don't know how I would be able to function without one. Not because I use it a lot (I don't really), but because if it isn't there then I am afraid I could miss out on something.

This was efficiently demonstrated today, when in my haste to leave my girlfriend's house so I wouldn't be late for the gig in Shrewsbury, I left my phone on her sofa. I had an inkling I might have forgotten it about ten minutes up the A3, but there was no time for turning back. I arrived in Hammersmith to meet Simon Streeting and realised I didn't have it. I was a bit early (dammit, there had been time for turning back after all). Usually I could have texted him to see how close he was, but not today. I was lost. Lost I tells you. The maddening slight inconvenience of it all.

And what if anyone was trying to get in contact with me, maybe to invite me to a last minute plush party in the West End? It's not important that I wouldn't be able to go because I was going to be in Shrewsbury. It would just be good to know that I had suddenly acquired a friend (or a stranger who'd dialled the wrong number) who knew people who had plush parties.

It also made me realise to what extent the mobile phone is a substitute for memory. Five years ago I would have known my girlfriend's telephone number off by heart, but now I simply have to press 'S home' or 'S mob' and I'm through. So I couldn't ring her to tell her that she had my mobile. Of course I was able to ring my own mobile, but S had gone out. What if the mobile lay hidden under a cushion and the battery ran out? Would I ever be able to speak to her again? Er, yes I would because her numbers are also programmed into my home phone. But I wasn't at home. I was in a car going to Shrewsbury. I might not be able to contact her for almost eight hours. She could have found someone else to go out with in that time, and with such lack of mobile phone contact there wouldn't be a person in the world who would blame her.

As it was, the battery didn't run out and I rang my phone at around 6pm and she answered (a bit presumptuously I thought!) I took the trouble to write down her number on something that was apparently used in the olden times, a piece of paper. Contact was re-established.

And apparently my fears were well founded. I had already missed a call from my mum and a text message from my cleaner – who surprisingly aren't the same person (well not any more).

You see how popular I am.

Monday 10th February

Now regular readers will know that I have an unhealthy streak of paranoia in me. And all the talk of terrorists and dirty bombs and ricin isn't really helping that. It's not that I'm particularly cowardly, I actually think I have it in me to be one of those tragic have-a-go heroes who get stabbed in the face for their troubles. I suppose I am just ultra-sensitive to potential trouble and, like most people in London at the moment, spend a small amount of my time looking round the tube carriage wondering if the Indian man and his five-year-old daughter sitting opposite me are actually part of an Al Qaeda death squad. This then immediately makes me feel like scum for the implicit racism of my imagination.

Today I got off the tube at Waterloo, so I could pick up my phone from S's workplace. In front of me was a man moving extremely slowly and blocking my way. He seemed to be looking around a lot, taking in his surroundings, without any particular interest in working out where he was going. From behind my racist imagination ascertained that he was of Middle Eastern origin (though he could have been Italian, or indeed British).

Now if I'm honest, most tourists behave like this. They loiter and look confused and come to a stop at the top of escalators or in doorways and generally get in the way of the grumpy local commuters (who nonetheless behave in exactly the same way when they find themselves on an unfamiliar underground system elsewhere in the world). But my paranoia had been pricked and there did seem to be something that slightly jarred with this fella. Firstly, he wasn't carrying anything. Tourists usually have a cumbersome bag slung over their shoulders in order that they can really effectively block your progress. Maybe not having a bag made him an unlikely terrorist. Where was he keeping his Sarin gas? But then again, the September 11th hijackers only carried those tiny little box cutters, and in any case, he might just be casing the joint, making a note of escape routes that he could use, or block, depending on his fancy.

Secondly his clothes all seemed a bit too new, and my Nazi imagination decided that they were almost like a parody of Western garments. The kind of clothes that an Al Qaeda instruction manual would advise its operatives to wear in order to "blend in". He had unscuffed, no-brand trainers, jeans and a denim jacket. Just the sort of clothes which would avoid suspicion because they were exactly the kind of clothes that an innocent, ordinary bloke would wear. He wanted me to think he was an innocent, ordinary bloke, but I wasn't going to fall for that trick.

At the top of the stairs he loitered (just like an ordinary tourist would. This bloke was good. Too good), despite the fact that the exit was indicated in either direction. I passed him and looked round at him. He looked at me a bit shiftily. And then I noticed the clincher. He had a scar right across his right eye. He might even have lost his eye. This was too much of a coincidence. Not only was he almost certainly foreign, he had an injury that was consistent with having taken part in guerrilla action in the caves of Afghanistan. How fascist was my paranoia being now? His skin is a bit brown and he's got a disability. He must be up to no good. My mind's eye was already typing up its CV for the Daily Mail editor's job.

He saw me looking at him and seemed to come to a standstill. Doubtless he was trying to pretend that he was intimidated by the attention of a stranger, on a strange underground system. As I rounded the corner to the escalator I decided to check him out just one more time. But he didn't emerge from the tunnel. He had taken flight.

Now I am taking the piss out of myself here a bit, aren't I? But in some paranoid right-wing cortex of my brain I was seriously considering alerting the police to this man. What was I going to say, "There's a slightly suspicious man somewhere in Waterloo station"?

"What's suspicious about him?"

"His skin is a bit tanned and he's lost an eye and his trainers are really new."

"In the old days that would have been enough to arrest him sir, but thanks to political correctness, one-eyed foreigners with clean trainers are allowed to walk the streets. It makes me sick too, sir."

So I didn't tell the police, but still went away feeling worried that if Waterloo station disappeared into a hole behind me, it would be my fault for not bringing the culprit to their attention.

Luckily nothing happened so I spent the rest of the day hating myself for my pathetic, reactionary paranoia. I kind of hoped Waterloo station would be blown to bits, just so I wouldn't feel so bad about myself. But alas it still stands.

Though there is always the possibility the man was just taking part in a practice run of whatever dastardly plot he had up his suspiciously denim sleeve. Just to be on the safe side I would keep away from Waterloo station for the next ten years if I were you.

Tuesday 11th February

In my thirteen-month crusade to lose weight (last week got down to thirteen stone, but put on a couple of pounds on tour this week. That elusive twelve stone something seems destined to remain just a dream) I have managed to overcome many of the psychological links between food and mood or occasion.

As I've said before, I realised that I used chocolate both as a reward or as a comfort (as well as quite often, something that tasted really nice) but I have managed to overcome that association.

One link that I find harder to conquer is the one between a long car journey and the need to stop at services to buy sweets and crisps and unpleasant pasties. So when we took a welcome break at a Welcome Break on the way to Leicester I couldn't resist the urge to head for the pick and mix (sorry, that should, of course be "pick 'n' mix", life is so hectic we can't waste our time with those two unnecessary letters) for some unpleasantly sugary confection. I chose two pink shrimps, three big yellow bananas, three gob stoppers (regular size, not giant), four liquorice allsorts, five toffees and three bits of fudge. Naturally I also stole a couple of sweets and ate them as I was choosing. You have to offset the inflated cost of the service station prices by getting a couple of bits of candy for nothing.

I took my nineteen sweets to the counter to pay for them and was told that they would cost me £2.03. Two pounds, three pence for nineteen sweets? Even taking into account the two pieces I stole, that's practically ten pence a sweet. How can Welcome Break possibly justify that?

OK three of the sweets were gob stoppers, which are quite heavy and you might expect to pay five pence each for them (though might still feel a bit ripped off), but the lightweight liquorice allsorts surely bring the average down. Yet I am still paying ten pence for one of those tiny bits of liquorice with a white filling (I don't believe they were even Basset's liquorice allsorts, but one of the inferior copies).

The woman at the till was clearly embarrassed "It's two pounds, three," she said, "Is that all right?" I said that it was, but I hadn't fully taken in the full horror of what she was telling me. I thought that that price included the newspaper and bottle of coke I was also buying. So I ended up paying for the over-priced fripperies.

Now you might expect that for ten pence a throw, those sweets would be fit for a king, and possibly have real diamonds at their centre, but although some of them had gone almost as hard as diamonds as they sat exposed to the air (and whatever else dripped into their plastic boxes) I'm afraid that your regal expectations would be confounded.

The liquorice allsorts were stale, one of the yellow banana things seemed to be mutated, as if it had been partially dipped in fluid and then dried out again, and the shrimps were a bit too pink and might possibly have been genuine sea creatures that had been found in a puddle by a sewage outlet and then dipped in sugar solution to be sold to children. OK, maybe not. But the sweets were not good and did not live up to their ten pence price tag.

So, how can I get Welcome Break back for their blatant theft of around £1.96 of my £2.03? I think that by stealing a couple of sweets each time I go I am just playing into their hands. All I am getting is a couple more horrible sweets and they have clearly factored such thefts into their prices and marked them up by about 10,000%. No, I have a better plan and you can help me implement it.

Next time I am at a Welcome Break and there is a "pick 'n' mix", I am going to fill a bag with sweets. And I mean fill it. I am going to take one of those big "pick 'n mix" bags and literally pick as many different sweets as I can and thoroughly mix them. But I am going to avoid any sweets that are already wrapped up. I want the sweets and their sugary coatings and their flavours to get thoroughly entwined. I am then going to take the bulging bag of sweetmeats to be weighed. I will presumably be asked for around fifty pounds for my purchase. The woman at the till will be embarrassed and say "Is that all right?" and I will say, "Oh no, that's far too expensive. I won't bother thanks," and then I will walk away, leaving the astonished employee with a massive bag of sweets. Welcome Break will then be left with the choice of throwing the sweets away or employing someone to un-pick and (sorry, 'n') un-mix them and put them back in their containers. If the contamination process has been effective then this will not really be possible. Very shortly the pick 'n' mix will look too unpleasant for anyone to buy.

Now if I do that alone it will not make all that much difference, but if we all do it, and we all e-mail our friends and tell them to do it too, then Welcome Break will have an annoying problem on their hands. I will write to them and let them know what is happening and tell them that they must

a) decrease the cost of their "pick 'n' mix" to an average of one pence a sweet (allowing up to three pence for large or novelty candy)

b) increase the quality of the sweets, so they are made by recognised major brand manufacturers and are in prime condition (neither hard nor water-damaged)

c) re-name the facility as "pick AND mix". We, their consumers, will not be short-changed and demand all the letters of the words used to be present.

I am serious about this, and urge you to join me in my crusade. For the moment let us concentrate on Welcome Break service stations. When we have won that battle we will move on to other pick and mix criminals.

It is your right to change your mind, so don't be swayed by any staff who attempt to force you to buy the bag of sweets that you no longer want. Let's see if we can make a difference.

I really thought this entry might lead to some nationwide campaign, but there was an overwhelming lack of response to this call for action. Though I think someone who worked in a shop with a "pick 'n' mix" counter did email to tell me that if anyone followed my instructions it would just mean that the staff had to then go through the bag and replace the sweets in the correct container. And it didn't seem right that they would be punished for their overlord's greed, so I let it drop.

On a more positive note, as I write this note I weigh about twelve stone ten. Admittedly I have been up and down a lot in the interim, but at least finally there's a twelve at the front there. Let's see if we can make it an eleven!

Wednesday 12th February

After the second gig in Leicester tonight, Simon and me decided to go out on the town. However, we couldn't really work out what to do. Disappointingly for a comedy festival there seemed to be no ascribed central meeting point for after-show fun (or if there was, no-one from the Festival had thought to tell us about it, or indeed make any kind of contact with us at all).

So instead we went and played pool in a pub near the theatre. This is what it's like on tour[16].

We decided to have a night cap in the hotel bar, though somewhat reluctantly as the evening had been sad enough already, and from what we had already seen of the hotel clientele, it was unlikely to be the swingingest spot in Leicester (but then again, it is Leicester that I'm talking about). We'd dropped the car back at the hotel after the gig and the only other people in the bar had been some businessmen and women having some kind of informal meeting.

But as we arrived back at eleven-ish there was a sense of excitement amongst the few people in there, and stretching out on one section of sofas were some rather cooler-looking patrons. There was a very glamorous young woman, and a couple of extremely trendy black guys, who were all apparently being videoed by a slick-

---

[16] This is a quote from an Ice T song. It seems fun to compare my experience of touring with its pick 'n' mix and playing pool with Simon Streeting, to Ice T's version of trying to get hoes off the bus.

looking older man. I felt I maybe recognised one of the younger men, guessing he was probably some kind of pop star, but I couldn't place him. Simon felt it was the girl who was the famous one, but I didn't recognise her, though she did look like any one of a hundred of those hopefuls from Fame Academy or whatever.

They were talking to, or rather being talked at, by a drunk, middle-aged man in a crumpled suit, who seemed to be pestering them. So much so, that within a couple of minutes of our arrival they all left.

From what I could hear from his conversation with the barmaid, the drunk was very impressed with meeting these celebrities (whoever they were). He was asking her what I considered to be rather intrusive questions about their movements, and how long they were staying and so on. He asked for another drink. I told Simon not to do anything to attract his attention to us. He was clearly slightly sad and lonely and I didn't want to give him an excuse to come and bore the arse off us too. Yet I had a sense of affinity with him, all too aware that we all have the potential to be the lonely drunk at the hotel bar. Many times when I've been away working, I've sat quietly in such bars myself, feeling miserable and alone, but not having the balls to talk to anyone. Mind you, the main reason I wouldn't talk to anyone is because I've seen too many drunks like this one, imposing themselves on strangers and spoiling their night.

A few moments later, the girl and the older guy with the video camera crossed back through the bar on the way to bed. "I didn't think she'd be with him, out of those three," said Simon. I made the same presumption, thinking the video fella must be another kind of slightly sad middle-aged sleaze bag (the video camera didn't help dispel that image). Of course there was also some element of jealousy, however much I'd like to claim otherwise.

Yet the next morning I was made to realise the error of my presumption. The video guy and the girl were sitting at the next table to me at breakfast. Out of her smart clothes and make-up the girl looked much younger than she had last night and my judgement of the sleaziness of the man went up a few notches. Until the girl went to the buffet bar and said "Do you want some cereal, dad?"

So, it was me who was the middle-aged sleaze bag, not him. He was just a father, proudly recording the meeting of his daughter (whoever she was) with some other blokes (whoever they were).

For the second time in a week I had made a horrible snap judgement, which said more about me than about the person I was stupidly judging. You know that Jesus bloke was quite smart on this subject, wasn't he? He should get more credit than he does.

Saturday 15th February

I had stopped playing on the internet casino because I had had a lucky streak, and then lost a couple of hundred pounds (still ending up over £600 up overall).

Today Ladbrokes tempted me back by sending me the software, that I had cleverly uninstalled, on a CD. I decided to give it another go.

Now I'd like to be able to use this entry as a cautionary tale, letting you see why gambling is bad and why you should never go back. But unfortunately I kept winning. I became a bit obsessed with it. I played on nine occasions. Here's a run down.

On my first go I took out £100, played for ten minutes and won £360 (a profit of £260), thought, "That's not bad for a day's work!" and banked the cash back on to my credit card.

About half an hour later I thought, "Well you've won £260, so you can afford to lose another £100." So I gambled £100 and this time won £190 (£90 profit – £350 overall. I was keeping a tally to ensure I didn't do anything mental.)

Within the hour I was on again. I gambled £100 and won £265 (now up to £515 profit). Something had to go wrong.

But the next two goes were even better and I made another £575. I was over a thousand pounds up.

I should, of course, have left it there, but if I'd done that when I originally said I would I'd be £800 worse off.

I played three more times and lost £290 pounds. I was still £800 up. But decided that enough was enough. My lucky streak was over and I uninstalled the software again.

So I'm around about £1500 up on Ladbrokes so far this year, which isn't too shabby. Beats working for a living. Certainly beats working in Leicester for a living!

But I have just been lucky. I don't want you all joining in with this one. This isn't like CNPS (nor is it as spiritually rewarding).

You can see from just this one day's gambling how addictive it is. If I had had a bad day I would be £900 down (though I probably wouldn't have played on if I hadn't done so well). I feel I should maybe re-install the software and have a really bad day, so I can leave you with a healthy moral to this story. But knowing my luck I'd win another £1000.

Sunday 16th February

Dammit. I was wrong. I only won another £750 (yes I reinstalled the software because I thought it was my duty to fail, to teach you that gambling is wrong). What sort of lesson is this giving out? Someone up there is fucking with me, by turning me into the jammiest bastard who ever lived.

I think it may be the CNPS Gods. These are genuine deities, who lived up on Mount Olympus with all the other fellas, but didn't really get all that much to do in the days of yore, largely 'cos number plates had not yet been invented. So they're making up for it now and are dicking with my mind in all kinds of weird ways (some number plate-based, others outside their official godly bailiwick). I wonder if I can use them as a defence when I am finally caught for my spree of ripping-based crimes.

Don't worry, I've only been ripping up objects, not any living creatures. There's no need to go mad. Those blokes who rip up people are giving us other rippers a bad name. I see myself as a suave, David Niven-style cat-ripper (not that I rip cats, though no-one would blame me if I did. They're asking for it, those cat whores! No, I am just saying that I am stealthy), only ripping things that belong to really rich people who deserve to have their more flimsy possessions torn up.

No, no court in the land would accept that the Greek gods in charge of consecutive number plate spotting had ordered me to rip stuff up on their behalf.

But is my religion any more stupid than any of the others? Just because I happen to believe that the world was created by some supreme beings, solely because they knew that one day men would invent the car, would make so many of them that each needed to be identified by a series of letters and (more importantly) numbers, then a very few humans would become obsessed with the idea of spotting all the numbers from 1-999 consecutively in numerical order (the chosen people), and then the Gods could screw around with their heads by sometimes engineering situations where the number required didn't come up for a while. That is the meaning of life. That's why we're all here.

Clearly that is a bit more stupid than most of the other religions, although similarly self-centred, "God created the world for ME! So, bum to anyone or anything that isn't me or people who think what I think."

I prefer the gods of more ancient civilisations, because they seem to make more sense of our chaotic life. The problem with an all-powerful single benevolent deity (even if he has an opposing sort of equal, but obviously in the end less powerful, malevolent enemy) is that it doesn't explain why life is so random, or why bad things happen to good people, or why evil can even exist if everything has been created by someone is completely good.

Yet with the Greek gods you have a reason for all this. There are lots of gods with lots of different personalities – some are good and wise, others are stupid and selfish, many are just mischievous tossers (definitely the CNPS gods who are bugging me at the moment) and some have shoes with wings on which means they can fly. They all pretty much like having a good time and making the most of life. They are essentially human beings (though some of them have shoes with wings on which mean they can fly) or possibly like in some rubbish old episode of Star Trek, they are more like children (but aren't most adults really?).

Another way to explain the randomness of life, is that life is just random. The reason it seems to be lacking control is because no one is controlling it. The reason that bad things happen to good people is because no one is keeping a tally of 'good' versus 'bad' deeds and because bad things happen to people (so good and bad will both be affected).

Of course, the reason this fails to catch the imagination of most people is because it's a bit scary and nowhere near as much fun as those shoes with wings on them.

So come on CNPS gods, stop playing with my head and turn me back into the unlucky loser that you designed me to be.

Monday 17th February

Won another £150. Bollocks. This really isn't working. Please don't copy me. Gambling is for jerks.

Some of the people I hate most in the world are estate agents. I hate generalisations, but all estate agents are slimy, money-obsessed, lying idiots, who went to public school, but still didn't get any A levels and so have to do an essentially unnecessary job for too much money. It's not a generalisation. Show me one estate agent who isn't like that and I will show you an estate agent who has lied to you to convince you that he isn't like that and has thus confirmed just exactly how much he is like that in reality.

I am currently having to deal with the rubbishy estate agents who are (half-heartedly) attempting to sell my flat for me and also the estate agents who are selling me my new house. The estate agents that are selling my place have annoyed me. They came round in late November and quoted me an asking price that was about 25,000 pounds higher than the estimate I had been given by a rival. The man (whose surname was Herring, so I thought I could trust him, but now I begin to wonder if this was some kind of trick. Maybe they print up cards in the office where they replace their real name with your surname, to make themselves appear like family) assured me that he would be able to get this amount. So what with him being related to me and being able to get me more money, I decided to go with his firm. A few weeks later they rang me and suggested the price was a bit high (like it had been my estimate: like I was the one saying that I could sell it for that) and that maybe if I dropped 5000 pounds more people would come round. So I agreed. I still thought it was probably a bit on the expensive side, but you never know your luck.

Then a couple of weeks ago they rang me and said they were having difficulty getting people to come and see the flat, what with the price being so high. They thought I should knock another ten thousand pounds off the asking price. Or maybe twenty. So essentially they are now telling me that the first estate agent who gave me an asking price had been nearer the mark, and that by putting my flat on the market with them I had wasted two months of realistic clients. I wouldn't mind so much, but the tone of the whole conversation was that this was my fault. Like I had insisted on asking far too much money and was mental. The horrible estate agent cunts.

I may move my business to the first estate agents, who although undoubtedly as evil as my current estate agents, at least didn't lie to me about how much my property was worth, in order for me to go with them, knowing that they would eventually drop the price, banking on the fact that I wouldn't be arsed to go with anyone else once the true price had been achieved, so they would get my custom.

I may do.

Or I may not be arsed.

Now the estate agent who is selling me my new house (who hasn't even had the intelligence to pretend to be called John Herring. Don't they teach these youngsters anything at Estate Agent school? Yes, they do. But the potential estate agents are too thick to be able to take it in) has been on the phone to see how things are going and when I will be ready to complete. Of course this is all really in the hands of the other group of people that I hate most in the world- solicitors. The non-false Herring (not that he's called Herring – he isn't – just that he isn't pretending to be called Herring in order to get in with me) estate agent wants me to ring my solicitor to see what the hold up is. It is probably that my solicitor is getting paid so much that he can afford to sit around all day eating caviar and can't really see the point of working all that hard.

To be honest it gave me great pleasure to know that a one of the kind of people I really hate in the world was being inconvenienced by one of the other kind of people I really hate in the world. So although I told John Not Herring that I would ring my solicitor immediately to find out what was happening. I didn't. I'm not going to ring him until Wednesday.

And thus I have my revenge.

Which I am sure will sour the massive commission that John

Not Herring will be getting for the sale.

Now I have to think of a way of getting back at my solicitor (as well as Paul Pretend-Herring at the Balham estate agents).

Tuesday 18th February

OK, now this is getting ridiculous. Today I won £620. I am really trying to lose. I am over £2000 up in four days and over £2700 on the year.

I rang my mum today. She said she'd been reading the diary and wasn't happy that I was gambling and that it was bad. I said "I'm two and half thousand pounds up!"

"That's not the point," she said.

I countered, "I have to carry on. I'm trying to prove to the people reading this that gambling is a bad thing, that it's a mug's game and that you can't win."

She voiced the suspicion that I was on some kind of deal with http://www.ladbrokes.com/ to promote their site and make the feckless idiots who read my diary (and who all love me and look up to me and want to be like me) throw their money down the toilet. I said I wasn't, that she was being ridiculous, though I had to admit that I was impressed by their tax-free winnings, their easy-to-use credit card system and the fact that any pay outs went straight back on to my card with no fuss or bother.

I'm joking. I'm not trying to promote them. Quite the opposite. I'm trying to show that they are evil shits who will steal your money (so it doesn't really matter if you don't pay tax, 'cos 25% of nothing is nothing). It's annoying me more than anyone that my plan isn't working, believe me. This lucky streak simply can't last. It can't. I will reduce myself to penury to save you from the evils of gambling, even if it means winning millions of pounds.

It's going so well that I begin to wonder if Ladbrokes are aware of this diary and are letting me win for the publicity. So don't fall into their trap. Do not go and play on online casinos. For the sake of my mum.

My mum was also keen to tell me of a new video that is hitting the shops soon that tells you what to do in the event of a chemical or nuclear weapons attack. I already know what to do, you run around screaming, flailing your hands in the air, shouting, "My skin, my beautiful skin. It burns. Aieee, I die!" I'm not paying fifteen quid to be told that.

I laughed at my mum and told her she was being paranoid (because as you know, that is not a trait I have in any way inherited from her). She spoke with a strange icy chill in her voice, "It's going to happen. It's definitely going to happen."

I began to wonder how she was so sure. Could my mother be part of some Al Qaeda sleeper cell? It would be the perfect cover. A 65-year-old woman from Cheddar who plays a lot of golf, helps out at Church events, has no criminal record and has never been involved in any major suicide bombing mission. That was definitely it. All this time suspecting strangers without noticing that my mother is Osama Bin Laden. The beard and the Kalashnikov should have given it away.

No, paranoia is definitely not something that runs in the family.

Now I'm a bit paranoid that the CIA or FBI or whoever it is, might have some internet search engine looking for the many key words that are in this posting and might not be tuned in to my unique brand of off-the-wall observations. If I wake up in the morning to find that Cheddar has been blown to smithereens by bunker-busting bombs (they'll need bunker-busting ones, because that's where my old mum usually ends up in her golf games! Boom boom! Literally boom boom in this case), I am going to feel a bit guilty.

She isn't really in Al Qaeda. At least I'd be really surprised if she was.

Adding to the slightly surreal sit-com-style life I am having at the moment (in more ways than you will ever know) my mother also informed me that my elderly Godmother, Aunty Joan – a respectable, elderly Christian woman from Halifax – has booked tickets to see my show in Burnley.

This is just disastrous on so many levels. She has already bought her ticket. The box office lady warned her that it was a bit of a racy show, but Aunty Joan said, "Yes, but you see, he's my Godson". My father warned her that the show might include knob jokes and she said that she had seen one (and probably only one – probably only once) before. I don't know if that will prepare her for the cavalcade of material about auto-fellatio, oral sex and Jesus enjoying the antics of lesbian nuns. Will Aunty Joan join in with the ladies shouting, "We love your cocks", I wonder? My mother asked if it was possible for me to tone the show down a bit for her. I said, "Only if I don't actually say any of it." Which might be the course of action I am forced to take. Perhaps for once the show will be about domestic fowl.

On top of this, Burnley is not selling particularly well and my fear is that I will be performing the show only to my Aunty Joan. If you live in the Burnley area then I think this might be a bit of a special show that's well worth seeing for all the wrong reasons. Maybe you'd like to buy a ticket for any respectable old ladies that you know who live in the area. Make a kind of theme of it.

Worse still, because the last bus back to Halifax leaves at about ten, mum has asked if I can give Aunty Joan a lift home on my way back to London. So there's going to be no escaping her reaction, whatever it might be. I will doubtless let you know how this goes!

Wednesday 19th February

At last, thank God. I lost £250. The nightmare is over. I got £50 up but then lost £300 in about five minutes without winning a single hand of blackjack (weird that this should happen only after I had called Ladbrokes "evil shits").

See, playing internet casino is a slippery slope and it's a mug's game.

I have taught you a valuable lesson that gambling does not pay and made £1800 into the bargain. Nice! We're all winners.

As I left the reading room of British Library this evening and crossed to the stairs to the cloakroom, I passed a young man having a heated argument on a mobile phone. He was seething with anger, trying to control the volume of the conversation, but still shouting, "You can't do that. You can't. Listen to me… listen to me… listen to me…. listen to me."

He had chosen a rather odd location for a private argument,

because he was projecting his half of the conversation out into the cavernous foyer of the British Library. His words echoed round for all to hear, yet still his body language was of a man trying to appear unperturbed, trying to keep the discussion between him and whoever was on the other end of the phone.

It wasn't exactly clear what the nature of the problem was. From outward appearances it looked like he was having one of those annoying arguments with a lover, where the importance of some minor problem get exaggerated out of all proportion and you blow your tops over it. It sent a chill through me as I remembered all such arguments I've had over the years, where deep-seated problems are not discussed and the resentment spills out over some unrelated and insignificant issue.

But as I passed him and carried onwards and shared a smile with a couple of library staff who were unwilling witnesses to one side of this spat, I could still hear his strangled protests rebounding off the walls. It didn't really seem like a conversation with a lover – there was talk of not bringing the authorities into it – it was clandestine. Was he being blackmailed? If so and he had some secret he wished to hide then he had chosen the worst place to have the conversation.

He started heading out of the building, down the escalator, but the further away he got, the more the booming echo of his words increased, heightened of course, because we were in a library and everyone else was respectfully quiet.

I descended into the cloakroom and he took his phone and his voice and his problems out into the freezing London night.

Thursday 20th February

One of the nice features of this website is that I have an administration page which has a traffic referral log. What this means is that I have a list of the sites that have a link to mine and a record of how many people have followed that link to find me.

This is interesting as it allows me to visit their sites and a) find out what they've said about me and b) read sites that I would otherwise never come across.

I hadn't really appreciated how many people kept daily diaries (or blogs as they are called by the internerd community[17]), and it is fascinating to get a glimpse into the lives and concerns of other people. As a history graduate (I feel a fraud calling myself that as I did very little work and learnt practically nothing at college, for which I have partial regret) I think it's ace that there is an accessible record of thousands of ordinary people's daily lives, something which is not true of any other historical period. We are restricted to the warped accounts of the lives of the great and the good and the evil, but know next to nothing about what life was like for the vast majority of people (only archaeology gives us an idea of some of the stuff they chucked away, not how they felt, or what concerned them. But hey, you can read *Excavating Rita* if you're really interested in this idea!).

Admittedly at the moment these accounts are mainly by teenage girls and strange men in their thirties who don't have proper jobs and spend too much time in a room on their own with their computer (do I mean me? How dare I talk about myself like that? I'm not a teenage girl at all), and possibly it's a bit grandiose to imagine that the alien historians of the future will be interested in anything we have to say. But it's a start.

Never mind the historical aspect, if nothing else it is incredible privilege for us to get a glimpse into the lives of people that we will never meet. I particularly like the random way that you can chance across a website. I notice that someone put the phrase "ten-pin bowling" + "oxford" into google, presumably looking for a place to bowl in Oxford, but instead chanced across my account of an evening at Streatham Megabowl with two other (similarly fraudulent) Oxford graduates!

In the last few days I've read about:

How a bi-sexual girl's boyfriend feels about her snogging another woman (amazingly he wasn't all that happy about it. Personally I would have been delighted);

How fantastic it was to be on the 'Stop the War' march (which will be an interesting historical source whichever way things turn out);

Someone getting an umbrella as a Valentine Day's present;

A man who is comparing singles from the same week in different

---

[17] *And isn't that charmingly 2003 that I felt the need to explain that?!*

decades (categorised by chart position);

Several people who have taken up the CNPS challenge.

People are able to express their uncensored opinions and get immediate feedback from the half dozen or several hundred people who visit their site. Yes a lot of it is irrelevant or nonsense or plain wrong, but I love it all the same.

For the first time I feel the web-like nature of this invention, and it's a web that connects us, rather than trapping us.

Friday 21st February

Things are all go at the moment. I have too much on and am getting tired out.

After a protracted tube journey home I went to Sainsbury's to get my dinner. I was feeling miserable and crotchety and on the point of collapse.

As I stood in the long queue waiting to buy my few items, there was a young couple standing behind me (probably both about thirty). They were quite cool-looking, but had that familiarity that comes of knowing each other too well, and they weren't really talking or interacting. After a lengthy pause, the man sighed, turned to his girlfriend and said "I'm just going to look at the raisins for a couple of minutes."

At least that's how my exhausted brain deciphered the sounds emanating from his mouth. He wandered off.

I chuckled to myself and almost made some comment to the girl about how interesting her boyfriend was, that even after he has been round the shop once, he takes a couple of minutes out to look at a limited selection of dried fruit. I was going to comment that he must think highly of her company if he'd rather be examining some wrinkled, dehydrated grapes.

But then I looked over at the bloke and he was nowhere near the dried fruit aisle. What was he doing? He was looking at shaving equipment. Why had he lied?

Then the pieces fell into place. He's said "razors". Of course, that made much more sense and meant he wasn't dull at all. Looking at razors for a couple of minutes is normal for a man. Looking at raisins would be odd.

My foolish misunderstanding resulting from stress and sleep deprivation made me openly laugh. In fact it quite cheered me up. I looked at the bloke looking at razors and then giggled, tried to hide my mirth behind my hand, but looked back at him, examining razors and laughed again. I worried that his girlfriend would think I was laughing at him for looking at razors, like this made him a dullard. But no, she would have misunderstood. It was the fact that he wasn't looking at raisins that was amusing. A man taking a couple of minutes of his time to look at razors is something that no one in the world could find funny.

Two minutes elapsed. He returned and said, "They're all so expensive and gimmicky these days."

He was right. The razor companies have cleverly turned the razor business into a massive profit spinner, by selling us razors with three blades, each cutting closer than the last, rather than razors with one blade. What they could do is make razors with one blade that shaves as close as the third blade on the new razor (the one that shaves much closer than the first blade and even closer than the second, thus making the other two blades surplus to requirements), but this way they get to sell three blades and they don't even have to sharpen two of them properly. Genius.

I walked home wondering if there was any similar scam that the raisin companies could pull on their customers.

I couldn't think of one. I'm not sure it's possible to be more raisiny than another raisin.

Saturday 22nd February

Thankfully my parents managed to dissuade Aunty Joan from coming to my Burnley gig. They read her my diary entry apparently and she laughed uproariously, sounds like maybe she should have come along after all.

Unfortunately my parents did not manage to persuade anyone else to come and it was the smallest audience of the tour by quite some distance. Only thirty-three in apparently, in a room that can hold up to four hundred.

But as can often happen in these situations they were a great and responsive crowd (who also gave more money to the charity collection per head than any other audience – thanks for that) and I really enjoyed making them laugh. There was a time when playing to such a small crowd would have made me miserable, where I may have taken my anger out on them (where of course, if anyone, it's all the people who didn't come who you should be angry with, not the ones who did), but it is gratifying to realise that I am learning and getting better all the time. I may have said this before, but the reason I love this job is because I am constantly discovering new things all the time. Just when I think I know what I'm doing, suddenly I have a revelation and find there's something new that I'd never thought of before.

But it was a long drive to perform to so few. A round trip of 450 miles, nearly fourteen miles per person. Nine hours in a car for eighty minutes on stage. It's surprisingly gruelling.

On the way home, with a pint-and-a-half of Boddingtons sloshing around in my stomach, I fell into one of those uneasy and painful half sleeps which make you more exhausted than if you'd just stayed fully awake.

Luckily Simon Streeting was driving.

Sunday 23rd February

Listening to Coldplay today. I have met Chris Martin a couple of times (I've been drunk and of course he has been sober on both occasions).

The first time was when Al Murray invited me round for dinner (maybe two years ago) and Chris was one of the other guests. At the time I had no idea who he was. I think I'd vaguely heard of Coldplay and knew one of their songs (the one about things that are yellow, not often enough celebrated in song in my opinion).

I have to say that he was a thoroughly nice bloke, genuinely modest and unassuming. He could do so much better than Gwyneth Paltrow. He should set his sights higher – this is obviously a kind of a joke. I have to say his attitude to his relationship with her (whatever it may be) is spot-on. It's no one's business. Contrast that with Zeta-Jones and Douglas, who sell photos of their personal moments to magazines and then get annoyed when other magazines are interested in showing more photos. They've put their personal lives in the public eye and so can't complain. But someone like Chris (or any normal person) would say, well that's my business, not yours, of course I'm not even going to talk about it.

Anyway, the reason I mention this dinner thing is not to name-drop about the only celebrities I have met who have not then immediately had me taken away by security, but because after dinner we played Trivial Pursuits.

Oh yeah, very rock 'n' roll. Well more sport 'n' leisure.

Now every time that Chris landed on the History square, Al and me would always (and I mean always) sing "He's gone for Yelloooow!"

It is a measure of how good a bloke he is that he didn't even get the slightest bit annoyed by this. Even though we did it EVERY time.

I can't remember who won, but I remember it wasn't me. I am a bad loser even when sober, so there's a good chance that Chris won and that I then stuffed all the yellow pieces of pie up his nose, whilst madly screaming, "You've got all the yelloooooows!"

Today I thought about emailing Al and asking if he could set up a re-match. The reason? Obvious. On listening to the new track, which I believe is called "The Scientist", I noticed another thing that I could sing at Chris Martin if I was playing Trivial Pursuits with him. There's a line that goes "Questions of Science, Science and" something or other. It doesn't matter what it says because if I could engineer a situation where I am playing Chris Martin at Trivial Pursuits again (unlikely after last time) then not only could I sing "Yelloooow" every time he lands on history, I could sing "Questions of science, science and nature" every time he lands on green.

It would be hilarious.

But I doubt that Chris Martin will want to play Trivial Pursuits with me after the possible pie-slices-up-the-nostril incident of two years ago.

So I put this into the public arena in the hope that one day one of you will be playing Chris Martin at Trivial Pursuits and so will be able to play this excellent gag on him – EVERY time he lands on green or yellooooow.

Or maybe I could arrange a match with Darius instead. 18

Incidentally, I am aware the game is called Trivial Pursuit. I am calling it Trivial Pursuits as a joke to amuse myself. It's the kind of thing your gran would do.

Monday 24th February

I went to the British Book Awards ceremony tonight. As usual with award ceremonies, I had not been nominated for anything (and as I've only written two chapters of my book I think it would be presumptuous to hope to win an award – though there was a part of me hoping I might do anyway). I haven't had much opportunity to cut loose recently, so I decided to get drunk. Why do I always do that when I'm in a situation where I am likely to meet people that I want to impress?

It was quite a star-studded event. Darius was there, funnily enough, but I was too drunk to think to challenge him to Trivial Pursuits. Lulu passed me on the stairs and clearly remembered me because she stuck her tongue out at me (though maybe Lulu does that to everyone). She didn't stop to chat though, which makes me think that she probably remembered me (and that night at Theo Fennel's) all too well.

But there were also quite a few comedy heroes there. Alan Bennett got an award (but I was so drunk by this point that I can't even tell you for sure that he was there in person), Michael Moore won best book and I got to say hi to him in the bar after, though he wasn't that keen to talk. Probably because I was drunk. I was also introduced to my absolute favourite comedian, Michael Palin. It is the first time I have met him. I wish I could remember what happened, but by this stage things are a complete blur. I don't think I was too embarrassing, but I was probably building up to it, (I think I might have been about to earnestly tell him that I loved him, no really loved him and wanted to kiss him on his mouth) when thankfully he realised he had something better to do and went away.

It's a shame I was too drunk to appreciate or converse with these people, but then I would probably have been a bigger idiot if I'd been sober. I am usually an affable drunk who becomes effusive with praise for people. You'd have to be a bit of a dick to be upset by it. I kind of like the fact that I am still a bit starstruck. I often think about how the fifteen-year-old me would feel if he knew the people I would end up meeting and the places I would go. Luckily I am not as much of an idiot as he would be, but I am almost proud of myself for still retaining the sense of wonder for the opportunities that my job gives me. I owe it to that fifteen-year-old comedy fan to get a bit over-excited!

As if to illustrate this point, earlier on I had seen Don "Did you Maclean your teeth today" Maclean in the toilet. How I used to love his antics on Crackerjack, especially the way he got Peter Glaze to say stuff he didn't want to by throwing in suggestions as Glaze was talking. He was on a table near to mine so I went up to him later, told him I was a comedian and how much I had enjoyed his work as a child. He laughed and took responsibility for my career choice and I left before I had the chance to say anything stupid. I think it made him happy. I think it's what the eight-year-old me would have wanted!

Tuesday 25th February

Now I remember why I stopped drinking.

I had a hangover which obliterated my whole day. With so little of my book written and so little time to finish it, I cannot really afford to waste time.

There was no point in even trying today. I realised I wasn't going to get anything done and so decided to relax and hope the sick feeling would go away

I felt a twinge of temptation to re-install the casino software, but resisted it. I realised the other day that I had made enough to buy a new laptop and that has been enough to make me think that I shouldn't go back.

Instead I did something equally stupid, which was to reinstall Civilisation II on to my computer. It has been a long time since I played this. It is a wonderfully involved and mesmerising game. It takes days to play and there's so much going on in it that even when you make a decision to have a break, you still need to take the next turn to make sure you caravan turns up in Heliopolis. Two hours later you are still playing, still having just one more thing to do before you can stop.

I have a book to write. I don't have three days to waste being the god-king of an imaginary civilization. Is there any way to justify it? I am currently writing about the cultural history of the penis, and playing Civilization does give me an idea of what it must be like for a burgeoning society with no knowledge, to grow into a modern day one. But although more people appear from somewhere, no one in this game is having sex, nor is it really relevant in any way.

As a kind of joke I played as the German nation and called myself Hitler (do you see what I did there? Naming myself after one of the most evil men who ever lived. Hilarious!), though I also enjoy calling myself a rude word like "Cunt" (very nearly a real leader's name anyway) and then being referred to as Emperor Cunt, or whatever my title may be. That is always amusing. I am thirty-five.

Ironically as Hitler I played a very peaceful game, choosing to concentrate on trade and democracy and giving my people Mass Transit systems and libraries. Then with the money obtained I would subvert the cities of other nations. And then occasionally have a war, but only if they start it. And with my superior technology I always kicked arse (not ass, I am English).

By midnight I had blurred vision. Tiny soldiers and engineers were still etched on my optic nerve and shifted along their imaginary way to nowhere whenever I closed my eyes.

It will have to go the way of Ladbrokes.

Wednesday 26th February

I have been disappointed to discover that the Cerne Abbas giant – the impressively cocked hill figure that features on my poster, book cover and talking cock website has not always been gifted with such an impressive cock.

I was aware there was some debate about which era he originated from. Most historians see him as an Iron Age figure, or possibly a representation of Hercules from the first century AD (he has a cloak on his non-club arm that has disappeared over the years), but he isn't mentioned in any records until the mid-eighteenth century, which has led some to suggest he was put there then as a joke to annoy the Puritans of the time.

Personally I think he probably dates from a couple of thousand years ago, but I'm not sure that that really matters anyway.

What I've just found out though is that prior to 1908 his cock was about six feet shorter than it now appears. Because the figure is cut into the chalk hillside, the lines have to be re-scoured every couple of decades or the grass grows back and the image disappears (hence the loss of the cloak mentioned above). Drawings of the "Rude Man" (as he is sometimes known) from before the twentieth century show him with a smaller (though still supernaturally erect – flat against his belly) penis, topped with what is generally taken to be his navel.

So some early twentieth century wag (or incompetent) decided to incorporate the navel into the phallus and one of the earliest and most successful penile extensions has been performed.

It makes me sad, mainly because I like to think of Iron Age men, delightedly carving this much too big dong, on their terrifying giant, which isn't so far away from the juvenile behaviour of school boys drawing similar impossibly gargantuan and spunking pricks on blackboards, overhead projectors and the condensation of sweaty school class rooms. A proportionately more average schlong is less humorous and thus the link I felt with those randy Ancient Britons is slightly broken.

But maybe the Giant being closer to the norm in the trouser department (not that he seems to care much for trousers) makes him more of an everyman figure (in all but the angle of his dangle). Perhaps in his original incarnation he is a better figurehead (in every sense) for my movement to celebrate the penis.

Or maybe what is taken to be his navel is in fact a slightly unusual bell-end. A lady in my show describes one penis as being like "a golf ball on a stick". Possibly he's still comically large and yet reassuringly unusual.

In any case I don't suppose it matters who made him, or who decided to give him a relatively painless extension. Whatever the truth for the last 350 years at least the citizens of that small Dorset town have ensured the grass never grows too long and re-cut the lines into the hillside (although he was camouflaged during World War II to stop German pilots using him as a navigational aid – should have left him up there, if the Germans had thought that was an average Briton they would have been too afraid to invade us!).

Let's hope he's still up there in 4003 and that by then his cock is up to his chin.

Thursday 27th February

My manager rang me early with exciting news. I have been asked to do a polish on the new Magic Roundabout movie script. That is to say they want me to take an existing script and work on it for a couple of days, in the hope of making it better and funnier.

Unfortunately my other work commitments mean it is impossible for me to take the job. Which is a terrible shame. As sarcasm doesn't always work in print I think I should point out that I am being sarcastic.

Don't get me wrong, I used to love the Magic Roundabout. I think Eric Thompson did a fine job of taking a French animation and then adding his own random and slightly subversive English script to images that he had no control over. I suspect the live action version (actually I'm not sure whether they are using the original puppets or actors dressed up or morphed through computer technology. I hope, at least it is the former) will not have the same subtlety and nuances. How can it? Unless they get a French bloke to make it and then get an English writer to make up a new script. Even if I was starting from scratch I would be hard pushed to think of a way of creating a fitting homage, but in forty-eight hours with someone else's script it would be a fool's errand.

What interests me is, why did they come to me? All these years never having been asked to polish a movie and suddenly out of nowhere the powers that be decide that I am the man to work on the Magic Roundabout project. Oh obviously, anything with a combination of necromancy and fairground equipment in the title, then Herring is your man.

Fair enough, that makes sense, so given those unique credentials, why didn't they come to me in the first place? Why did they get someone else with no interest in the occult or complicated machinery designed to spin you around for a couple of minutes for no particular reason to have a go at a script that had my name written all over it? Clearly they are regretting cutting corners (not something that is even possible on even the most magical roundabout) now, because they've been forced to come to me with their tails between their legs and say, "Yeah, the other fella wasn't up to it. Could you give it a spin, so to speak? Ha ha ha ha ha. We should use that in the film."

Doubtless the finished product will, against all obvious logic, go on to be a massive success and the person they get to polish the script will be snapped up and taken to Hollywood to write movies about all manner of enchanted carousels. But you won't catch me in thirty years' time, sitting on a park bench, drinking meths, shouting, "That should have been me." Oh no. I have more pride than that. If the Magic Roundabout is a successful film I will simply kill myself.

You have my word on that.

Luckily my razor sharp instincts proved to be correct about this project. How did I possibly foresee that?

Friday 28th February

The drive from Cardiff to Stratford-upon-Avon reminded me of the coach trips we occasionally took from my school in Cheddar in the early 80s to see various Shakespeare plays at the RSC. My main memory is not of the plays (though I do recall that the black woman from *Blake's 7* was one of the witches In Macbeth and I also remember Phil Fry showing me how you could release the catch on the opera glasses using the strap of a digital watch and thus save yourself ten pence) but of the journey. In the high street of one of the towns that we passed through on the way (I have no idea where it was, now there's a challenge for someone) there was a shoe shop called 'Richard Herring Shoes'. I remember that we all found this impossible and hilarious and that after the first trip me and my friends would anticipate the sighting of the store and there would be a rousing football-style chant of "Richard Herring, Richard Herring, Richard Herring Shoes! Richard Herring, Richard Herring, Richard Herring Shoes!" to a tune that would be very familiar to you, but I don't know if it has a name.

Now it strikes me that it would have been quite funny if it was a shop that either just sold the kind of shoes that I wore or alternatively would only sell shoes to me. As I was a thirteen-year-old schoolboy who lived a hundred miles away at the time, neither venture was likely to be very successful. I can't imagine many people in this anonymous Midland town, coming into the shop and saying, "I want to wear the same kind of shoes as a nerdy Somerset teenager, what can you offer me?"

They are more likely to have come into the shoe shop and asking for some cool trainers or whatever, only to be greeted by a weary shop assistant saying, "Sorry we only sell black Dr Marten shoes, not boots like Rich's friends wear, because his mum won't let him. Just the shoe version. Ironically in a few years' time such a shoe will go through a brief phase of being trendy, but as you know, now in 1980 they are laughably un-cool. Do you want to buy some? We only do the one size of course and Rich has freakishly small, yet wide feet."

And had the shop just sold shoes to me it would have had a similar stock, but been similarly unsuccessful. Perhaps cannily the shop owner had opened the shop on the route between Cheddar and Stratford realising that I would pass by in a coach at least once every two years, and that my curiosity was bound to be piqued. Unfortunately he had forgotten to factor into the equation that I was going to be in a bus which I had no power to command to stop, that I was a teenager who carried only two pounds maximum, which I planned to spend on ice cream in the interval (or opera glasses if I had forgotten my watch) and that in any case my mum bought all my shoes. Maybe had he called it Barbara Herring Shoes he might have had a better shot at success.

I think I passed through the town some years later (though I may have been mistaken) and the place I remembered Richard Herring Shoes being was now occupied by a different shop (possibly Simon Harris Pillow Cases), so clearly the rather specific retail enterprise had floundered.

 The touring continued and S was distant both literally and figuratively. At the end of the month I was heading off to the Melbourne festival for five weeks. The chances of us keeping things going when we were on the other side of the planet from each other seemed small. I think I must have been quite self-obsessed at the time, because although I knew she was going through various troubles that were nothing to do with me, I took her detachment very personally and don't think I was very helpful. I knew she was unhappy, but it was only years later when she wrote about it in the paper that I discovered she was actually suffering from depression. Despite my broad gestures of buying a home for us to live in and helping out with her son, I can see that I wasn't showing the necessary emotional maturity required for such a massive commitment. At the time I was a bit bamboozled by S's lack of appreciation of how brilliant I was being, but again with that wonderful luxury hindsight I can completely understand what her reticence was about. In any case she had enough problems to mean that I was never going to be that high up her list of priorities. We were as doomed as Romeo and Juliet, though the consequences would hopefully not be so dire. Am I trying to create some dramatic tension here by implying that we might both end up dead at the end of this? Because if so I am being quite short-sighted, given my all too evidently being alive five years later.

Saturday 1st March

It was in Cheltenham, it turns out. Here's the website – http://www.herringshoes.co.uk/about.html

It seems now to be called 'Herring Shoes' (or 'Herrings Shoes' with no apostrophe according to the shop canopy). And they call that progress.

I went to the wedding of a friend of S's, which was in a barn near Oxford, but luckily one that was nicely decked out, rather than one full of cows and stuff, like where I imagine Jesus would have got married if he'd ever found the right girl (but with such a perfect mother he didn't have a chance. Imagine it, "In my day you weren't only a virgin when you got married, you were still one when you had your first kid". No wonder he took to hanging around with prostitutes).

Apart from the barn setting, the only slightly unusual aspect of the wedding was that, because the two families involved were of different religious persuasions, it was presided over by both a Christian Bishop (the Uncle of the groom) and a Jewish priest (or at least a Jewish bloke, not sure what his background was). Although undoubtedly erudite, the Bishop got on my nerves by emphasising the importance of God in relationships and also seemed to see marriage as something that is created only to create children and to remind us of God's wrath if we do something wrong. He also told a slightly patronising story about how he used to preach at Cambridge University in the term time, but had a parish in lowly Hemel Hempstead in the holidays and seemed surprised that love was the same for the common people as it was for the intelligentsia. To be fair he did make some good points too and was keen to include examples that applied to both Christianity and Judaism.

The Jewish stuff all seemed a lot more casual (especially as the fella doing that part of the ceremony wasn't dressed in religious robes. Thinking about it, he might just have been a passerby who took a chance and no-one realised he wasn't meant to be there), but also more celebratory of love than of God. But maybe I'm only saying that because I am more inclined to be dismissive of the religion of my own upbringing, but more capable of being charmed by something that is more alien to me. In the same way that the

Indian culture and religions seem so much better than our own to students on their year off.

But there was no call to plight troths in the Jewish bits. Instead they shared a glass of wine (showing the importance of alcohol in getting through any long term relationship) and then the bride circled the groom seven times, which apparently protects him from evil spirits. The evil spirits element annoyed me in the same way as the Christian stuff, but the actual enactment was rather romantic.

Not only was it pleasing to watch and nicely symbolic, there was also the jeopardy of whether the bride would miscount how many times she'd been round. If she ended up doing eight circles, would that scupper the whole thing, or would the groom be slightly more protected? Maybe if you do too many they start cancelling each other out.

As it happens she got it right. So no evil spirits will get the groom now.

Then best of all, the groom stamped on the wine glass that they had drunk from, at least theoretically. I think they used a different one, 'cos they didn't want to break the nice one. How Jewish can you get?

That's theatre. I think the Jewish stuff was better regardless of my own prejudice, but I am a firm believer that marriages should be about love rather than religion and be a celebration of the bride and groom, rather than the parents of either.

Then I got outrageously drunk for the second time this week and in doing so reminded myself that I am not always effusive and jolly when drunk. I can also become unpleasant and then behave like a petulant child. Luckily I was not alone in this and in the morning all was forgiven! Love conquers all. If only I'd been circled seven times I may have been saved from the evil spirits (which in this case was whisky, the kind of alcohol that breaks long term relationships!)

I am actually quite surprised that I came so close to admitting my bad behaviour in that entry, as I generally attempted to keep more personal things to myself. Though I didn't get anywhere near going into how childish I had been. This should have been a great day for S and me, as we hadn't

been getting much time together at all, and precious little where
we didn't have a young baby to look after. So this was a welcome
weekend away, staying in a posh hotel, P's grandparents caring
for him at home – it was a chance to be romantic and relax
and repair the damage. But things were fractious from the
start. After checking into the hotel, I had been keen to find an
internet café to update Warming Up, already a little obsessed
with getting the daily bulletin in as soon as possible. Clearly it
could have waited, but I was quite insistent. It was at this point
that the mote seemed to fall from S's eyes and she looked at me
with new eyes and commented, "You're a bit of a nerd, aren't
you?" I don't know how she hadn't spotted this before – I had
been playing CNPS for over five months by now.

The wedding itself had not been much better for us. I was
self-conscious as I didn't know anyone there apart from my
girlfriend and bizarrely perhaps given my job, find it quite hard
to interact with strangers. So we both proceeded to get horribly
drunk and failed to really engage with one another. I think I
upset her by spending a long period of time talking to another
woman on our table, and even though there was no flirtation
going on, it was still inconsiderate.

Things came to a head on the bus that had been hired to
take us back to the hotel in Oxford. Months of frustration
poured out thanks to our drunkenness and we had an
embarrassingly loud and public row. I don't remember too much
of it right now, but I certainly accused her of being ungrateful,
after I had bought a house for her and her son to live in and
disingenuous for complaining about its location when she had
done nothing to help when I had been searching for it. Back
then I really couldn't see how I might have been wrong about
that and so her subsequent fury just made me angrier and even
more juvenile.

When the bus got to Oxford I pushed my way off ahead of
her, made my way back to our room and proceeded to pack my
stuff. I was out of the room and heading for the car park before
she had even got back to the hotel. I don't seriously think I was

*planning to drive home. I am very much against drink driving,
even when tiny amounts of alcohol have been consumed, but
at this point I was too drunk to walk let alone drive. I am sure
I was just trying to make a point of some kind, burning with
indignant fury, crapulously convinced that the relationship was
over and thus unable to bear being in the same room as this
selfish woman. Luckily, in any case, I wouldn't have been able
to get the car out of the car park to inevitably crash it in the
narrow lane outside, because the barriers operated on a token
system and no-one in their right mind would give a token to
this swaggering red-faced idiot and even if they had I would
never have been able to get it in the slot.*

*I think I had decided to sleep in the car, though must have
known that this attention-seeking strop would not be allowed
to go unchallenged. Some of S's friends came out to calm
me down and finally coaxed me away from the car and into
the hotel bar, where they potentially unwisely gave me more
whiskey and talked me through things, trying to smooth it all
over. I can't remember how it was all resolved in the end, but
enough of a truce was called for us to spend the night together
in the same room and the same bed. Though I guess we both
passed out pretty quickly and I was not thus able to dwell on the
humiliation of behaving like such a prize knob in front of all of
my girlfriend's friends.*

Sunday 2nd March

I read on Ceefax today that some of the people who went out
to Iraq a few days ago to act as human shields in case of attack, are
coming home over "safety fears". I wonder if they fully appreciated
what they were doing when they went out there. There's a clue in the
job title, "human shields". The reason that humans generally need
shields is because human flesh is a poor protection against swords,
guns and bombs. So to make a shield out of a human is only going
to lead to problems in the long run, most especially for the human is
being the shield, and then after a very minimal time for the person

who is being protected.

It's a bit like agreeing to be a suicide bomber and then expressing safety fears later on.

Although I suppose I admire the bravery of these people, risking their lives for a cause they believe in, I think it was always a rather naïve policy. I actually think the Americans are super-conscious of the necessity to hit as few civilian targets as possible. If they do (and they will) it will almost certainly be by accident (with one of what Al Murray calls "their wedding-seeking missiles"). If the target turns out to be militarily important then I don't think having a Westerner in the building is going to stop the bombing of it. Let's face it, America and Britain are sending its citizens over to face death already (in the form of the Armed Forces). They are able to square a minimal loss of life with an objective achieved.

It was also fairly inevitable, as seems to be the case, that Saddam Hussein would use the protestors as pawns and put them in places that suited his needs.

I am against war and the murder of human beings (whatever their shields are made of) in general. But then who isn't really? Sometimes a war is necessary in order to stop even more killing (or at least in the hope of doing so). If someone was attempting to harm my family or friends then my anti-murder stance would change. There are no absolutes here.

So I don't know what I think about this potential war. Whilst being suspicious of Bush, I infinitely prefer him to Hussein. Yet I don't think America or Britain has any kind of moral right to determine the governments of the world even if by doing so they make the country involved a better place. I would like it if there wasn't a war, but then I wouldn't like it if a few years down the line Hussein starts bombing the crap out of people, because no one tried to stop him. Imagine agreeing to be a human shield for the Nazis in 1939. That would be an embarrassing thing to justify today wouldn't it?

At the moment I don't see that either side has proven its case. It is good to be aware that our governments can lie to us, but that doesn't mean that they always do. I don't think this is a war about oil and I don't think Blair would risk this level of unpopularity unless he really believed in what he was doing. But it is frustrating that he won't share the supposed "proof", if it exists, with us.

I suppose I am saying that the level of certainty some people have (in both directions) is somewhat suspicious. But if there was any way of getting round this without bombing the shit out of an already oppressed people, (which common sense says there must be) then I would be all for it. Sending some shields made out of some kind of bomb-proof material might be a start. Or at least human shields who understand what being a shield involves and don't come home again because they think they might get hurt.

All of which biting (pedestrian) satire ignores the quagmire that my emotions were going through on this day. I had driven S back to her house in near silence, both of us no doubt with aching heads and mortified souls, both of us still unable to communicate properly, just trying to ignore the events of the previous night in the hope that the causes of it all would somehow magically disappear. I was very much assuming that we'd reached the end, briefly feeling that soaring liberation that comes at the death of a broken relationship. I had to head back to London and so dropped her off in Hampshire before driving back to Balham. The internal euphoria was short-lived and now I couldn't bear to think that this union, which had begun so intensely and so romantically was falling apart. I was listening to Coldplay's Parachutes and found the situation so tragic and the music so moving that I began weeping uncontrollably as I drove, my tears bouncing off the steering wheel. This was something I chose not to mention to Stewart Lee a few days later as he railed against this band and its music. But then he's never played Trivial Pursuits with Chris Martin, so maybe that was what swung it.

Somehow, unbelievably, S and I papered over the cracks, ignored the elephant in the room and the relationship continued, for the moment at least.

Monday 3rd March

I am ridiculously busy at the moment, trying to get as much of my book done as possible before I go to Australia. So I am rushing around from pillar to post and then back to the pillar, then to a different post, then back to the same pillar, then to a different pillar and then thinking I should really stop rushing around between pillars and posts and go to the library and work.

This morning I dashed out of the house so quickly that it wasn't until I was half way down my road that I realised I hadn't put a shirt on. Don't worry, I wasn't bare-chested, I had a T-shirt and a coat on, but normally (in the winter) I wear a long sleeved shirt for show and a T-shirt for warmth. There wasn't time to go back, but I was slightly annoyed as I was wearing my Scrabble T-shirt (that Stew had bought me from America as a joke, so that I would look like the all-the-eligible-two-letter-word-knowing nerd that I am). I thought now I am going to have to sit in the British Library with everyone looking at me, saying (oh no, not saying – it's a library) – rather, thinking "Look at that all-the-eligible-two-letter-word-knowing Scrabble nerd. He's such a nerd that he doesn't even know that being an all-the-eligible-two-letter-word-knowing Scrabble nerd is an embarrassing thing.

Fortunately I had momentarily forgotten that I was headed for the British Library, which outside of Dr Who book signing season is Nerd HQ. A faded, stretched Scrabble T-shirt is the height of sartorial elegance. There's a bloke there who wears a pair of glasses with a giant magnifying glass attached to the rim. These people don't care. Thank God for them.

I worked until just after 7pm, and then was tired and hungry. I didn't want to wait until I got home to eat, so I popped over the road to Pizza Express to treat myself to a spicy chicken pizza. As I was alone I sat at the table playing my Gameboy and drinking a cold beer.

Then it struck me, I was sitting in a Pizza Express on my own, playing Scrabble on a Gameboy, wearing a Scrabble T-shirt. How much of a sad idiot must I look? People must have been thinking (or even saying this time, as Pizza Express unfortunately does not operate under the strict no-speaking rules of the British Library),

"Hmmm, a middle aged man in a Scrabble T-shirt, playing Scrabble, not against another human being, not even against another sad nerd, but against a (not very powerful) computer. One wonders why on earth he finds himself unaccompanied this evening."

Two men had been employed to play musical standards on an electric guitar and saxophone respectively. No-one was listening to them. No-one applauded them. Normally I would have found their efforts a bit pitiful, but what position was I in to judge? The guitarist tried to catch my eye. Was he laughing at me? Or did he also like Scrabble? Or did he like Scrabble a bit, but not enough to wear a Scrabble T-shirt whilst playing Scrabble on a Gameboy?

I thought "Fuck it" and had another beer and carried on playing Scrabble against an imaginary old man.

Surprisingly none of the women in Pizza Express this evening tried to hit on me.

The obsession with Scrabble continues, though I now play a newer and in many ways inferior version of the game on my futuristic Nintendo DS, as well as playing all kinds of cheating idiots on Facebook. As I write this I am supposed to be working on the pilot episode of a sit-com about Scrabble players, provisionally entitled Absolutely Scrabulous *(many thanks to Johnny Maitland for that title). Which means that playing Scrabble is now research. So I don't feel guilty at all for wasting so much of my time doing just that.*

Tuesday 4th March

I arranged to meet my old friend Stefan[19] at Macnab's in Balham tonight. When we were both single Balham men, we often used to meet here for some food and a bottle of wine, before heading on to

---

[19] *Stefan Stern is a financial journalist and was director of the Oxford Revue 1988,* Waving at the Pigeons *which I co-wrote with Stewart Lee and also appeared in, to general indifference.*

Goblins[20] on Bedford Hill for some illegal late night drinking. Sadly Goblins closed down a couple of years ago, a sad loss, which left a gaping hole in the social lives of about eight, slightly odd, Balham men.

Now Stefan is married (incredibly meeting his wife in Goblins, which is all but impossible as no women ever went there) and living in Collier's Wood and I have a girlfriend and am shortly heading out west, so we decided to meet up for old times' sake in Macnab's and relive the old bachelor days, where we would morosely sit in the wine-bar for two hours, looking at women, but not talking to them (or each other), before heading back to our respective unpleasant Balham flats, drunk and alone. Happy days!

But when I got to Macnab's tonight, it had gone. The building was still there, but it was dark and empty and the sign no longer said Macnab's. The sign was for an Indian restaurant. By the looks of things that restaurant was either some way away from opening, or had already opened and gone bust before I'd even realised Macnab's had closed.

First Goblins, now Macnab's, the glittering night-spots of my youth were disappearing. The symbolism was not lost on me.

Instead we went to the Duke of Devonshire and then on to a new posh Balham restaurant, Lambert's. In my day such an establishment would not have been tolerated by the unpretentious folk of Balham. They would have burnt it to the ground, found Lambert and put him in the stocks and thrown his 'Oxtail and clapshot' back in his astonished face.

But Balham has changed – there's a Marks and Spencer's Food Hall opening here for goodness' sake – and Lambert's was reasonably well patronised for a Tuesday night.

The food was delicious. The wine was excellent. The service was friendly. We had a lovely time.

It just wasn't like the old days at all.

You can't go back, Stef. You can't go back.

---

[20] Goblins not only inspired Stewart Lee to create a bar called Pixies (I think) in his excellent novel The Perfect Fool, it also bears some similarities to the bar Hobbits in Absolutely Scrabulous.

*Balham continues to gentrify and on my rare visits back
I am always slightly dumbfounded to see the changes being
made to this once shoddy and non-descript suburb. Whilst I
am generally a fan of progress I think that Balham should have
been preserved as it was in the mid-1990s for all time, as a kind
of heritage experience.*

Thursday 6th March

I went to Jane from Avalon's leaving drinks last night (Avalon is my evil management agency, which has the twin aims of promoting comedy and killing Third World orphans). We were in the basement of a natty bar, so it wasn't a private do.

I was talking with the comedian Stewart Lee, when a man approached me. He looked a bit familiar and, as there were people there who had worked for Avalon over the years, I wasn't sure if I knew him or not. "Are you Richard Herring?" he asked. I confirmed my identity. It became apparent that I didn't know him, but that he had seen me on TV. He told me how much he enjoyed my work, and also commented on the fact that I had put on weight (but as with always this observation very much depends on when you last saw me!), but he was a little drunk and I feel I would be hypocritical for chiding him for being both rude and effusive to a comedian he likes, whilst under the influence of alcohol.

Then he asked, "Is it true that you are no longer talking to Stewart Lee?"

I said something along the lines of, "No, that isn't true. In fact, look there he is," in his excitement at seeing me, he had failed to notice Stew was right in front of me, "I was just talking to him a matter of seconds ago. That's how far from the truth that statement is." That rather put that rumour to bed, I thought.

The fact was that the only reason I wasn't currently talking to Stewart Lee was because this man had interrupted our conversation. I didn't mind – Stewart is very boring, I wish we weren't speaking – I just found it rather satisfying to be able to demonstrate the fallacy of the statement so effectively.

I was joking about Stewart being boring, in case you were feeling like spreading more false gossip. He is anything but that. Next time you see him ask him for his opinion on Coldplay.

> *I really love this story, which clearly demonstrates people's*
> *ability to make up the story that suits them, even in the face*
> *of the evidence in front of their eyes. If anything, Stewart and*
> *me are better friends now than we were when we were working*
> *together, given that we now don't have to spend up to fourteen*
> *hours a day, six days a week, in a small office with nothing to*
> *look at but each other's stupid faces.*

Friday 7th March

In Jersey the car number plates all consist of the letter J followed by a number. Each number is obviously different (or there wouldn't be much point in having the number plates) and range from 1 right through to numbers with six or seven digits.

I spent most of my day in St Hellier thinking what Hell (or Heaven) it would be to play a Jersey version of CNPS.

It would take many life-times to complete (I once read that it takes four days just to count out loud from one to a million) and also, as each number is represented only once you would have to wait a long time to progress onwards. Plus, of course if a car and its number plate are taken out of use then you would be stuck on whatever number you had reached.

I was slightly concerned about this problem before it struck me that no-one would ever play CNPS in Jersey and that no-one in the world thought as much about number plates as I currently do. Well maybe they do, but I don't think there is anyone who thinks as much about number plates and cocks as I do. I am the world expert on those two subjects combined.

The significance of the different number plates was heightened by the fact that aside from the number plates everything else on Jersey is the same as on the British mainland, though there are more French road names and the town centre seems curiously old-fashioned and individual (largely because it is not full of all the same shops and department stores that have turned other UK town centres into weird clones of one another).

So for me, with my number plate obsession (which started out as a kind of joke, but is swiftly becoming a genuine preoccupation) being in a place that seemed familiar but where the number plates were weird (and useless in my quest) was slightly unnerving. I felt like I was in an alternate universe, with only one very small and insignificant alteration. Like I had been zapped here by some malevolent force to stop my dream of spotting numbers 1-999 in order before I die. It was my personal Room 101. What if I got home and all the towns had adopted this insane un-CNPS friendly version?

My attempts to bury the failures of my childhood would be smashed into the dirt.

My mind is so used to checking number plates now that I still couldn't get out of the habit, even though I knew there was no chance of me seeing the number I required (even if I had seen J80 I would classify it as a foreign number plate).

It is great that I have had the chance to travel to a new and unfamiliar place and that this is my only observation about life here.

Saturday 8th March

As someone who understands much about probability it is ridiculous that I treat every plane journey as a chance to take stock of my life and prepare myself for oblivion. Statistically I am much more likely to die when I get into a car (especially if I am driving and even more especially if I start playing CNPS), but something in me still believes that every plane journey will be my last.

Or possibly something in me believes that if I openly state that the plane is going to crash then there is no probable way that it could. The coincidence would be too great. So by preparing myself for death, I am actually protecting myself, because everyone knows if you say something out loud, then in fact the opposite will happen.

Clearly this is even more ridiculous and embarrassing to admit for someone who claims to be an atheist, rationalist.

I don't fly all that much though, so it is good to make my occasional peace with the world (which would just get annoying if I had to do it every time I got in the car), to be thankful that I have beaten impossible odds to be alive in the first place and have been lucky enough to live in a time and place where I am generally happy and comfortable and able to do the ridiculous job I do.

There was a Muslim couple sitting in the seat in front of me, and the woman had a video camera on her lap. I thought this was odd and desperately tried to stop myself thinking that they had somehow got a bomb disguised as a camera through the fairly tight security. I knew that she couldn't have and that I was once again just being horribly paranoid and racist. I also knew I didn't really believe it, but still hated my brain for having imagined it and was still thinking, "Why have your video camera on your lap on a plane flight?"

But I didn't complain. I accepted my death like one of those idiots who believes that everything happens for a reason. Even though I am utterly confident that practically everything happens for no reason.

Despite the worries of death and destruction I do actually like flying (and especially the privilege of being able to get anywhere in the world so quickly) and am a much less nervous flyer now that I have realised that you just have to accept you are in a situation you have no control over. There's nothing you can do, so you might as well enjoy the flight and the freedom from responsibility. It is such a wonderful and ridiculous achievement to be able to fly above the clouds (that so few people in history and even living today have ever experienced) that I actually believe it is worth the slight risk of death. And there is even a part of me that would kind of like to witness a plane crash from the inside, especially if I had some kind of *Star Trek* force field around me... and a parachute. Planes have taken me on some wonderful adventures (even better than the current trip to Jersey) and it would be terrible if irrational fears had stopped me from boarding those planes. I am ready to die the minute the good lord Enki[21] wants to take me.

As it happened the lady in front had her video camera out so

---

[21] *This is the ancient god of Sumeria who I mentioned in Talking Cock most notably creating the Euphrates by having a wank and proclaiming, "Let now my penis be praised!"*

that she could film our take-off out of her window. As electronic equipment isn't meant to be used on take-off this was possibly as disastrous as her coming on with a bomb and I began to wonder how much damage Al Qaeda could do with some strategically placed mobile phones and Gameboys (I thought Scrabble could only be used for good, but it could bring down a plane).

We also had a slightly bumpy ride thanks to turbulence and I realised that much as I am ready to die, and much as watching my own flesh being burnt off would be academically interesting, I would much prefer to stay alive with my unburning skin covering my non-excruciating pain-filled insides.

This paranoia, though embarrassingly faintly racist, was probably shared by many people at the time, in fact I think I felt it more acutely before the 2005 London bombings than I do now. But maybe this is down to personal change as I am nowhere near as nervous about flying as I was then. Nowadays, in a wonderful show of treating all humanity as equal and ignoring racial and religious differences, I tend to move down the tube carriage away from anyone carrying a large backpack or suitcase. Which is of course much healthier than just being suspicious of people who look like they might be Muslims.

Sunday 9th March

The thing I most admire about babies is their ability to be constantly amused by exactly the same 'joke' (and I put that in inverted commas, because often the thing that makes a baby laugh has no real humorous value to a grown-up). If human beings only carried this trait on into adulthood then my job would be very easy. All I would have to do is go on stage and sing the one line "I'm Ms Dynamite...ee ee" over and over again and the crowd would be rolling in the aisles. (I mean, what's the joke there? I don't think P is laughing at the sophisticated mismatch of supposed and actual gender. It's more likely that he enjoys the silly way that the "ee ee" sounds. I have to admit, I do do it very well.)

It would certainly save me from the living Hell that is writing a show, but I guess if I chose the wrong initial 'joke' then I might be in trouble. What if I sang "I'm Ms Dynamite…ee ee" and the audience just stared at me like I was insane, or worse just not of any interest to them, which is P's reaction to many of the things that I imagine would make him laugh.

Then I would be stuck with an hour of "I'm Ms Dynamite…ee ee" and no back-up material to get me out of it. If everything else about these adults had remained constant from babyhood, then I would have an audience full of crying, screaming, chatting and sleeping people, many of whom had inadvertently pissed themselves (but not in a way that the comedian usually hopes for) and shat themselves and been sick. So rather like my recent gig in Wellingborough then (I thank you).

My sister bought P a musical book of nursery rhymes for Christmas. As well as having the words and pictures of a nursery rhyme inside, it also has little buttons you can press at the side, which play you the tune of each of the songs in the book. P really likes *Old MacDonald* and has worked out which button plays that song. So what he does is presses the button and then looks at you and expects you to sing the song. Then when you comply he laughs (briefly) and waits for the song to end. Then he immediately presses the button again, looks at you again and expects you to sing the song again. Of course you do it. He's a baby. You want to please him. It does please him (though not as much as the "Ms Dynamite…ee ee" thing) and so the second you have finished the song he will press the button again (sometimes in the interim he has crawled a little way away from the book to do something else, but he always returns and hits the right button).

This goes on and on and on.

It is the repetition of the 'joke' that makes it more amusing for P.

Very occasionally he presses the wrong button by accident and you get to do *Three Blind Mice*, which is a welcome change for me, but he doesn't like it as much. It's not at all funny. Of course not. It's violent and ultimately tragic: it's not bad enough that these mice can't see, the farmer's wife has to cut off their tails as well. What kind of message is that to our children about the plight of the differently abled? "They can't see? Well cut off their legs as well, that'll teach them!" – all right, the farmer's wife was provoked, the mice after all, all chased after her, but when you think about it they can't really have been doing that deliberately can they? Unless she had some cheese in her pocket that they could smell. Then she's only got herself to blame.

So P's soon back on the one true path that is "Old MacDonald".

S has had to endure this for a few weeks already and today wearily asked P to stop quite early on, but I was up to the challenge. I am a grown man, he is a tiny baby. I could outlast him in this game. I was going to keep singing *Old MacDonald* until P no longer found it amusing.

It was an old-fashioned 'musical nursery rhyme book' stand-off.

I had two advantages. Firstly unlike the dire *Three Blind Mice*, *Old MacDonald* has an important piece of variety every time you sing it. That's right. The animal and the sound it makes varies each time. Thus the song is not quite as monotonous and boring to the singer as it might have been.

Secondly, P is a baby and can't understand English, so some of the time I could just sing "Blah blah blah" and he'd have no idea that he had been duped. The tiny idiot.

I didn't want to use that second option though. I wanted to beat him on a level playing field. I could get through this. I would win.

But I'd done cow, sheep, horse, donkey, dog, cat, chicken, cockerel, goat (though I had to make up a noise for that one, because I wasn't really sure what goats say) and duck and P's tiny finger was still returning to the *Old MacDonald* button. I was given some time, P's finger had slipped and the book was playing a nursery rhyme that I had never heard before (it sounded a bit like *After the Ball is Over*, but it can't have been that, surely). I said "Sorry, can't help you there, boy" and tried to think of another animal. I could probably have repeated, he wouldn't have known, but it was becoming a challenge and it's not like I'm stupidly competitive or anything, but I had to beat this baby. I'd wipe the delightful smile off his face.

"Pig" said S, which I took as a suggestion for the song, as I hope it was intended.

Of course, how could I have forgotten pig?

Far from being unamused, P was laughing more than ever.

I was in trouble. He hit *Three Blind Mice* by mistake. The fool. He'd given me an idea. A farm can have mice and mice go "Eeeek". I was not to be defeated. I could see P was kicking himself for making the mistake. But he still pressed on.

Surely I'd done the lot now. But I thought of rats and voles and moles and stoats and ferrets. All thanks to that mice mistake. Ha ha! But still, I felt I was getting in a bit of an "eeek" rut though that didn't bother P at all. His hand heading back ever quicker to the button. I thought of tractor. P looked at me dubiously. I admitted I was possibly stretching the rules, but as long as it was on a farm and made a noise I think it counts.

But I'd been stupid. Who was to say that Old MacDonald only had domestic farm animals and traditional vermin? Perhaps Old Macdonald's many years on this earth had turned him into a loveable eccentric, like Lord Bath, who has a safari park within the grounds of his 'farm'. I had every animal in the world to choose from. I laughed at P's giggling face. I had the upper hand. He'd soon be bored.

Forty-five minutes later, I had got to zebra, which I imagined made a noise a bit like a horse, but with an African accent and P was not remotely uninterested yet.

I on the other hand was going insane through tedium and was losing my voice. Even if I could have thought of another animal then I couldn't face having to sing the same bloody song again. But that was what P wanted and expected.

I could only think of dinosaur and I gave it a go, but I knew in my heart that after a life-time's farming Old MacDonald would not have had time to perfect the technology required for a Jurassic Park-style addition to a farm that was already putting Noah's Ark to shame (though interestingly Old MacDonald only had one of every animal, which must have caused him some problems and made his farm somewhat unprofitable). I was crying into the sofa. But P pressed the button and looked at me. I shouted, "All right, all right, you win. Leave me alone. Stop playing *Old MacDonald*. I admit it, you are better than me."

The music stopped and P pressed the button again. "Didn't you hear me? I said you've won."

P pressed the button again. Maybe he was playing his inability to understand language card. Or maybe there was more to it than that. He pressed the button again.

"Please stop it. I can't take any more. Please."

P pressed the button again.

It wasn't enough for him to have won. He wanted to show me that he could have carried on this test forever. He pressed the button again.

So then S took the book and put it upstairs and hid it. She had spotted his one weakness. His inability to walk.

We all have an Achille's Heel. P has Achille's legs.

The room fell silent.

But it didn't matter. P had proved his superiority. He simply crawled over to his box of toys and played with some squeaking eggs instead.

I wondered if Old MacDonald might have had one of those on his farm.

Monday 10th March

I have some amazing news that may revolutionise the diet industry.

For the first two months of this year I ate healthy food, drank much less alcohol than usual and did thirty minutes exercise for five or six days a week and I consequently lost over half a stone.

For the last ten days I have eaten when I feel like it, drank copiously to numb the pain of living and done no exercise at all and have put nearly all that weight back on.

Now I know that my experience does not prove anything scientifically (and some other factor may be the cause of my weight gain), but what this suggests to me is that taking more calories into your body than you burn off, may result in obesity.

I don't want to put all these faddy protein diets and unpleasant shake drinks out of business, but losing weight might all be to do with getting off your fat arse once in a while and stopping stuffing your face with chips.

I am going to attempt to put this information to the test by starting to exercise again and to lay off the Pickled Onion Monster

Munch and Werther's Originals on tour. I will let you know what I find out.

> *I am back on a diet again as I write this and pretty much following the credo of this brief entry, which is entirely correct. Of course in the intervening half a decade my weight has gone up and down by two or three stone about five or six times, showing that there is slightly more to it than this. But I'd still quite like to bring out a diet book that essentially made the above point on page one and was followed by 200 blank pages. It's really up to you if you're going to decide to use the above knowledge to regulate your weight, or if you don't care and just eat what you want. It's working for me so far in 2008, but it's early days and experience would dictate that my will shall be broken. As always I enjoy the liberating power of placing hope above experience.*

Tuesday 11th March

Being a writer gives you a taste of Heaven and an eat-all-you-can buffet of Hell. There is nothing to match the exquisite pleasure and satisfaction I felt last week, when I finally completed the first draft of a difficult chapter on the cultural history of the penis. But the next day I was plunged into the abyss of despair as I struggled to get my next chapter even started. And a week later I am not much further on. The annoying thing is that I kind of know what I want to write, but for some reason seem totally incapable of sitting still long enough to give it a go.

I caught a bit of the fly-on-the-wall documentary about Rob Newman's attempt to write a novel last night and recognised much of the torment he was going through. How he spent a day changing his office and his bedroom around, hoping this would give him a fresh start, an impetus to carry on, but most importantly a feeling of actually having achieved something. The way he got a new desk in the belief that that would somehow exude magical ideas. All the sticking bits of paper on the walls – I've been there, believe me.

All the procrastination, the totemism.

I also empathised with the changes in appearance, weight and mental state. This job can surely take its toll (although Rob seemed to look better the further he got).

Writing can be like pulling teeth. Not out of your mouth. That would be easy. Writing is like pulling teeth out of your genitals. It's like being bitten in the cock and testicles by a massive radioactive rodent and then trying to prise its jaws away from you, only to find that when you finally manage to (after a week or so of struggle), its adamantine teeth have come loose from its gums and are still piercing your bleeding and mutilated genitalia. And when you attempt to pull them out you find they are burning, white-hot and also have little barbs on them, like fishing hooks and they are exuding acid and the AIDS virus into your blood.

It's exactly like that. If you can't be bothered to try writing, just do that instead and you'll know what my job is like.

The problem is that finishing writing is like waking up to find that the whole radioactive rodent thing was a dream, and that far from being mutilated and full of acid and disease, your cock has miraculously doubled in length and is studded with strategically placed jewels which simultaneously make you the greatest lover in the world and the richest man who has ever lived.

Which is why the very next day you willingly and arrogantly place your knob into a cage of leprous monkeys with eyes that shoot lasers and which live on a diet of over-sized jewel-encrusted genitalia.

Really this metaphor may sound ridiculous, but it is uncannily accurate (and also demonstrates the extent to which male genitalia now rule my world).

Unfortunately (or fortunately because this was a bit like living the nightmare of my own life as entertainment), I fell asleep part-way through the Newman documentary, but apparently even though he got his book finished, he hasn't got a publisher yet, which is a shame (though I am tempted to say he should just put it up on the internet, none of us needs publishers any more. Though the downside of that is that you won't get paid. That's the good thing about publishers).

When I awoke I spent a day of harrumphing around, eating bagels and watching *Diagnosis Murder* and totally failing to make any progress. I thought about buying a new desk.

Which I think you will find when you die (if you've been bad) is exactly what Satan has waiting for you in Hades.

When will this torture be over?

> *This idea made it into the stage show* The Twelve Tasks of Hercules Terrace. *It is, I believe, the first* Warming Up *entry that would then be turned into a routine on stage. And satisfyingly this first draft written in without revisions is pretty much how the bit ended up on stage (though the radioactive rodent became a radioactive dog). It had only taken three and a half months for this thing to start paying for itself!*

Wednesday 12th March

One of the thing that amuses me about being on tour is that wherever you go you are guaranteed to get a massive laugh if you take the piss out of the next town along to the one you're in. Tonight I was in Birmingham and so was able to get cheap and effusive laughter from implying that the men of Wolverhampton have extremely smelly cocks.

Of course when I was in Wolverhampton a few weeks ago I got a similar level of appreciation for making exactly the same disparaging comments about the genital hygiene of Birmingham's male population.

The audience will cheer and applaud, even though in their hearts they must know that I am simply playing to local sensibilities. I love the fact that our greatest disdain is reserved for those who live closest to us and who essentially to an outside observer are practically identical. Of course, hardly anyone is really taking any of this seriously and they are aware that they are participating in what is essentially a massive joke (it's like in my heart I know the people of Sistova Road are essentially the same as the people in my street, but I would never admit that in print, because they are all idiots).

Recently I've been enjoying pointing the stupidity of this out to the partisan crowd. But despite this, I did acknowledge that I genuinely think Birmingham is superior to Wolverhampton.

Although it is probably only superior in the sense that shit is superior to diarrhoea. I didn't mention that to the audience though. See how deceitful the comedian can be.

Although in honesty most people love jokes about how crap their own town is. Nearly everywhere is a shit hole to be honest. I am sure that is why we find knocking our local rivals so much fun. "Yeah, that's right, I do live in Birmingham, but at least I'm not from Wolverhampton." We are laughing at each other and ourselves. This is what comedy is for, in my arrogant opinion.

Unfortunately, as with most good jokes, there are a few people who take these things seriously and think it is a good idea to beat someone senseless because of their postcode, or because they believe in a slightly different form of the exact same religion.

But all the people who are like that either live in Wolverhampton or Sistova Road or [INSERT THE NAME OF YOUR LOCAL ENEMY HERE]

Thursday 13th March

After the gig in Derby, Simon Streeting and me popped into a pub near the hotel for a wind-down pint of Guinness. Not knowing the local pubs and not being able to see through the windows we took a chance, hoping we wouldn't end up in the hardest bar in Derby. Because once you've made that commitment to go through the door, you can't really go out again. Oh sure, you can exaggeratedly look around as if you're pretending to look for a mate and then say to yourself in a stage whisper "Oh, he isn't here," but no-one will be fooled and they will come after you with crowbars anyway.

It was a bit of a rough looking pub on first impressions, but there weren't that many people in there drinking. Probably because there was an extremely loud punk/heavy metal style gig going on in the back room. We chose not to join the throng of sweaty men who were attending and played pinball instead. Simon Streeting then spotted a *Who Wants To Be a Millionaire* machine on the other side of the pub, so we thought we'd have a go (hoping that some other punter in the pub would cough at the appropriate moment to help us out – has anyone else pointed out that that is what happened in that old

Morecambe and Wise Harsenel Mastermind sketch? Hilarious if it is true that someone has tried it for real[22]).

On the way across to the machine, a wild-eyed man caught my gaze and said, "Hey, I saw you coming out of somewhere earlier." I said, "Oh right. Good." And carried on my way, unsure if this was someone who had recognised me as a minor ex-TV star, or had just seen me exiting from an unspecified location at some unknown point in the past.

So Simon Streeting and me started to lose at *Millionaire*, but when Simon Streeting went up to get us another drink, the wild-eyed man again caught my gaze. He came across and offered to help out with the game. He was fairly drunk (there may have been more than alcohol in his system, but he was drinking Newcastle Brown which is the strongest hallucinogen known to man, so that might have been it). We played a few games, losing every time, but it filled some of the aching chasm between our births and our inevitable deaths.

Eventually the touch-screen of the computer went a bit haywire and we were forced to stop having added about ten pounds to the already bulging coffers of *WWTBAM*. Our new wild-eyed friend, although initially a bit scary, was quite a sweet fella and went and retrieved his Newcy Brown to come and sit with us.

He was obviously alone and a bit lonely and asked us what our plans were for the rest of the night. We answered honestly that we were very tired and were going to bed. It became apparent that he hadn't recognised me from the telly, but he repeated his earlier assertion that he had seen me coming out of somewhere earlier, but did nothing to clarify where or when this might have been. But I think his brain was struggling to keep up with the stimulants in his blood stream, so he probably didn't have much chance of remembering.

We sat and chatted and Simon Streeting produced a pack of strong Gauloise cigarettes that he didn't want, but had surmised that our new friend might enjoy. Although I don't smoke and can't

---

[22] *This is, of course a reference to Charles Ingram, who apparently cheated his way to a million pounds on the popular quiz show with the help of a coughing accomplice, but was caught and lost his prize. I later interviewed him and his strangely alluring wife on my little known poker based TV show,* Heads Up With Richard Herring.

smoke and feel ill if I smoke, I decided to have one out of a sense of the camaraderie of lost souls.

He tried to persuade us to head into Derby in the search for excitement. But I was tired and now feeling sick from smoke inhalation, and the pub staff were kicking us out, so we headed back to the hotel and left him to down his full pint of Brown Ale and contemplate his demons.

Friday 14th March

I have been using hair gel to keep my girlish flowing locks out of my face whilst I'm on stage. In the shower this morning I was struck by an idea of pure and brilliant genius. When you wash your hair, the gel obviously dissolves and is washed away. Which seems like a waste.

My idea was to invent a hair gel that doubled as shampoo. That is, it had all the properties necessary for holding and styling your hair, but when you stepped under a shower the gel would lather up and you would be able to wash your hair. Why take one bottle into the shower, when you could take none? With the right marketing and an endorsement from Gareth Gates this could be the greatest time-saving invention since sliced mushrooms.

I was considering writing to Wella or someone to tell them of this brilliant idea, and already spending the money I would make for such a ground-breaking notion. I told Simon Streeting about it in the car on the way to Oldham. He didn't seem that impressed, but I knew he was just jealous.

Then he said, "Yeah, but what would happen when it rained?"

Dammit, he was right. Your beautifully crafted hair would dissolve into lather and you would be a laughing stock. In one second Simon Streeting had destroyed a whole morning's worth of work.

Back to the old drawing board.

I did contact a shampoo manufacturer to ask them about the efficaciousness of such an idea, but as with so many of my more fanciful missives, whoever received the email chose to ignore

it as the work of a madman. But they said Einstein was mad
when he said you could split the atom, they said the Wright
brothers were mad when they claimed they would be able to fly,
they said the Yorkshire Ripper was mad when he killed all those
prostitutes. And they were right about that last one. But they
were wrong two out of three times, so if anyone wants to give
my Shamgel a go then please let me know.

Saturday 15th March

Yeah, but what if you have to massage your hair vigorously for
the shampoo to work? My dream is not over! It's my idea. Don't
steal it.

There was a big party of ten-year-old (maybe a little older, but
prepubescent anyway) kids from Northern Ireland staying in my
hotel last night. I was watching *Comic Relief* and the World Poker
Championship (which opened my eyes to a new gambling avenue[23])
to wind down after the gig. At about 11.30pm the kids all arrived
back to their rooms and for the next forty-five minutes they were
shouting each other in their shrill unbroken voices, running up and
down the corridor and banging on each other's doors. My heart sank,
it was going to be a disturbed night's sleep. The grown-up in me got
a bit huffy. It's not what you expect when you book into a nice hotel.
You deserve some decorum for your £82 (Yes, £82 – that's how nice
a hotel it was).

But I didn't want to complain. They were, after all, only children
and who amongst us didn't behave like that when we were young?
It's exciting being away from home. Of course you're going to shout
and run and play rubbish practical jokes without a care in the world
for the boring businessmen (and extremely interesting stand-up
comedians who nonetheless are in bed at 11.30 on a Friday night).
Every now and then an exasperated teacher's voice would call for
calm and issue mild and impotent threats and things would be quiet
for approximately thirty seconds. But then the noise would start

---

[23] Indeed it did - poker was to become one of my major obsessions over the next few
years.

up again, rising from whispers to shouts in the time it takes you to make the same shift in volume on a TV remote control.

It was annoying, but my inner child instructed me to let the shenanigans be. It would be hypocritical to complain when I had been culpable of the exact same crimes as a youngster.

In fact the incident gave me rather fond memories of the camping holiday I had in Minehead with my school mates (which later provided the inspiration for much of *Punk's Not Dead* [24]). One night we had stayed up until about 3am, drinking cider and making up tortuous and impossible puns for new versions of the "My wife went on holiday last year" joke. We'd done that for about two hours and amazingly the fun had started to dull, so Steve Cheeke started doing an impression of the son of Satan for some reason. Suddenly there was a heavy rapping on our tent roof and an angry, threatening, French male voice rasped, "You can keep your blurdy, sheeety mouths closed!"

We were immediately silenced by fear, but within a minute we were laughing and imitating his ridiculous accent and his poor (yet strangely more effective) command of English swearing.

Yes, it must have been annoying for him to have his holiday in Minehead ruined (if it's possible to make camping in Minehead any worse than it is already), but could he not remember a time from maybe twenty years before, when he had been young and exuberant and suddenly released from the rules and regulations of his parents? Hadn't he wanted to laugh and joke the night away as well, without even a thought for another human being?

In Oldham, I decided to break the cycle and so I didn't ring reception, though alas someone else did (Simon Streeting as it turns out, the party pooper) because the noise ceased around about 1am.

I felt proud of myself for letting it ride, but couldn't sleep anyway as it happens. So I was less inclined to nostalgic empathy when I was woken at 6.30am by the same happy, shrieking and swearing voices (they had a better command of serious curse words than my French adversary of twenty years ago, though an equally amusing accent). And I was even more annoyed when I was woken again at

---

[24] *You can read this play in the Downloads section of www.richardherring.com - I am very proud of it.*

9am by the maid who had entered my room because one of those rapscallions had found it amusing to turn my "Do Not Disturb" sign around, so that it read "Please Service my Room".

If I could have got hold of them I would have wrung their blurdy, sheeety necks.

Sunday 16th March

The thing with studying history is you usually know how things turned out in the end. So Neville Chamberlain and his piece of paper seem in hindsight like the worthless and misguided things that they both were. Of course what you don't know is how people felt when they heard about what Chamberlain had done. Did they think, "Good, that's Hitler sorted then, there will definitely not be a war" or "That piece of paper isn't worth the piece of paper that it is"? (Ironically I bet that piece of paper is worth a lot of money today, if it's still around and if Hitler didn't ask for it back so he could wipe his arse on it.)

The point is that at the time no one knew what was going to happen, though they may have had suspicions, and until you reach one of those turning points in history you can't really judge.

So today I watched Bush and Blair and some Spanish bloke with a nice moustache basically inform me that it's time for war, with a sick feeling in my stomach. Because we don't know how this one turns out yet, do we? Though my guess is it's not going to turn out very well for any of us. I also suspect if the war didn't happen that it's not going to be that great for any of us either. I reckon we're pretty much fucked in the long run, whether Saddam Hussein is around or not.

There's no way to deal with three blokes with a bag of anthrax or a box with a bomb in it. Eventually between now and the end of history it's inevitable that someone succeeds.

So let's live a bit of history and hope most of us are still around in thirty years' time to work out whether Bush and Blair's decision was a good one, a bad one or whether it made little difference in the long run.

Hope you have a good week.

It turns out that the anti-war protesters were pretty much
on the money about this one. At the time I actually believed
that Blair was doing the right thing – I assumed he must know
something that he wasn't telling us and that's why he acted so
decisively, when he had been so wishy-washy about everything
else. He had been so keen not to offend anyone about anything
that I thought that in making such a bold decision he had to
have some serious intelligence about our imminent destruction.
I was also suspicious of how the anti-war protesters could be so
sure that he didn't. But I was wrong, wasn't I? Though glad we're
still here, if only for the short-term.

Monday 17th March

Someone has suggested that the gel to shampoo transformation
could be heat activated, thus normal cold rain would not be a problem.
I am beginning to suspect that the manufacture of such a gel would
outstrip the cost of just buying shampoo and gel separately, but I'm
going to press on. They laughed at the idea of toast once upon a
time, and now look at them. Marmite all over their faces.

On the way back from Hereford tonight we stopped behind
another car at some temporary traffic lights. The traffic lights changed
to green (green is the frog all covered in slime – GO![25]) but the car
in front of us didn't move. It then indicated left and pulled into the
kerb. Naturally Simon Streeting (who was driving) pulled round to
the right and overtook the car. But the driver seemed perturbed by
this action. He immediately pulled out again and flashed his lights
at us, full beam, for several seconds. We tried to work out what we
had done to annoy him. Surely his actions suggested we should over-
take. Had Simon Streeting inadvertently had his headlights on full
beam at some point along the road and this was a sophisticated and
grown-up revenge? Was he just a bored youngster looking to make
trouble and incite a needless road rage incident? Was he drunk and
acting irrationally? Or was he just trying to shit us up?

---

[25] *I am self-indulgently quoting a character I played in BBC2s* Fist of Fun. *But then*
what is this book if not a monolith to self-indulgence?

The car hung on our tail as we traversed the winding A-road, just outside of Gloucester (I suspected that possibly the ghost of Fred West was driving the car looking for fresh victims, but as you may have noticed I can get a little paranoid). Although there was no real danger unless the other driver decided to run us off the road, his bizarre and intimidating behaviour was a little frightening. Even when we started pulling away from him, I could still see his headlights behind us in the left-hand wing mirror. One of his headlights was slightly brighter than the other. He was behind us for quite a good long while. It was a bit sinister and suspenseful. It would make a good film. But only if the bloke behind had started attacking us with knives. This didn't happen.

Luckily we shook him off before Swindon. But if the bloke who was driving the ghost car is reading us could you please email me and tell me why you behaved so oddly? Please reveal the make of your car to prove that you are the real twat-face.

There is a prize of 1p for the genuine driver.

This offer still stands.

Tuesday 18th March

I am off to Melbourne surprisingly soon. In preparation for the Festival I've been doing some press interviews to publicise the show. I was informed that I would be rung at seven o'clock tonight to do a pre-recorded radio interview for a breakfast show. No call came at seven and so I went out for the night.

At ten o'clock I was in the pub and had had a couple of pints and my phone rang. They wanted to do the interview now, so I went out pissed into the streets of Balham to talk to some people on the other side of the world who were settling down for breakfast.

This would have been disorientating enough, but because I was on my mobile there was a massive two-second delay on our conversation (as is much loved by the sketch writers of comedy TV shows).

And it was quite funny. "Who were those girls laughing?" asked one of the presenters. I didn't know what he was talking about, but then I remembered that some girls had walked past me, what seemed like ages ago to me, but because their laughter had taken a few seconds to get to him and his question had then taken a few seconds to get back to me, and because the alcohol in my blood stream had caused the words to take a few seconds to get from my ear to my brain, the girls were well up the road before I realised what he meant.

"Is this live?" I asked, imagining how shoddy and unlistenable it must be.

I got an affirmative answer back eventually, though it might have been to a different question.

Within thirty seconds the presenters were bailing out and saying they'd organise something when I was in the same time zone as them!

I was left thinking that the people of Australia would be left with the impression that I was a confused, drunk man who took about five seconds to answer any questions. It seemed to me that this was unlikely to help ticket sales. Although they do like Paul Hogan out there. Ha ha! I am funny.

I went back into the pub and sat down with Mackay, Simon and Dave. I told them what had happened. "So you've just been talking live on Australian radio?" Sitting in the dingy old man's back bar of the Bedford Arms this did seem like an extremely surreal thing to have just happened.

It seems this incident shows the wonders and limitations of technology.

Wednesday 19th March

I was packing for Melbourne today and as I was looking through my wardrobe for what stuff I should take, I noticed a familiar smell. It wasn't unpleasant, and was pretty faint, but it was the musky smell of the suits and jackets in the wardrobe, which I suppose is really the smell of me. Yet it was very specifically the same aroma that I recall from the wardrobe that my dad kept his clothes in when I was little. It took me straight back to games of hide and seek (wardrobes are such good hiding places, so always look there first if you are a seeker and want to ruin a child's fun) and stifled laughter. But it also reminded me of those fleeting early years of your life when father and son are not afraid to be close to one another and we could cuddle and I could fall asleep on his lap. Although I don't particularly hanker to repeat that scenario now that I am thirty-five, it was comforting to be taken back to those days through that amazingly accurate olfactory memory.

But whether hiding or hugging it really is a smell of security and safety.

It was a telling reminder of the days before adolescent rebellion when your father meant everything to you. The older I get the more that I realise that kids get it right on so many things (apart from finding good hiding places, which they suck at), and that the self-consciousness that comes with puberty, though necessary, blinds us to a lot of what is true and good.

The father/son relationship is a bond that we have to break in order to become men ourselves, but hopefully one that will repair itself once our own manhood is established. It embarrasses me how long it has taken me to realise just how much my parents did for me.

But it was weird to realise that his smell is also my smell. Though perhaps not surprising given our genetic similarity. However much I still try to rebel against it I am more similar to him than I like to acknowledge. Though I don't know why I don't want to admit that. If I could be half the man he is then I would have every right to be proud of myself.

Tragically I am still only able to express my love for my father when writing about him, never to his face. In fact I show him nothing but rudeness in real life. But, you know, he reads this shit, so he knows, so I can still be an arsehole to him in person, right?

Thursday 20th March

The British Library can be a bit like being at school.

As there are a lot of things to sort out before I go away and I was expecting some calls, I had my phone on silent today so I could see if anyone was calling and receive texts. I got a few calls, but put them all on to the answer phone knowing I could ring them back. My manager Jon rang. I went out to try and ring him back about five minutes later, but he was in a meeting. Exactly the same thing happened a couple of hours later. So around about 5.30pm when I got a call, I figured it would be him, so not wanting to miss him again, I answered, whispered "Hold on, I'm in the library" and then walked to the exit so I could continue the conversation.

As I passed the entry desk, at a part of the library where conversation is acceptable in my mind as you are asked for your pass and to show your bags there etc, I whispered to Jon's PA. "OK, I'm ready to take the call now," and left the library and headed for the lobby.

When I came back in, I showed my pass and walked through as usual, but the woman on the desk called me back. "Can I have your pass," she said.

I gave it to her, not understanding why she suddenly needed to inspect it and she started writing down my membership number.

"Is there a problem?" I asked.

She didn't look up, but grumpily remarked, "You were using your mobile in the library."

I said, "I wasn't. I was leaving the library so I could have a conversation on my mobile."

She looked at her colleague, "He was using his phone wasn't he John?"

The pudgy-faced and miserable man remarked, "Yes".

Neither of them looked me in the eye.

I said "I started talking as I was leaving the library. That's hardly using the mobile in the library. I am yards away from anyone working and they couldn't have heard."

In fact we were making much more commotion by simply having this conversation. But they didn't listen to me and although I thought about arguing I couldn't really be bothered. It reminded me of those occasions you get in trouble for doing something at school, but are in fact innocent (for once) but there's nothing you can do to prove it. The security guards were being self-important and going by the exact letter of the rules in order to make themselves feel important and brighten up their humdrum lives. It's a shame, 'cos most of the fellas who do the job are very personable and like to have a laugh with me over my bag of personal books which are all to do with the penis.

I don't know what my punishment is. I am guessing it's not serious as they gave me my card back immediately. But I still feel aggrieved because I was trying to do the right thing and was made to feel like a naughty little boy (you know, in a bad way).

I suspect if I commit this terrible crime again that I will get into trouble. But maybe I'll get back from Australia to find the place festooned with photographs of me, with "Do not admit" written across them. Or possibly there'll be a burning effigy of myself in the lobby and I will be chased out by librarians shouting "shush" (on the delicious irony). Or maybe an old woman will come to my desk next time I'm in and tut at me. Quite loudly. The worst punishment of all.

Friday 21st March

I have a very tiring few days ahead of me.

Tomorrow I am off to Gloucester to do *Talking Cock*, then on Sunday we have to drive to Heathrow to get a plane to Glasgow to do a gig at the Tron theatre. I will be getting up at 5am on Monday morning to catch the flight back to Heathrow and then will have two hours before my trip to Melbourne. It's another piece of organisational genius. Though my first gig in Melbourne isn't until Thursday, one has to take into account that it takes more than a day to travel and around about a week to get over the jet-lag (even without the early morning flight from Scotland). Essentially I am doing three consecutive gigs in three different countries (the first two of which are pretty close, but the last one being as far away as is humanly possible without booking me a gig in outer space).

I imagine my diary entries for the next few days will be largely unreadable gobbledegook. So no change there etc.

Anyway today was largely taking up with packing my suitcase. I was aware that I needed to be sure to have everything I would need for the next six weeks (though rarely taking into account that they do have shops in Melbourne). This is slightly more complicated than usual because I also have to bring everything I need to complete my book (which is due to be finished on the 24th April – dream on, Ebury Press! Haven't even got half way through chapter three yet).

I can't wait to arrive in Melbourne and discover what I have forgotten, nor indeed to look at some of the bizarre items I have deemed that I can't live with and think "Why the fuck did I bring this?" The suitcase is almost too heavy to lift, so I'll probably have to shed some items at the airport anyway. I have a feeling the plane might not be able to take off if any of the other passengers are inconsiderate enough to bring luggage.

I shouldn't complain. I am going to Australia. This is my job. I am surely the luckiest man in the world. But I have to go to Gloucester first. The dark and light in this world are always in balance.

Looking back on all this it is hard to work out when I would have got any time to see S, who lived a good hour-and-a-half's drive away from London, especially given that the tour meant I was rarely at home anyway. I think the truth is that we weren't seeing each other any more and on the rare occasions that we did we were behaving more like friends than boyfriend and girlfriend. After our recent troubles and our literal and emotional distance I am surprised that we didn't make the decision to break up before my trip to Australia. But I think we were both hopeful that we were just going through a phase and that things would improve. Or maybe we were just stumbling on in the dark and not really thinking properly about any of this. Having been to Australian festivals before I knew how many comedians' relationships and even marriages had fallen apart – you're away from home for over a month, the sun is shining, the beer is flowing and there are other illegal distractions if you care to partake of them. As an overseas visitor you are also treated with a degree of deference that as a middle of the bill comic you might not be used to in the UK. I remember when I was at the Adelaide festival in 1997, as we sat in the hotel jacuzzi, drinking beer in the sunshine, surrounded by attractive and easy-going Aussie women, we felt a bit like plumbers who

*had been mistaken for Hollywood superstars and didn't want to
risk ruining it all by telling anyone about the error.*

*S and I both knew there would be temptations and so
broken was our love that she even told me that she thought I
should give into them if I wanted and we'd pick up where we
left off when I got back. But things were not broken enough for
me to wish to cash in on this offer. I still hoped that we could
rekindle the romance and that everything would work out. But,
of course, I would have five weeks in paradise to mull over the
state of our union. I wonder if you can guess where things were
heading...*

Saturday 22nd March

I have been the victim of a rubbish and annoying crime for the
second time in four months.

We arrived in Gloucester with everything we need for the next
six weeks in a rented car (so that we can dump it at Heathrow
tomorrow when we fly to Glasgow). Gloucester seemed to have a
surprising air of menace, like many smaller towns where the youths
have nothing much to do. But also, of course, the ghost of Fred West
haunts the streets, which possibly adds to the awkward atmosphere
in my imagination, at least. Simon Streeting and me were reluctant
to lug our heavy suitcases into the hotel, so thought we'd risk leaving
them in the car in the hope that anyone strong enough to lift them,
would find paid employment as some kind of circus strong man.

I also had an empty bag which I planned to transfer some of my
stuff into, because my bag was almost too heavy to lift (I'd filled all
remaining space with programmes in the hope of taking a few over
to Oz). But seeing the kids aimlessly bashing a football around the
car park as we went to the hotel, I must admit I did worry that we
were making a mistake. Arriving in Australia with no clothes or
possessions would be annoying.

When Simon went to the gig, he parked the car in a backstreet
behind the Guild Hall. He was uneasy about doing this, but there
was nowhere else to park, so he hoped for the best.

We had a lovely gig and afterwards I chatted with several very friendly and pleasant Gloucester residents. They are not all like Fred and Rosemary West as I had (possibly unfairly) expected – though one of them did tell me that her dad was a policeman who had met Fred several times in the course of his job (for minor crimes before the extent of his work was revealed) and he'd said Fred was a lovely, friendly bloke. So I wasn't going to fall into the trap these smiling Gloucester fools were setting me. You can't trust them. You certainly wouldn't one of them moving in next to you. When it was time to go we carried the props back out to the car. We were relieved to see it was still there and our suitcases remained untouched (but visible through the window) in the boot. It was only when I moved round to the passenger door that I noticed the small back passenger window had been smashed. We looked again at our possessions in the boot and it seemed that nothing had been touched. It would have been such a nightmare if we had lost everything. So had the thief just been disturbed mid-theft?

Then I saw what had gone. It was my completely empty transfer bag. So some sneak thief had spotted it on the back seat, smashed the window, opened the door, grabbed it and run off, unaware of the suit cases in the back which contained quite a few saleable pieces of electrical equipment, DVDs, clothing and programmes about cocks[26]. Maybe they'd attempted to take them, but realised the bags were too heavy for a human to carry.

Instead they'd run off with the nice light piece of hand luggage. So light, of course, because it contained nothing but the air that was in any case in plentiful supply all around the criminal mastermind.

I had planned to just dump the bag in any case, if it hadn't turned out to be necessary to use (which was the case as we used up more programmes than expected at the gig tonight and would need the extra ones for Glasgow), so aside from the broken window the thief had done me a favour. Though like the blokes who got my bike, I suspect the thief just dumped his booty when he realised how rubbish it was! From my experience it seems that these criminals

---

[26] We were forced to dump nearly all of these at Heathrow as they took us over our baggage limit. I wondered at the time if anyone found them and wondered what the hell they were doing there

might make as much money if they just went round asking people if they had finished with stuff. And in that way they wouldn't cause the expense of repairing the damage caused by their heavy-handed crimes.

And though it was quite an exciting end to the evening (rather than the usual depressing anti-climax) I had to admit that it was hardly the worst crime that had ever been committed in this town. I doubt very much whether this was the work of a certain curly-headed, grinning-faced ghoul.

Sunday 23rd March

The Tron Theatre in Glasgow definitely wins the award for the best pre-gig meal of this tour so far. Yes it was even better than the egg mayonnaise (heavy on the mayonnaise) sandwiches in Swindon.

Genuinely the café attached to the theatre is brilliant. The lamb I had was one of the nicest bits of meat I have ever eaten (remember fifteen of my years fell to vegetarianism, so that's not as impressive at it could be). It was worth flying up to Scotland and having to get up at 5am tomorrow morning just to eat here.

I am a born-again meat eater I am both proud and ashamed to say, though my previous life means that when I eat an animal now, I at least appreciate the sacrifice it has given for me and I try to make sure I eat it all. Which was no problem with the lamb at the Tron. I could have eaten another two. Even though two more innocent lambs would have had to die.

So essentially I suppose I am recommending that you eat at the Tron and that if you are a vegetarian you give it up (at least for the one meal you have here!)

Sorry if I offend any of my previous vegetarian brethren, but it's a man-eat-lamb world out there.

(This entry written on no sleep at Kuala Lumpa airport with twelve hours to go before I make it to Melbourne).

That meal remains the single best pre-gig food I have ever
been provided with in my twenty-year career. If the Tron want

to put a plaque up to that effect then I am happy for them to
do so, though I have to say on my next visit the menu (and
probably the chef) had changed and, whilst still better than
most theatre catering, the meal was not a patch on that lamb. It
may have been the best meal of my life.

Monday 24th March

I spent most of today above the clouds. It fills me with wonder
and gratitude that I am able to write that sentence and mean it
literally.

Like most people, if I am flying somewhere alone I much prefer
to have no-one sitting next to me. Sitting next to a stranger on
a long haul flight means that you are in danger of getting into a
fifteen-hour conversation with someone who is boring or stupid or
insane and often all three. Of course you might be next to someone
interesting and intelligent and erudite, but then the chances are that
to someone like that, you yourself are boring or stupid or insane and
you'll be ruining their day.

All in all, it's best (though unlikely) that you get to sit alone.

The man next to me on the first leg of this unbelievable trip (well
second leg for me if you count the flight from Glasgow) initially did
not seem interested in conversation, but was more keen on drinking.
Which is fair enough. He was around about fifty and English and
seemed affable, sane and had good bodily hygiene, so things didn't
look too bad at all.

I took advantage of the fact that for once I was going to be sitting
in one place for twelve hours and did a bit of work on the book.

A few hours in though we fell into conversation. The man wasn't
boring or stupid or insane, but I think he must have been a little
drunk and was certainly a bit deaf. He had seen me writing, and so
I had to tell him I was a comedian. This is always something I do
reluctantly as it usually results in the other person saying, "Comedian,
hey? Tell us a joke then!" or "Really, I know this great joke……"

Unfortunately I don't know any jokes and I don't really like being
told jokes. Especially the kind of jokes that people who like to tell
jokes like to tell. They usually involve Irishmen or worse still "Pakis"

(which seems to be a word that you thankfully only hear these days in the form of rubbish jokes). Also there aren't that many jokes and so chances are you've heard what you're being told before.

This man chose to tell me a joke (and threatened to email me some more). It was the joke that ends "Because every time I fuck your wife, she gives me a biscuit." I suspect you know it. I certainly did. As jokes go it's reasonably funny (ie it's not totally unfunny), but it's annoying to have to sit and listen to something when you know what's coming, but are also aware that you are going to be expected to register surprise and hilarity when the other person finally stops saying the thing that you already know.

After I had registered surprise and hilarity, we had a chat. He is a retired engineer who now works on a freelance basis advising firms about engineering (mainly in Malaysia). Despite being told this, I didn't then say, "Engineer hey? Do some engineering for me then!" Nor did I say "Really, I did this great bit of engineering the other day and now I'm going to make you look at it, even though I am not a professional engineer and doubtless anything I can tell you about engineering you will have heard before, what with you being a professional engineer and all that." No, instead I said his job sounded quite interesting and it must be nice to get to travel the world.

Anyway, he'd seen me writing and when he found out I was going to the Melbourne Festival, he asked "So you've been writing some new jokes for your act." I explained that I was actually writing a book and that the show was a male answer to the *Vagina Monologues*, but he didn't seem to hear or want to listen. "Yeah, with everything going on in the world you must have to keep on writing new stuff and coming up with fresh angles on the war and so on." I explained that I was actually writing a book and that the show was a male answer to the *Vagina Monologues*, and so wasn't all that much influenced by war-based topicality. I thought he must have registered the facts this time. But wasn't sure.

He asked if I was based in Australia or the UK and I told him that I was from the UK. He asked where I lived and I said "London".

"Whereabouts?" he asked.

"I'm moving to Shepherd's Bush, but I live in Balham."

"What part?"

I was surprised Balham wasn't specific enough (it's too specific for most people) and figured he must know the area pretty well, so I said "Not far from Sistova Rd, sort of between Balham and Streatham."

And he said "Not quite kangaroo country then!"

I thought that was an odd thing to say. I'd expected him to reveal why he was so interested in knowing the exact location, presuming that he must have lived in Balham at some point. But instead, there was just this kangaroo country comment. I don't think anywhere in South London could really be classified as kangaroo country. Given that the nearest significantly large number of kangaroos is about 14,000 miles away. But I let it go.

As the conversation went on and he began telling me how much better my cricket team was than his and I realised that he had somehow got the impression that I was Australian. I don't know how, what with me not having an Australian accent and telling him I was English and all. So I presumed he hadn't been listening to me, or was a bit deaf. That would make sense of his "kangaroo country" comment. Maybe he thought I had said I lived in the Bush, not Shepherd's Bush. But you'd think all the specific London place and street names may have tipped him off.

I decided to let it go again. The conversation had gone on too long and it would be more hassle than it was worth to correct him. To be honest as long as he wasn't telling me jokes then I was happy.

He soon fell asleep, which was a relief (though he was an all right bloke aside from the not listening/deaf thing).

As we prepared to land I packed away my computer.

"So written any good gags for the show?" he asked.

I considered reminding him that I was writing a book, but couldn't be bothered.

"So you write most of your act on the plane over, then!" he stated.

It's obviously what he wanted to believe. He wanted to think that comedians are so laid back and cool that everything is thrown together at the last minute. He wanted to believe I was Australian. I don't think he was deaf, I think he just wanted to have his preconceptions confirmed. So I confirmed them.

"Yes that's right, we write most of it on the plane, mate."

And for the only time on the flight I spoke with an Australian accent.

Tuesday 25th March

Annoyingly after the flight from Glasgow to Heathrow and then Heathrow to Kuala Lumpur, the flight from Kuala Lumpur didn't go directly to Melbourne, but instead stopped over in Sydney. Which meant at around 8pm local time Melbourne passed some way to the right of our plane. I was tempted to knock on the door of the cockpit and ask the pilot if he couldn't just drop us off as he was passing and all. But I think that might have been considered a hijack situation.

Despite the fact that the plane would arrive at Melbourne in about three hours time, to ask for it to go there a bit early would be a criminal offence.

So there was an unwelcome further stop in the widely perceived as, though actually not, capital of Australia before just one more flight on this thirty-two-hour journey.

But by now it felt I had spent my entire adult life either on a plane or sitting in an airport. To actually arrive at my destination and be able to go to other places and meet other people was actually a bit frightening. I was like one of those lifers who gets so acclimatised to life in prison that they have to top themselves when they are finally released.

In my tiredness and confusion I managed to almost board the wrong flight to Melbourne, though unhelpfully the departure screens only listed one flight and so I had assumed that that must be mine. I had thought they had said to get back on at 10.30pm, but the screens had said 10.50pm and now realising my error I rushed from gate fifty-five to fifty-one, fairly sure that I would have missed my plane.

But luckily they had waited for me, though it was slightly embarrassing having to walk back in to all the rows of people who had been intelligent enough to get on the right plane at the right time.

But the woman sitting next to me (the non-listening man had

got off at Malaysia to advise people about engineering and then not listen to what they said back) who hadn't said a word between Kuala Lumpur and Sydney told me that a few people had been confused and that as I was a comedian (I don't know how she'd found out – maybe the flight attendants knew and had speculated that my late arrival was some kind of joke) I could keep them all entertained during the rest of the flight.

But she was joking herself, fortunately and we managed to have quite a long and interesting chat about the war. About half an hour in though, she decided to read her paper and the conversation ended and I realised that as she had been quite interesting, this time I must be the one who was boring and stupid and insane.

So I drank my complimentary champagne and speculated what my new life back on the ground would be like. I decided that although it would be hard to adjust back to those old days that I would give it a try.

Wednesday 26th March

Being back in Melbourne is both wonderful and disorientating. It is familiar yet strange. Best of all I didn't feel at all jetlagged after the best sleep I've had for months.

It so doesn't seem a year since I was here, which is such a cliché of getting older, but some places I would pass and think, I was there just the other day surely. Yet on the other hand I would get confused and lost for a while in a city that I lived in for a month, only this time last year.

I managed to locate the street that the supermarket was on and was ambling down it, feeling a bit hot in the somehow unexpected sunshine (though you'd think I would have remembered that it was quite hot here and left my leather jacket in the hotel), when suddenly I saw Dave Gorman. Now there are quite a few Dave Gormans in the world as this particular Dave Gorman has gone to great lengths to demonstrate, so I think I should point out that this Dave Gorman is the British comedian, perhaps best known for his show *Are you Dave Gorman?*

Initially I was very surprised to see Dave Gorman. Meeting

someone I knew in somewhere so far from home seemed an incredible coincidence and I was momentarily shocked (my insides jumped) at the impossibility of seeing a familiar face on the other side of the world.

But then I remembered that Dave Gorman is here because he's doing a show at the Melbourne Comedy Festival, so there wasn't really any need to be surprised.

After a pleasant chat with the bearded obsessive comedian (a sentence that applies from both perspectives, I hope) I concluded that maybe I was a little jetlagged after all.

Thursday 27th March

I had a couple of radio interviews to publicise the show. One of these was just before my first show, on PBSFM, Melbourne's second largest community radio station (though I feel that it is unlikely that there are more than two community radio stations in Melbourne).

The interviewer was a slightly eccentric and pleasantly camp fella called Hugo, who remembered interviewing me last year for my *Christ* show. He told a story (I think on air, but it was such a whirl that this may have been during a record and he didn't really change modes in between) about his male friend coming back from England recently having had the best sex of his life with a pommy with the biggest cock he'd ever seen. He added that this was no mean feat as the friend in question was an air steward. I felt this was a shocking generalisation to make about male air stewards. To imply they are all gay and promiscuous. Ridiculous. I am sure one of you will be able to email me and tell me about your heterosexual and/or monogamous air steward friend. But I won't hold my breath!

Like all the interviews in Oz (I think the radio is very good out here) we had a lot of fun. Hugo asked me if it was the kind of show that he could bring his mum too. After his air steward story I felt pretty sure that he would be fine to bring his mum!

The interview ended and I had to get back to the theatre to do my show. Pru, my publicist out here, was talking to someone on the radio station phone. Someone had clearly rung in wanting to talk to me. It seemed he was a fellow Englishman who supported

West Ham and wanted to know which team I barracked for (or supported). As we were in a rush she told him to ring back on her mobile, which I was a bit unsure about as he sounded a bit eccentric even from Pru's side of the conversation.

Sure enough five minutes later the phone rang and it was my new English friend, who still retained a cockney accent, but with a strong Aussie twang (which was quite a weird combo as the Australian accent is similar though not quite the same as the London one).

He told me how much he liked listening to community radio (which made me more convinced that he was mental, but possibly only because I associated the concept with care in the community radio) and told me personally he supported West Ham. Although I am not all that interested in sport, I made the required laddish retort of "Well someone has to!" and he made the required laddish noises of amusement and chastisement.

Then he said he had a proposal for me, which made me a bit worried about what was coming up. This, after all, was a stranger who had rung to talk to me after I had been talking about penises, seemingly only because, like him, I was English. But it's not like there aren't any English people in Australia.

He said that if I gave him free tickets to my show he would invite me round to his place for a slap-up roast beef dinner, which he felt would be something I was missing now I was away from home. I pointed out that it was only four days since I had been in England, so hadn't yet managed to get all that homesick. I don't know if he'd noticed but the food in this town is so amazing, that eating a traditional English dinner is one of the last things I wanted to do.

Plus of course this was a man I had never met, and my mum told me never to accept sweets from strangers (though she didn't mention what I should do if a stranger offered me meat). Although I think he was clearly very sincere (possibly a bit lonely, but maybe just nostalgic for his home) and the invitation was well-meant I had to turn him down. Just in case he was the Australian version of Jeffrey Dahmer. Though it's a nice idea to think that you could ring up anyone you've heard on the radio and invite them round for dinner. Might try it myself some time.

Friday 28th March

I got to do a face-to-face interview with the breakfast crew at Triple M radio. These were the guys who I had attempted to speak to from the dark streets of Balham last week. I have to say that the interview was a great deal more successful when I was in the same hemisphere as them. Being in the same room was an extra bonus.

The lady one on the team told me that kangaroos have corkscrew penises, but I was under the impression that the penis of the kangaroo was forked. Can anyone settle our argument? Please email to richardherring@richardherring.com[27]. Please mark your email 'I know the shape of a kangaroo's penis, but only through academic study. I am not unnaturally interested in marsupial genitalia and anyone who says that I am is lying.' If you know about the shape of a kangaroo's penis through unnatural interest then I do not wish to hear from you.

I met my second Python participant in as many months on the way into the interview. As I pulled up in my cab, Neil Innes was waiting outside and asked if the driver was free to take him. It seemed he was, so we swapped positions and I shook Mr Innes' hand and told him how nice it was to meet him. He looked confused and certainly didn't know who I was. So it seems I don't require alcohol to behave inappropriately in front of my comedy heroes.

Then again, I was pretty jetlagged still, so I can't be totally sure it was Neil Innes. Which explain the man's confusion.

> *A quick browse through Google suggests that most of the kangaroo species have birfurcated (forked) penises, but a couple of the larger ones have single tipped prehensile ones, which may or may not be corkscrew. To be honest I have done enough research into this subject to last a lifetime, so if you really want to know you're going to have to look it up for yourself.*

---

[27] *Don't bother. And my email now, should you wish to tell me how brilliant/ unnecessary this book is, herring1967@googlemail.com*

Saturday 29th March

My body clock is still seriously out of sync and I am spending my days in a bit of a blur of lethargy and confusion. I seem to remember the same sense of disorientation and depression from last year.

Similarly I am slightly worried about whether my show is going to get an audience. I am certainly getting more people in than last year, but the theatre is about four times bigger and I don't know how many people are paying for their tickets. It is too early to worry about it too much and I am hopeful that word of mouth will get round, but there are over 200 shows on in this festival and unlike Edinburgh they are all on in the evening, so there is a lot of competition. And of course no one really knows who I am out here (not that that many do in the UK either to be honest), though I was informed yesterday that a church venue who usually give a room for a festival performance have withdrawn that privilege this year, specifically because the Festival had booked my *Christ on a Bike* show in 2002. So it's good to see that the show had some kind of effect on Melbourne, even if it wasn't to actually get people off their arses and into the venue. In fact by making such a gesture the church in question has probably made more people aware of the show than actually came to it. But it's good to make a stand. I know Jesus would have approved of their action. It's not like he thought it was important to turn the other cheek or anything.

Surely as Christians they should not only have allowed the venue to be used, they should have given another room as a venue as well. As Jesus said, "If someone nicks your coat, fuck it, give them your trousers as well. That'll show them." Look it up, it's in there. Ian 14:2, I think.

I just hope that the genito-urinary department of the local hospital won't take similar action after this year's show.

The whole of this year's Melbourne Festival is a bit of a blur to me now, I must confess. I spent a lot of it unhappy about my disintegrating relationship and the poor attendance at my gigs (actually, as I admit, it would have been respectable if I hadn't been in such a massive venue, but not sure the city that spawned

Puppetry of the Penis *was ready for another cock-based show)*
and got drunk most nights and slept through most of the day,
so I doubt I will have much to add to the blog for a while.
In fact I am quite amazed that I managed to find something
to write about every single day. I do remember that on the
crucial opening night of the show, where I had a decent-sized
audience including journalists and other influential people,
Simon Streeting was stuck teching Dave Gorman's overrunning
first night and didn't arrive to set up the show until after the
supposed start time. I felt that as Dave was at fault and because
he was pretty much in control of the technical elements of his
own show that Simon should have had the common sense to
leave, but Simon, flustered and haughty said, "You can't expect
me to choose between Dave and you!" as if he was in the centre
of some love triangle. I argued that he had chosen between us
by electing to stay at the other show, but he felt he would have
disturbed the performance had he left.

Even once at my venue, Simon was too overwrought to get
his job done and because he was rushing ended up setting up
the projector incorrectly and nothing was working. Meanwhile
the audience were waiting impatiently outside and I found
myself in the unusual position of being a performer attempting
to calm down his techie before the first show. We went up a
good twenty to thirty minutes late. It would be unfair to blame
the subsequent poor attendance of the show on this incident,
but I am going to do it anyway. It was all Simon Streeting's
fault. The arrogant twot.

Sunday 30th March

Twelve hours sleep makes the world look a lot better.

After my show I bumped into excellent Aussie comic, Sarah
Kendall, who was talking to another girl I hadn't met before, who
was called Prudence (I think). Prudence was wearing both a thin,
feminine scarf and a chunky beaded necklace. Someone commented
that her neck was overdressed. Prudence replied that she had put on

the necklace to make day become night. I think she meant this in the sense of making a psychological distinction for herself between day and night. Putting on the necklace meant it was time to go out.

But I wondered aloud whether she believed that by putting on the necklace she actually caused the day to turn to night. And what a responsibility it must be to make sure she puts the necklace on every day at the right time. It's no wonder that occasionally in her haste she would end up wearing a scarf as well.

I think she was being arrogant if she really believed that. I think it is much more likely that day and night are due to the earth revolving around the Sun, but as long as she puts on the necklace at the correct time each night there is no way to prove that she is wrong.

Yes, sure I could steal the necklace and throw it in a big burning bin. But then what if by doing so I doomed Australia to perpetual day (and presumably the Northern Hemisphere to perpetual night, though I don't know if they run on the same system, possibly someone has to put on some special socks to turn the night into day there, so it might continue to run smoothly)?

I would be in trouble, that's what would happen. Everywhere I went there would be tired people pointing and saying, "There he is, the day/night necklace burning bloke. Yeah, I liked the daylight, but not twenty-four hours a fucking day. Thanks a lot for ridding us of the night, you chump. I am being sarcastic in my thanks."

It would be quite freaky if everyone said exactly that, but I think that they would all be so annoyed that they would probably send a card to everyone with that written on it and tell them all to say exactly that to me if they saw me. You know, just to rub in how stupid I'd been.

Yet this is how most religions started up. Someone noticed that when something happened, it caused some cosmic event and began to believe that if the first thing wasn't done, then the second wouldn't happen. In Ancient Egypt priests masturbated each morning in order to recreate the day. But that's one custom I'm happy to keep going, just in case.

Monday 31st March

I am always on the look out for new songs to sing to P. Anything to avoid *Old MacDonald* again. This morning I woke up early and watched a bit of telly.

On one channel there was an Australian man dressed up as an old woman singing a song I had forgotten about: *There was an old lady who swallowed a fly.*

I don't know how it had slipped my mind. It used to be one of my favourites and is an excellent number. Not only does it have slight variations in each verse (as well as that old standard, repetition of a list of all the verses – excellent), it is also a very witty song. It takes an illogical idea to its logical conclusion and is a telling satire of the fears and neuroses of human beings.

First comes the jeopardy, an old woman swallows a fly. Understandably she is concerned. It could result in her demise. Although she has already lived for longer than an average life span she is still afeared of death (though interestingly there is an implication in the song that the act was deliberate. "I don't know why she swallowed a fly," says the narrator.) Like so many of us, she seeks a short-term solution without considering its immediate and long-term consequences. She swallows a spider. Spiders, she has reasoned correctly, are the natural predators of flies. The spider will seek out the fly and eat it and her problems will be over.

Yet as soon as she has ingested the arachnid she realises she has a new problem. The spider is probably more hazardous to her health than the fly she initially ate. She now has a spider wandering around in her system. Sure he has just eaten, he is satiated for now. But there will come a point where he becomes hungry and has no choice but to eat her old lady insides. She could keep eating flies to dampen the spider's appetite, but such an action would surely make a mockery of her decision to swallow the spider to catch the fly in the first place. She would have to admit that swallowing the spider was a mistake. She is human. She hates to be wrong. In any case the spider could be pregnant (she forgot to check) and then her insides may become clogged with spider children and grandchildren and the flies required to feed them within a matter of days. Instead she chooses to rid herself of the problem in what some might consider a short-sighted fashion. She swallows a bird.

Birds of course, eat spiders (also worms, but that is not the concern of the old lady at this juncture, though if she has worms this could prove to be an additional and unexpected bonus). Even if the spider has spawned a hundred tiny spiders, then one small bird could soon make short work of the family. At last her intestines are free of creepy crawlies.

But in an elaborate satire of the arms programme, her problems have escalated. She now has a bird flying around inside her. Hitting her with its wings, nipping her with its beak, burrowing into her pancreas in a vain search for worms. She is in pain and though by now she may have noticed a pattern emerging, she has no option but to find a creature that will bring about the demise of the bird. She either has to swallow Colonel Sanders or a cat. She takes the more humane option, largely for fear of Colonel Sanders refusing to eat the bird before covering it in his secret blend of herbs and spices. She may be desperate, but not desperate enough to have KFC batter in her stomach.

Her choice of a cat is logical, but clearly insane. The cat does not like to be confined anywhere, but especially in places that are damp. A cat is also angered when bile and stomach acids are squirted in its delicate cat eyes. The cat eats the bird, but is now writhing around, biting and scratching, ripping the sensitive tissue of the foolish old woman. She knows her death is inevitable, but her survival instinct is too strong to let her go down without a fight. She swallows a dog.

Up to now her choices have been sound. It is once the dog has dispatched the cat that things start to go wrong. The old lady now has a living dog inside her (which itself presumably contains a living cat which contains a living bird which contains a living spider which contains a living fly). So, how does she choose to counteract the dog? She swallows a cow.

This seems like an odd choice to me. The old lady's logic has broken down. The dog and cow, whilst not particularly friendly, are not enemies. The cow is a herbivore and you should only really swallow one if you have previously swallowed a life-threatening quantity of grass. It is difficult to think of an animal that would be prepared to eat a living dog though. I can only think of a tiger, but

I believe the old woman considered this and realised that though a tiger may attack and eat a dog, it would also be as likely to attack and eat an old woman. He would swallow her long before she could swallow him. I think by this stage she's pretty much given up and thinks "What the fuck! May as well go out in a blaze of glory." I think she had another option that she missed. She should have realised that dogs really love to chase things. What she should have done is taken off her pants and bent over, had her anus clamped open and pointed it at a field of sheep. The dog would have been so desperate to worry the sheep he would have jumped out, with the cat and other creatures inside him and the old woman would have been saved (though possibly had severe anal injuries. Maybe Michael Barrymore could use this as a possible scenario in his defence. Sorry. But not so sorry that I have deleted what I have just written).

Instead, the old woman swallows a cow (I don't know how she swallowed a cow) and is astonished to find that she is still alive. Maybe she begins to think she is immortal or maybe she simply likes a challenge, but her last choice of animal shows that she is really not interested in solving her problems. Perhaps she has seen that there is no way out of her predicament. If she wanted to be rid of the cow she should certainly have swallowed something that ate meat. But instead she goes for a horse. Why has her logic let her down at this point? Is she just confused by a stomach full of animal, or is there a more sinister explanation?

It is only in over-analysing this child's song that I begin to wonder if this was her wish all along. As I've said she possibly swallowed the fly on purpose – we at least do not know why she did, which heavily implies it wasn't an accident. Maybe she knew all along where this would lead. She was an old woman, she was tired of life and frustrated by her frailties, yet she did not wish to commit blatant suicide aware that this would be upsetting for her family. So she chose this eccentric path, which would make her look a little crazy, but nonetheless would certainly kill her.

She died, of course. Of course. It was clear she'd die. Only a deliberate desire to end it all can explain this logical (and yet illogical) progression of events.

Though I had fully intended to stay true to my sweetheart while I was away, my resolve was beginning to crack. Talking over the situation with other people gave me a perspective on how badly things were going. Also S, with problems of her own, was not replying to my emails and our very occasional phone conversations were brief and terse. My lack of appreciation of S's emotional state meant that I took these snubs as a clear sign that our relationship was over. But I did my best to resist the temptations on offer anyway and can be proud that I managed to get through the first fortnight before I cracked.

Tuesday 1st April

I was flying back from Sydney where I'd been doing a TV interview to publicise the show. Australian internal flight security seems fairly lax, given the current world situation.

I had had an e-ticket (electronic ticket, though if I was a different kind of comedian I could spin this out into an hilarious routine about drugs. How you would laugh) bought for me by my promoters, which means that I just had to turn up at the boarding desk, present some ID and then I was given my boarding pass.

I had my passport so gave that to the lady at the desk and she looked at my picture and then looked at me and said, laughing, "It doesn't look anything like you."

She was right. The picture was taken in 1996 and showed a chubby faced, clean-shaven youngster with sad and nervous eyes (though this could just be the effects of wind) and strange, short hair. Seven years on I am slightly thinner and have a beard and the kind of long hair that would ideally be styled with Sham-gel. Look into my eyes and you see what appears to be the benign wisdom of advancing years, but which is in fact still the effects of wind.

I do look like a completely different person. She was right.

As she passed me my pass I commented on the passage of years, though in truth I look a hell of a lot better than I did back then. This is where men get lucky, improving with age (though I suppose conversely you could argue that women are lucky in that they get to look more attractive when they are young, and so get to be sexually attractive at a time when they actually have the energy to do something about it).

But what concerns me is that in such a case, where someone presents you with identification that doesn't really match the reality, is it the right thing to do to just laugh and then give them their boarding pass anyway? Shouldn't you at least ask for a second bit of ID?

Or had she looked into my eyes and seen the unmistakeable continuity?

Wednesday 2nd April

The best new thing I have noticed about Melbourne are the Boost juice bars. I am sure these aren't a new phenomenon, but I didn't really appreciate them last year.

Essentially they are just little take-away shops that make extremely delicious and healthy smoothies, but it is also quite a spectacle as you get to see a team of four or five people making the smoothies as you wait.

The shops are incredibly popular and so the bloke at the front has four food mixes which he whizzes into action like a man spinning plates. Behind him other young people prepare ingredients, load the ingredients and ice into a mixer jug, or wash up the spent jugs. When you consider all the people who go into making just one drink it is extremely good value at around five dollars (under two pounds).

It is hard for me to capture the mood and the colours (remember I am from Somerset and thus possibly overly impressed by such things) in a brief entry, but suffice to say the shops are well worth a visit and the smoothies themselves are just brilliant.

Someone please bring this to the UK. There may be less call for such cold drinks in our climate, but they'd still do really well. If only because I would be in there all the time, looking at the whizzing shakes.

> *These drinks became my pre-gig lifesavers, literally boosting my tired and hung-over body enabling me to get through the show, before I then subjected it to another alcoholic battering. I don't know how I got through the Sundays and bank holidays when the juice bar was not open.*

Thursday 3rd April

In my ongoing campaign to destroy innocence and beauty wherever it may flourish I took promising comic Francesca Martinez[28] to Melbourne casino. It wasn't her first time gambling. I had already taken her to the casino in Edinburgh last year. Now she was hooked, I just had to reel her in, get her addicted to this insane pastime so she will lose all her money and possessions. By eliminating the comedy competition I can guarantee myself a career in the laugh biz for life.

In Edinburgh, Francesca had been pretty lucky, but we lost $100 in about three minutes at roulette and blackjack. You have to remember that these are Australian dollars and thus largely worthless, but it was still a disappointing start. And I suddenly saw the flaw in my plan of comedy domination as we were only gambling with my money.

We played some more blackjack and lost another $100. The magic was gone, but then had some luck on roulette and scraped back most of our losses. As we were walking out Francesca said she had a good feeling about one of the blackjack tables. So we had another go and indeed had an impressive run and so I ended the night $150 up (enough to buy a can of coke in the UK or a small house on the outskirts of Melbourne).

So my good luck continues and we left the gaudy confines of Melbourne casino where the desperation and pain of the other gamblers hung palpably in the air. I felt like calling out to them "Don't you understand? You can't win! You can't! Just by being here you are confirming your status as a loser."

But the casino fell silent and the lights stopped flashing and they all looked at me as one as and chanted, "How can you say that? With your crisp new $150 in your pocket. If you can do it, so can we," and the casino burst into life again. The pokies (slot machines) sang out their tinny tunes, the cards flapped onto green baize, the roulette balls jumped and danced their furious dance around their wheels looking for somewhere to rest for just a second and the croupiers pushed the hundreds of dollars of losing chips down the hole in the table, where they fall directly into the bank vault of the laughing man who owns the Crown Casino.

---

[28] *Francesca appeared in TV's Grange Hill as a youngster, but continues to take the stand-up world by storm. She has cerebral palsy and successfully challenges and subverts audience's prejudices towards disability, in one spectacular routine, using her cheeky and flirtatious demeanor to persuade a young man to come up from the audience in order for her to cut their hair. I once saw her doing this to flouncy haired ponce, Lawrence Llewelyn Bowen, who tried to pretend he was OK about it all, but*

Friday 4th April

The shows in Melbourne have been going pretty well, though the Aussie audiences are much more reserved and easily shockable than I had imagined they would be. This is possibly because the crowds are still pretty small. I probably had about sixty in tonight, which would be OK if I wasn't in a 600-seater theatre.

I think the people who have seen it have enjoyed it and I've had three good reviews and lots of great preview press, but that isn't translating into bums on seats. Though to be honest it would be equally disappointing if I had to play to a theatre which was just full of disembodied bums on seats. I dread to think how they would show their appreciation. Also a bum on its own would have no sense of sight or hearing and so couldn't enjoy the show on any level. In fact a bum disembodied from the rest of the organs of the body would probably be unable to survive the sixty minutes of the show. I think I would be faced with a theatre full of 600 arses writhing around in agony. It would be horrible. Though as long as they'd paid, I wouldn't mind – though how would they pay?

Thinking about it, this is unlikely to ever happen and so probably isn't worth wasting too much time pondering over.

Despite the audience being a bit quiet and the lack of numbers I think I did a pretty good gig tonight. I really enjoyed it anyway and I am still finding new stuff in the material and new ways of doing things. It would be great if the numbers picked up over the course of the run, but I sort of think that things would have had to get better this weekend if that was going to happen. Last year I let the small audiences get me down, until the last week or so, when I managed to adapt and enjoy playing to twenty or thirty people. This year I am determined to have fun from the start, though I have to admit my head has started to drop on occasions in the last week.

I was talking to Dave Gorman last night (yes, again, the comedian one, not any of the other ones you may have seen) and he postulated that people might be being put off coming to the show, because without knowing me or my previous work you might imagine you're

---

was apparently apoplectic afterwards about having his locks lightly clipped. The gigantic cock. Do catch Francesca's act if you can. She's terrific.

going to be treated to an hour of just knob gags. He suggested that this wasn't helped by the fact that one of the publicity stunts for the show is having some men dressed as sperm, roaming the streets, handing out condoms with a *Talking Cock* sticker on each packet. Dave says that that would be the kind of thing that would make him decide not to see the show being advertised. He may well be right on that one.

At the end of the day I do have to remember that I am in Australia, having fun and making new friends and that this is my job.

And also that my job isn't to get dressed up as a sperm and hand out condoms to strangers.

Saturday 5th April

The deadline for the completion of my book has been extended until 1st June. This is a bit of a relief as I think I would have had trouble completing it in the next nineteen days, but it's bad news in some ways as I was gearing up to at least give it a try and now the lazy part of my brain (which is a significant majority. It is my belief that lazy brain cells never die) is thinking I can take it easy.

So although I was supposed to work today I mainly sat around playing backgammon on my Gameboy or reading the newspaper.

But because I knew I should be working I didn't feel I was able to go out and do something fun with other human beings. That would be to publicly acknowledge my laziness, so as long as I stayed in my hotel room and did nothing I was at least closer to getting some work done.

It feels wrong that I am on the other side of the world, in a country with wonderful weather and I am stuck inside failing to buckle down.

But the wastefulness has made me determined to not be so pathetic for the next couple of days. I am going to finish chapter three, which I've been (largely avoiding) working on for over a month, by the end of Monday. This will mean working hard but is by no means impossible. Then I can reward myself with a usefully spent day of sightseeing or socialising.

That's the theory anyway. I'll let you know how it goes.

Sunday 6th April

After a good show yesterday and a reasonable crowd of over 100, numbers dropped sharply again today and I let my disappointment affect my performance, which is deeply annoying to me. It still went OK, but I found the shocked responses of the audience a bit dispiriting and wasn't my usual jolly self, which makes for a different kind of show. I don't suppose anyone really noticed, but I was cross with myself afterwards.

In the bar across the road someone commented on the men dressed as sperm who are still patrolling the Melbourne streets, handing out condoms (even though this is nonsensical, the condom is the natural enemy of the sperm. If a sperm every gives you a condom I would treat it with suspicion. It is in the sperm's interest to give you a defective prophylactic.) They said that the sperm had teamed up with another troupe of leafleters who are publicising a show where actors dress in cartoonish suits that make them appear nude (made of see-through tight-like material with false genitals and breasts and stomachs attached). Apparently they were creating quite a spectacle and Japanese tourists were stopping to have their photos taken with the sperms and 'naked' people.

I commented in my post-show misery that it appeared that the sperm were creating more of a buzz than the show that they were supposed to be publicising and I could envisage a scenario where the sperm get snapped up by a big American producer to take their show to Broadway. "See how the sperm satirise the fragility of their own existence by handing out the very objects that will prevent them from reaching their goal. A goal which is almost an impossibility in any case given the sheer volume of sperm in an ejaculation. It is a telling metaphor for the counter-productivity of our own lives. Of the certainty of our own failure... Plus the suits are real funny."

Those sperm will end up advertising soft drinks and crisps and have their own cartoon adventure series and I will be left performing in cavernous theatres to a few dozen easily shockable Australians.

I am pleased for the sperm. They deserve it. Sperm get such a bad deal in our society, it's good to see a couple of them rising out of the sewers and making it big.

On a similar, but tangential point, I am reading about masturbation at the moment and it struck me that if God didn't want us to waste sperm, why did he make us produce so many in each ejaculation? Even if one is successful, around about 500 million more are wasted every time anyone spoufs up. Why didn't he make just one super-efficient gigantic sperm, about the size of a trout which was guaranteed to make it to the egg[29]? Plus it would give men some notion of the agony of child-birth. Maybe that's why God didn't do it, because he knew men would never participate in reproduction if it was likely to do them any physical harm.

Maybe the human sized sperm wowing the people on the streets of Melbourne at the moment are all part of God's plan to move towards that system.

Tuesday 8th April

I thankfully got my comedy mojo back tonight and did one of the best performances of the show yet. This cheered me up a lot.

It is pathetic how much a below-par gig can ruin your day, and that a good one can turn you into the king of the world. How insecure and childish comedians are!

I love Melbourne and when I'm sitting in a café drinking a latté and eating the most beautifully prepared focaccia you have ever seen (with a combined cost of about three pounds) I think that it might be good to live here.

But things are generally so perfect and there is so little to annoy one, that I wonder if I would ever come up with any comedy here at all.

I am finding it hard to think of anything to write about for this *Warming Up* section (which is partly because it's a festival and so the daylight hours are largely spent either asleep or in a hangover-induced blur). If I lived here all the time I would still only be able to write about the high quality and low cost of the food and service in

---

[29] *This notion is explored in my show* Someone Likes Yoghurt

this city. And about how friendly everyone is.

Which would soon become boring.

So I am looking forward to returning to damp and dingy London, with its expensive coffee and limp sandwiches, which are all the fuel I need to be amusing.

> *I may have blanked out a lot of this month in my mind, but I still really remember that focaccia. It was awesome. The food in that city is unbelievably good. Do visit if you get the chance.*

Wednesday 9th April

Been doing another round of radio interviews in a desperate attempt to drum up interest in the show. At the second one today I was greeted by the presenter in the waiting area. As we walked to the studio she asked me, "Do you want a glass of water?"

I said that would be good and she stopped by the water dispenser and filled a plastic cup. Assuming that when she offered me a glass of water she had intended to procure it for me, I reached forward to accept the drink, but noticed she was already apparently moving on without offering me the cup. She in turn noticed my outstretched hand and stopped in her tracks. There was a moment of awkwardness where neither of us budged an inch.

"Is that for me?" I asked.

"Yes," she replied unconvincingly, and gave me the glass.

We then walked in silence to the studio, where the last record was still playing. The atmosphere was a little strange. I was feeling embarrassed for assuming that the woman was being polite enough to pour me the water that she had offered me (or at least to let me pour my own before she pushed ahead and thought of herself). Presumably she was either feeling embarrassed by her faux-pas, or more likely I felt from her attitude, that I had been rude and presumptuous by expecting her to actually pour a glass of water after she had offered it. I wondered if perhaps I was reading too much into this. Maybe I had misunderstood the signals. But I still felt uncomfortable.

The woman then introduced me to a man in the studio, (but didn't say if he was a producer or a co-presenter) and then said, "I'm just popping to the bathroom."

The man and I sat in awkward silence. And he couldn't even know about the water incident that had caused all this bad blood. He'd just taken a dislike to me for no reason at all (unless this was a test that the woman always played on her guests. So him seeing me walking into the booth with the cup in my hand would be enough evidence to confirm my guilt).

After a minute or so of silence, the presenter walked back in. Tellingly she had a fresh cup of water in one hand. So unless she had just become thirsty in the last ninety seconds, (and I am not convinced that she had been gone long enough to both urinate and fill a new cup of water. I would say this was only possible if she had urinated into the cup, but the smell and colour of the liquid was not consistent with the presence of uric acid), this proved to me that she had fully intended to take the first glass of water for herself and that I – her guest, remember – had been expected to pour my own, AFTER she had selfishly got her greedy hands on her own cup of water.

Also she had shown she wasn't embarrassed, nor that the getting-her-own-water-first incident had been an absent-minded mistake. Anyone suffering guilt for the rebellion against all social niceties would have kept up the pretence that she didn't want any water, at least until I had left the building. Then she would have blushingly quenched her thirst saying, "I can't believe I offered him water, then just took a glass for myself. How rude am I?"

No, she was bringing in the other glass of water in order to say to me, "No, of course that water wasn't for you, how dare you presume such a thing? It is you, not I, that is the rudest person alive and have forced me to lie about needing the toilet, so that I can get the cup of water that I craved."

The strange atmosphere continued throughout the interview. I notice that her opening gambit to me included no actual question or conversation starter and I was forced to dig myself out of the hole she had dug for me. She didn't say it, but her face said, "Yes, my failure to ask a question is entirely due to the cup of water incident. Not so clever now, are you, cock boy."

I had no chance of recovering. The interview was strange and stilted. Also assuming it was a co-presented show I had sat in the wrong seat and was much too close to the moisture-coveting woman who hated me so much. To make matters worse this was most popular community radio station in Melbourne. This was the kind of mistake that would have gone unnoticed at the second most popular community radio station in Melbourne, but not the first most popular community radio station in Melbourne.

That night I had the smallest and quietest audience of the run so far. I fear that these two events are not unconnected.

So, as you have learned, my unpopularity in Melbourne is not due to me being shit, but to giant sperm men and selfish women who think they are too good to pour me water.

Thursday 10th April

As I was walking down the sunny Melbourne streets I saw three young women walking towards me. They were all wearing those T-shirts with outrageous/provocative phrases on them that are currently in vogue.

The girl on the left's T-shirt read, "Don't Tempt Me!" an instruction which I think I managed to comply with extremely effectively as she didn't even notice me. It was good to have given her what she wanted.

The second girl's slogan interested me more. It read, "I have an attitude!"

Two things struck me about this. Firstly, people who have an attitude don't need to advertise the fact on a T-shirt. If you have an attitude then you let that attitude speak for itself. If you have to given people a written indication of your attitude, then your attitude is not working properly. People who wear a T-shirt saying, "I have an attitude!" are actually saying "I would like to have an attitude, but I am not interesting enough to have one, so instead I've got a T-shirt."

Secondly, in a sense we've all got an attitude, haven't we? If you're shy or friendly or polite then that is still an attitude. Again, she might as well just have had a T-shirt saying, "I am a human being".

If she meant a bad attitude then she should have got a T-shirt saying that. Though again, if she had a bad attitude she wouldn't need to advertise it. The T-shirt should have read "I would like it if you thought I had a bad attitude, because that would make me appear interesting and exciting, rather than a slightly sad figure who is desperate for attention".

Maybe I could market a line of T-shirts for people like this woman simply reading "Idiot. Please avoid. Unless you are also an idiot. In which case, let's be friends."

Although there are so many kinds of idiot in the world that you might need to say "I am the kind of idiot who would wear a T-shirt saying 'I have an attitude!' If you are a similar idiot, or think that someone wearing that kind of T-shirt is cool and sassy (even though in reality they are clearly an idiot) then talk to me and we may become friends."

This might be a bit involved. I guess the "I have an attitude" T-shirt is already doing this job rather effectively.

Friday 11th April

I was talking about those logo T-shirts with some female comics tonight.

One of them had seen a girl wearing one that had an arrow pointing upwards and said, "My face is up here!" But the girl wearing this T-shirt had extremely small breasts, so the T-shirt took on a whole new dimension of desperation. It would have been better if she'd painted an arrow pointing downwards on her face and written, "My tits are down here."

It seems churlish to have a T-shirt castigating men for looking at breasts when it seems the whole raison d'etre of these T-shirts is to say "Look at my tits".

As if men need any encouragement do to that more than they do already.

Saturday 12th April

I went to an Aussie Rules Football match today.

It would be very easy to take the piss out of this game, in a "What's all that about?" kind of a way. Although any such observation would have to ignore the fact that any game which you are not familiar with seems bizarre compared to the ones you are familiar with. And that in fact most sports are pretty weird if you can stop and look at them with fresh eyes. But once you get the hang of the rules it is actually a pretty good sport.

The most impressive thing about the experience though was what a great time the crowd had. It was an entirely mixed audience with all generations happily attending and what seemed strange (but again with a bit of consideration actually makes the UK seem strange and fucked up) was that the fans of the opposing teams were not segregated. They sat alongside each other and though there was a little good-natured barracking, there was no trouble.

The Australians have realised that sport is essentially an entertainment. That if your side beats another, it gives you an opportunity to feel superior, but that in your heart you know that their victory is nothing to do with you and is not important enough to hurt anyone over. Perhaps in the UK we have so little in our lives that the fate of a game involving twenty-two men kicking a ball about is worth smashing someone's face in for. But in Melbourne they have things in perspective.

It was simply marvellous to see a sporting event where women and children made up a significant proportion of the crowd. The game was close until the last quarter. We all enjoyed it. Then one of the teams of men won (I was pleased because I preferred the colour of their jerkins). Some of the crowd cheered, others sort of screwed up their faces, tutted and said, "Ah well. Never mind."

Then we all walked out of the stadium in an orderly and trouble-free manner.

Maybe the autumn sunshine that we basked in as we left was enough for us all to know we didn't have to take the game seriously.

But the pitch was circular and it was a bit like rugby but different, what's that all about?

Sunday 13th April

Although Melbourne is great, it is not perfect. Like anywhere it has its fair share of strange men offering to sell you drugs (unless they actually are just offering to smack me), and alcohol-ravaged tramps (and after four straight days on the lash I fear I may be in danger of joining them by the end of the festival).

But even the tramps are friendly. One of them asked me if I wanted one of his beers when I was enjoying a burger outside a fast food restaurant. I declined.

Though homelessness is a tragic thing and a subject that one shouldn't be flippant about (so sorry that I am being) I would have thought Melbourne was at least a comparatively nice place to sleep outdoors in, if you have to be a tramp somewhere.

Yes, I know I'm being crass, but even so. At least it's warmish most of the time.

It set me to wondering whether living on the streets might be an option for everyone. Would it be possible to do it without the begging and drinking aspect? If you could keep the rest of your life exactly the same (ie keep your job and friends and everything), think of all the money you'd save in rent, council tax and bills. Your bank balance would soon start to look very healthy, with the minimal outgoings you would now shell out for. Obviously you wouldn't be able to have many possessions, but that would just save you even more money. I think we all have too many possessions anyway. We don't use half the stuff we've got.

You may think that you'd become scruffy and dirty and lose your job, but you would easily be able to afford to go to the gym every morning and wash there. If you were well organised you could also afford to have all your clothes dry-cleaned. You could pop in each morning and give them yesterday's clothes, and then pick up a complete fresh set each day. You could store quite a few different outfits at the shop and then just collect them when you needed them.

You'd easily be able to afford to eat out every night and could still socialise in pubs and clubs. With the money you had saved you could lavish drinks on everyone. A big spender like that would probably manage to pull every single night, which would mean you wouldn't even have to sleep on the street most of the time. If you were alone and the weather was really bad you could always book into a hotel.

With the money you saved you could also afford to go on expensive holidays and you could save even more money by sleeping rough on the streets of your holiday destination.

I may be ignoring the danger and the lack of sleep one might get in a cold shop doorway, but no system is perfect. And how much would it cost to buy a blow up lilo and some nice bed linen, which could be stored at low cost in a locker somewhere? Additionally it would still be relatively cheap to employ a security guard to watch over you while you slept for the requisite eight hours (probably about fifty pounds a night, still cheaper than most rents and if you put a hat down beside you as you slept you'd probably get given some money by passers-by anyway).

Yes, I think it would definitely work. I can think of no drawbacks. I will let you know if I decide to stay in Melbourne and give it a go.

Monday 14th April

Easter is a difficult time for a recovering chocolate addict. When I have given up chocolate in the past I have usually fallen off the wagon (and landed in my own equivalent of the river of chocolate in Willy Wonka's factory) when Easter eggs appear in the shops.

Although they are made of chocolate, which is available in shops all year round in many forms, there is something about Easter egg chocolate that is especially delicious. Perhaps it is just the comfort of memory of childhood (and I was very much one of those kids who ate all their Easter eggs within five minutes of receiving them, even though this made me sick. I hated the bastards who only ate a bit each day) or perhaps the evil chocolate factory owners add some kind of drug to the chocolate they use in the eggs (as if chocolate isn't a dangerous enough drug on its own).

Whatever it is, the eggs in Australia are not as appealing. They do have Cadburys and Mars chocolate here, but go for more fancy chocolate for their Easter eggs generally.

Somehow that doesn't do it for me, so maybe that childhood

association is the key.

But although I still get a pornographic pleasure (or whatever the equivalent is for stomach-related rather than sexual appetites) from discussing my life-destroying relationship with chocolate (and have just this minute made myself smile with specific memories of the special and distinctive sound that an Easter egg makes when you crack it), my days of dependency are over. I have been clean (ie not have chocolate smeared all over my chin) for almost sixteen months now, and when I was offered inferior Australian eggs at a party last night, I only had the slightest of pangs of regret and longing.

Part of me wonders if I can ever go back to just enjoying chocolate on a social basis, but in my heart I know that like any addict, just one Cadbury's mini egg could send me reeling back into a habit that cost me upwards of one pound twenty a day.

My name's Richard and I'm a chocaholic.

Tuesday 15th April

By the third week of a comedy festival your brain becomes a fried quagmire of fused nerve endings. It's not just the alcohol that does this to you (I was fairly restrained in my alcohol consumption last Edinburgh and it still happened), but the whole experience is emotionally and physically exhausting. A festival starts to take on its own reality and returning to the outside world is a bumpy and disorientating experience.

So many times I've gone to a festival thinking I would be able to work during the day, and every time I have managed to do a small amount in the first week, followed by an hour looking at a blank piece of paper in the second, followed by a third week which involves waking up fifteen minutes before your gig and then standing in a dark room, shouting at someone you don't know very well, being unable to hear what they are saying (no, it's not in a bar. Just a strange room that they have at festivals.... which is run by strangers..... who don't talk very loud).

That I have managed to keep this *Warming Up* section updated is a minor triumph in itself (so let's not discuss the quality of recent entries).

To call it warming up at the moment is somewhat of a misnomer. By the time I am done I have to go back to bed for two hours.

Burning Out would be a better name.

Somehow, magically the book will get itself finished by 1st June. Thank God for those little elves who work at my computer at night in return for an acorn cup full of beer (the idiots. Don't they realise how little that costs me? Though getting the acorn cup presented some logistical difficulties).

I nearly built up some enthusiasm for work today, but when I got back to my room *The Simpsons* was on and it was the Stonecutters episode ("Who Made Steve Guttenburg a star?"... worth having another look for the faux-modest reaction of Guttenburg to what is in fact a clear insult to his abilities), so I watched that instead.

Remove the stone of shame. Attach the stone of triumph.

Wednesday 16th April

What I like about *Talking Cock* is that instead of hecklers, I tend to get people asking questions in the middle of the show.

Tonight, after I'd listed the places where men had put their penises for fun and was about to deliver the punch-line to my favourite joke in the show (the one about the abyss. It often doesn't get a laugh at all, but I think it's brilliant. When I wrote it I was so proud, I had to run downstairs to tell my director[30]), a woman chipped in, in a crisp voice, "Did anyone say they had put it in the ground?"

Slightly annoyed at having had my favourite joke spoilt I answered that I didn't think they had, but was sure that that had happened. As Lenny Bruce said, "Men will fuck mud".

She then started asking about moss and ferns or something. I am always conscious that the show is a bit too long, so don't want to get into digressions or I'll bugger things up for the start of the next show. So I moved swiftly on.

---

[30] *After listing two dozen bizarre objects that men have tried to couple with I said, "I could go on for hours. There are thousands more and they're worse than the ones I have told you, but I will spare you the terrible details of what I have had to endure on your behalf. I have stared into the abyss... knowing that someone, somewhere has definitely tried to put his cock into it."*

But in hindsight I wish I'd asked her why she was so interested. It was clear from the piece in the show that men will put their penis into anything that could possibly accommodate it (as well as in many things that couldn't possibly accommodate it). So why was she so obsessed with men wanting to make love to the moss covered earth?

And why did she feel the need to share the question with the group?

It's good that the show makes people curious, and that they can't keep their questions to themselves. But sometimes you have to wonder what's going on in their heads.

My favourite audience comment of this run was from a woman who suggested that the man who had sex with a hollowed out cucumber was doing it for vegetarian reasons.

Again that raises more questions than it answers. I'll leave you to work them out for yourself.

Thursday 17th April

With only three more shows to go after tonight I think I have to accept that *Talking Cock* is not going to take off and fly at the Melbourne Festival.

I had just over fifty people in tonight and they were the quietest audience I think the show has ever had (at least Elton John interrupted the pre-Christmas performance by loudly talking to the person next to him).

With six hangovers catching up with me, I could feel myself squinting under the bright theatre lights. I put as much into it as I could, but it's very difficult to remain enthusiastic when the audience don't give you anything back.

One woman laughed very hard at the joke about the man bleeding onto his girlfriend's sheets and I asked if that had happened to her. "No," said her friend, "she's just bought $600 sheets."

So she was just laughing at how annoying that would be if it happened to her. Even me pointing this out didn't make the rest of the audience laugh.

The professional inside me wants to do the best show that I can. After all, I might have had an audience of fifty mutes who are really enjoying the show, but cannot outwardly express it. But the temptation is to put your head down and rattle through it. I found myself cutting a few gags that I guessed these people wouldn't like.

But it's important to remember once again that it isn't the audience's fault. It's the other few million inhabitants of Melbourne that I should be berating, if anyone. I only needed 550 more of them. Was that too much to ask?

I decided that maybe I should have an early night for the first time in a week and I slept like a baby with a massive hangover.

Friday 18th April

I was woken up at around 8am by the sound of a car alarm going off in the street below.

Strangely it was exactly the same type of car alarm that often goes off outside my house in Balham.

I was still half asleep and for several seconds I was extremely confused and couldn't work out where I was. I felt like I was at home, but something wasn't right. This wasn't my bed. This wasn't my bedroom. But I couldn't remember where I was.

I don't think this sensation is something I have experienced since I was a child. It was very disorientating and I couldn't claim that alcohol was responsible as I hadn't had any the night before.

Then it came back to me. I was in Melbourne. But I was actually really happy to have had the chance to go though that confusion again.

It reminded me of waking up at my grandmother's house at some unspecified point in my early life. It was only a shadow of a memory, a fragment of a shared emotion, but I smiled to myself and went back to sleep.

Nostalgic for the past, nostalgic for home.

Saturday 19th April

Finally got a chance to see Dave Gorman's new *Googlewhack Adventure* show as he did an extra performance this afternoon. As usual it is a consistently interesting tale of obsession bordering on insanity (and then often stepping over that border and revelling in its own madness). He's doing it in Edinburgh, so make sure you book early because its bound to sell out.

More than anything it made me consider again how much of my life I waste. Especially given that I had had to peel myself out of bed at five o'clock in the afternoon to get to the Town Hall in time. (Maybe I should have given up alcohol, not chocolate. I think that will have to come next!)

Not that Gorman's adventure is a massively constructive use of his time. It is, as he admits, just an extremely elaborate displacement exercise to get him out of having to write his novel.

But it does make one realise how easy it is to get out and see the world. How instead of sitting round the flat in your pants, you can jump on a plane to China, have a chop suey in Beijing and then head home again.

I don't even really have the constraints of a proper job to stop me doing that at almost any point. The world is my oyster. No, actually, I think it's better than that. To compare the world to an oyster (even one that is owned by me) is to undersell it a little, I think. If you had an oyster, what would you do with it anyway? Prise it open, see if there's a pearl in it? Find out there wasn't? Maybe eat the oyster and then wish you hadn't really bothered because it just tastes of seawater? Keep the shell and use it as an ashtray? Maybe try and buy another oyster and set up an oyster farm that breeds oysters which are then eaten by disappointed people, some of whom pretend to like eating them to justify the expense and make themselves appear interesting? How interesting do they imagine it makes them? How boring must they be to be so desperate for that extra slight degree of interestingness that they will eat an oyster without pulling a disgusted face?

The world is clearly much better than an oyster, not least because the world already contains all the oysters (that we know about) and loads of other stuff. You could exhaust maybe two minutes doing all the things you could possibly think of doing with an oyster and then move on to some of the other great stuff that is available: mussels, cockles, limpets.

Then maybe even away from shell-based life forms all together.

You could go bungee jumping.

That's just one example.

When we die one of three things will happen:

a) Nothing. We will be dead.

b) The Gods of CNPS will take great delight in taking us back through our lives, pointing out how close we came to an 88 in the four days it took us to spot one.

c) We will be made to account for our wasted time and shown what we could have won if we'd made the effort to make the most of this precious gift of life.

It's probably a) I think, but in the seconds as a) rapidly approaches, it would be a shame to do a quick mental version of c) and think "Oh!".

At the end of the day I don't think it makes much difference if you spend your time looking for Googlewhacks or helping the poor children. The only real insult you can give, having received this unrequested, but nonetheless pretty impressive gift of life, is to do nothing.

You'll have plenty of time to do nothing when you're dead. In this brief window of mortality, let us resolve to do something.

And don't waste any of that time on oysters. I did and I already regret it.

Sunday 20th April

I don't know what it is about final festival performances that brings out the eccentrics. In Edinburgh last year, there was a bloke in my last show who started saying "Yes!" loudly after anything I said that was remotely like a question (and a few things that weren't). I put him down quite well and asked him to stop, but it became apparent he was drunk and had no intention of stopping. So I said I couldn't be bothered with him, offered him his money back and asked him to leave. Thankfully he went (without taking his money) shouting, "You're bollocks" as he left. I replied, "No, that's next year's show."

Tonight in Melbourne a fittingly small crowd watched a slightly flat show. There was some early disapproval from women (which is unusual) and the "Lazy Lesbians" line got some tuts. As happened at my first gig at the Battersea Arts Centre this year, there was some consternation when I implied that women were to blame for men's feelings towards their genitalia. "It can't be men's fault," I teased (most audience's recognise that I am taking the piss), "so whose fault is it?"

"It's men's fault," said a female voice.

"No, I've said it isn't men's fault. So whose fault is it?"

"It's the fault of males."

It was the last show. I thought I'd run with it and see where it took me.

"That's the same thing as men," I countered.

"Males isn't the same as men," the unfunny conversation continued.

"Well it is." I said.

"But not all males are gentlemen."

I could see we were heading into a comedic dead-end and no-one was laughing. I told the woman that maybe I would be subverting my statement in a couple of seconds, that perhaps I didn't believe what I was saying.

I was maybe a bit aggressive (no I definitely was) and I could feel the experience inexplicably getting to me. I felt hot and my voice raised a few tones. I pressed on and got through another difficult show (though some bits went better than they ever have here).

It was with some relief that I ended my season here. I would hate you to think that I have had a bad time, because much of it has been great. Most of the shows went really well, but being the person I am I enjoy writing about the bad ones more. The people who saw it mostly seemed to like it. It was a shame that more people didn't come, but as one of the women from the Festival pointed out tonight, had I not been in such a massive venue I would have actually sold pretty well and would have come away feeling I had been a success.

And it certainly doesn't feel like a failure. At least I've learnt that being a man isn't the same as being a male.

Monday 21st April

Luckily I have a week and a half before I have to go home. I am going to have to use the time to catch up on the work I have failed to do on the book, but it is good to have some time in this wonderful country outside the excesses of the Festival.

I got up typically late today and headed to St Kilda for a 5pm breakfast, lunch or dinner, depending on your perspective.

I had forgotten how close to the sea I have been all this time. Watching the sun go down over the ocean is like nature's Prozac. I have spent so much time indoors it has been easy to forget that I am on the other side of world to my home.

It's going to be good to be awake during daylight hours and enjoy the wonders of this remarkable city again, without having to talk to 100 strangers about cocks.

But if I want to talk to 100 strangers about cocks I can still do it, though I may be arrested.

Tuesday 22nd April

I am writing my chapter on masturbation at the moment. This is my job.

I asked on the website whether men were ever discouraged from masturbating and if so, how. One man said his mother told him that every time he had one off the wrist it made Jesus cry.

Poor old Jesus. If that's true, he must be constantly in floods of tears. He's got to be the most miserable bugger in the Universe. At any one moment there has got to be several million men shaking hands with the unemployed. It must be unrelenting.

You'd think Jesus would become immune to it. Surely he would reach a point where he thought, "Well all this crying isn't doing anyone any good and it doesn't seem to making any difference. Maybe I should just accept that all this wanking is going on and isn't doing any real harm to anyone. Then I could choose something important to get upset about. Like the starving babies in Africa."

Turn the other cheek, Jesus. Let he who is without sin and all that.

Wednesday 23rd April

I went for lunch at the Botanical Gardens. Even the pigeons are classy in Australia. There was one strutting around by my table, shining with health, glistening purple plummage around his neck. It's not like this in Trafalgar Square!

A small toddler of just over a year old was on the next table. He threw the pigeon a tiny piece of red pepper. The pigeon went over to it, sniffed it (if birds can sniff) and then turned up its beak and walked away (these Aussie pigeons are classy I'm telling you).

The little boy was disappointed that the pigeon hadn't accepted his gift and rather sweetly thought that the bird hadn't seen where the vegetable had landed. Unable to speak to express himself the child helpfully pointed. The pigeon, feeling that his intelligence and class was being underestimated, pranced off to look for food that hadn't been dropped on the floor.

Thursday 24th April

When I came to Australia my producers sorted out my visa. As I had requested it to last to the 4th May (and as it was an electronic visa and thus there was nothing in my passport) I had assumed that this was the case.

Today I got a phone call from Emma, one of my producers saying that the visa had only run to the end of the festival and that I would need to go and apply for a visitor's one.

This had happened last year too, so I wasn't unduly concerned, but I had known in advance last time and had got the new visa whilst my old one was still valid. Emma didn't seem to be quite sure when the working visa ran out or if it had done already. We joked uneasily about me being kicked out of the country. Our laughter was forced.

I had a three-hour wait in the relevant department as I waited for my number to come up. Ross Noble was also there. His effortless Geordie humour helped pass the time.

Eventually I got to go to desk eighteen. The woman there greeted me in a friendly fashion. Even the bureaucrats are better in this country! I explained the situation and she called up my details on screen.

She then did something that I hadn't expected of a civil servant. She sang that small descending refrain of music that you get in horror films when something bad has happened – "Duh duh duhhhhh!"

That would immediately make you think that something bad had happened, but not something so serious that you have to worry too much.

She said, "Your visa ran out yesterday."

In the interim I had been back to my hotel and found a piece of paper that had told me this, so I said, "I know, but no-one had told me this until today."

She said, "I can't give you a visa, unless you have extreme circumstances that stopped you from getting one before yesterday."

My heart leapt into my throat. Was I about to be sent home? Her cheery demeanour suggested not, but then she was Australian, maybe they are cheerful even when breaking bad news.

I said, "Well I only found out about it today."

"That isn't enough," she replied, "You are expected to know the dates of your own visa."

I was waiting for the, "But it's OK, because you can do this...." that her attitude suggested would soon follow. But it wasn't looking good.

Eventually she asked when my flight was and said that if I went to the fifteenth floor I might be able to get an extension to those dates. Still anxious, I asked whether that was likely. She seemed to think it was and told me not to worry, that I wasn't going to get thrown in gaol in anything. I wasn't really worried about that. I was going to be sent somewhere much worse. Balham.

That would have been such an anticlimax.

I went upstairs, was seen to immediately and was given a paper visa extension within ten minutes. If I had got a visitor's visa, it would have cost me $160. I was expecting some kind of similar remuneration and possibly a fine. But the man handed over my visa, told me I had to inform him if I stayed anywhere else other than my hotel and wished me good day. "Is that it?" I tentatively enquired, almost adding, "Don't I have to pay you something?"

He said that was all that was required.

I went back to my hotel, realising that over-staying on my working visa had actually saved me around about fifty quid and in fact had I realised in advance that I just had to go up to the fifteenth floor I would have been in and out of the place in fifteen minutes, rather than the three hours or so the whole thing took.

Who said crime doesn't pay?

Friday 25th April

I went out for dinner with the comedian Lee Mack.

As we arrived in the restaurant the waitress said to me, "You've been here before."

She was right. I'd been a couple of times. The last occasion was a couple of weeks ago with the comedian Dan Antopolski.

Then the waitress added, "Mr Pork Bellies."

Again she was right, both Dan and me had eaten pork bellies on the last visit. But of course to anyone listening to that conversation you would think she was commenting on my (sadly increasing) gut or on my gluttony. She realised what it sounded like and immediately tried to cover "I don't mean anything personal. That's what you ate." But by now I was holding my stomach sadly and Lee was laughing. She tried to flannel her way out of it, but it just seemed worse. Luckily I found it amusing, but even so it was quite embarrassing.

Of course, she was trying to be nice, and showing off that she remembered both me and what I had ordered. But by adding the epithet Mister, she had immediately changed the meaning. If anything it sounded like I was memorable to her because I was always in there, stuffing my face with pork bellies. To achieve a nickname like "Mr Pork Bellies" one would have to imagine that I came in one night and ordered pork bellies, then ate it, then ordered another pork bellies, which I devoured before asking for three more pork bellies. Possibly ending in some kind of real life version of the Monty Python sketch where Terry Jones's guts explode.

You'd remember me then wouldn't you? Everyone in the kitchen would be saying, "Hey remember that pork bellies bloke who ate all the pork bellies and who also had a belly a bit like a pig might have? Let's think of a nickname for him. How about Mr Pork Bellies?"Then for the next fortnight it would be a running joke in the restaurant. Gluttonous customers would be compared to the disgusting Mr Pork Bellies, and come off favourably. Someone would put a pig carcass down the front of their apron and say "Who's this?" and everyone would shout out "Mr Pork Bellies!" and laugh until they wept.

Then one day Mr Pork Bellies would return to the restaurant, with a different friend who knew nothing of his Pork Belly fetish and the waitress would remember him and before she could stop herself she would blurt out the secret, satirical nickname and ruin another friendship.

That at least is what I'm sure Lee Mack was thinking.

The fact is I had only eaten one pork belly (and so had Dan Antopolski, but did he get an unfair nickname? Oh no) and on my previous visit I had steak (But she didn't chose to call me "Mr Rare Sirloin With Mustard Mash", did she? No because that wouldn't make me sound like a gluttonous pig). Yet here I am marked for life as Mr Pork Bellies or Porky B to some of the younger chefs.

I ordered the duck.

Saturday 26th April

I went out tonight with a few stragglers who are still in town after the comedy festival. We were having a drink in a club at a table near the toilets.

It was quite dark there and there was an unexpected step down and it was amusing me greatly to observe all the people who didn't spot the step and then staggered. The look of surprise on their faces was good, but better was their attempts to regain dignity after their childish error. I think it was probably especially funny when it was a woman, partly because they were all dressed up in their Saturday night finery and there's something hilarious about a sophisticated-looking woman nearly falling on her arse and partly because they had clearly just finished preening themselves in the ladies and were making their big entrance to the club.

Anyway you probably had to be there, but it was very amusing, especially when I realised how many idiots made the same simple mistake.

After a while I tired of the game and chatted away drunkenly to the other comics. Eventually I had drunk enough liquid to require me to empty my bladder. I find this easiest to do by going to a toilet and urinating through my penis, so I excused myself and carried out my plan.

On the way back to the table I had forgotten about that extra step and it caught me by surprise and I stumbled on it. "Oh no," I thought, "I have done the very thing that I have been laughing at others for. What if the other comics have seen? They will laugh at me for my double stupidity."

I thought all that as I stumbled.

I regained my composure and found myself doing exactly the same kind of pathetic attempt to regain my composure that had made me laugh when others did it.

Luckily no one else had seen me, although I wish I could have had the incident on film, because my expression as the realisation of my own stupidity must have been hilarious.

Sunday 27th April

On the wall of the bar we were drinking in tonight there was a picture from the 40s or 50s of a topless woman, wearing a ship on her head. She held her arms out triumphantly and showily, and though initially my eyes were drawn to her pleasant 1940s bosom and I pondered on the sad effects of the passing of time in a manner that was reminiscent of Keats (though I'm not sure he ever pondered, "Sad isn't it? Imagine what her tits look like today," but that in essence is all he was on about), it wasn't long before I became distracted by the ship.

Now I don't want you to get the wrong image, it wasn't a real full-size ship, it was just a model of one. In essence it was a hat. But the hat was shaped like a ship, complete with rigging.

Of course the obvious thing to wonder is what was the occasion that saw that particular outfit being worn? It's not often that a lady forgets to put a top on, but remembers to put on a ship. But if, as one would assume the picture came from some kind of vaudeville stage-show, that would explain the bare bosoms, but what was the significance or point of putting a ship on the lady's head?

I could only conclude that to whoever it was who put the show or photo-shoot together, found the idea of a woman having a ship (and it was a nice ship) on her head, sexually arousing.

Now I don't find that arousing myself – I liked the bit with the naked breasts. I could see what they were getting at there – but the ship just didn't do it for me. It confused me. I would have been looking at the pretty lady, but then become distracted by the ship and it would have put me off.

However, I started to imagine what it would be like if I could only get sexually aroused by a woman wearing ship on her head. I figured that that woman from the 1940s was probably the only woman who would be prepared to do something so strange and perverse. That's a long way to go, to put a ship on your head. Something would have to be dead inside you to allow someone else to degrade you in such a peculiar way. Even if the woman was still alive she would be too old by now (not that I'm saying ninety-year-old women aren't sexually attractive. I'm not a body fascist like you. I'm saying that a woman of ninety simply wouldn't be able to support the weight of a ship – even one fashioned from balsa – without snapping her old woman neck).

Imagine how difficult it would be to ever fulfil your dream of having sex with a woman with a ship on her head, if that was all that could get you going.

You'd have to date a girl, try and win her trust, yet avoid going to bed with her, as you would be useless without the ship. Then finally you might get her back for coffee and turn the lights down low and start kissing. Before you got to the crucial moment you'd have to say, "There's just one thing. Would you mind wearing a hat while we're in bed??

"A hat?" she'd say.

"Yeah, just for a bit of fun. I'd like it if you wore a hat."

She would probably laugh a little nervously, but be happy to go along with it. You've won her trust and it's just a hat.

But then you'd get the hat out and she'd say, "But that's a ship."

"No, it's a hat in the shape of a ship.

"It's still a ship. I thought you meant a beret or something."

"Yes, it's a lovely ship though isn't it? Look at the rigging and the mast. You'd look so lovely with that on your head... oh and with no top on."

There isn't a woman in the world who wouldn't turn on her heels and flee. Not for the first sexual experience. Probably not ever, not even if she'd done every filthy thing you can imagine. The ship-hat would be a hat too far.

But if that was all that could arouse you, then it would have to be the first sexual experience. It would be ship-hat or nothing.

Even a prostitute would baulk at doing something so strange. It would just be too disgusting. There are some things money just can't buy. And topless ship-hatted women is one of the things.

It would be a lonely life for you if you were a man afflicted with that peccadillo. Unless you had been lucky enough to have met that one ship-hat whore from the 1940s. Who was not only prepared to do it, but hold out her arms and smile. Like she loved wearing the ship-hat. Think how happy the ship-hat-loving, yet otherwise impotent, photographer must have been. It's a wonder he could keep the camera steady.

And imagine being a topless ship-hat-loving, yet otherwise impotent, man who has wished all his life to meet a topless ship-hat woman, who happens to chance upon this bar in Melbourne (so many miles away from his home) which has an ancient photo of such a creature. How momentarily he would be pleased, and probably aroused, but how as the seconds passed he realised that the ship-hat woman would be dead, or too old to support a ship-hat (and he's not prepared to force it onto her head and risk breaking her neck. He's not sick) and is in any case probably untraceable.

How his momentary arousal would fade, how his torment would double, how the ship-hat back in his flat would continue to gather dust.

That man isn't me though. I just imagined what it might be like. It's the kind of thing anyone would imagine if they'd seen that photo.

And the ship-hat in my flat is from an old *Fist of Fun* sketch. Oh no, you won't have seen it. It got cut from the final shows. I just kept it as a souvenir. You can come round and try it on if you like. If you're a topless woman. Just for fun. There's nothing funny about it.

Monday 28th April

Every day as I walk out of my hotel I pass a Chinese restaurant (well I pass quite a few as my hotel is in China Town), which has fish tanks in the window.

One of these is home to ten or more lobsters. They are pretty crammed in anyway, but accentuate this problem by pretty much all crushing themselves into the right-hand corner of the tank. It is a somewhat tragic, rather than appetising, display.

Every day I wonder if the lobsters at the bottom of the pile are still alive. It's hard to tell, as living lobsters are essentially just skeletons anyway.

After living here for over a month I see those lobsters as kind of friends, though I have no idea of the turnover of lobster in the restaurant and am aware that it may be a totally different bunch than the ones that were there when I arrived – a couple of them must have remained unchosen even in that time, probably the ones at the bottom of the pile who look like they've been dead for two months. No one would choose those.

And I have to say the sight of those friends imprisoned in a tiny tank makes me a bit sad.

Which is stupidly hypocritical as a) I like eating lobster, it is delicious and

b) I have no problem with eating the dead carcasses of other animals, which are kept out of sight in fridges at the back of the restaurant.

But every day as I pass the lobsters seem to be shouting out to me "Kill me! Please! I am in such lobster Hell! Let me die!"

And that might be one solution. I could go into the restaurant and order ten lobsters. This would have the dual result of releasing my friends from their purgatory and me getting to eat lots of delicious (and oh so fresh) lobster.

Of course, in a sense this would merely lead to the restaurant buying more lobsters. Lobsters that would be kept in the confines of that tank (that doubles as a kind of perverse abattoir-zoo), lobsters that I would have to eat to free, which would make space for more lobsters. It's a vicious circle, though one whose viciousness is slightly lessened by how much delicious lobster I would get to eat.

Alternatively I could creep over there under the cover of night and smash the restaurant window and break open the tank and let those lobsters out to roam free in the streets of Melbourne.

Yes, they may all probably be soon captured, or run over, or eaten by passers-by. But if just one of those lobsters made it back to the sea it would make it all worthwhile.

Alternatively I could probably just buy the lobsters and take them back to the sea myself. But where's the fun (and lobster jeopardy) in that?

Tuesday 29th April

As you know no-one could accuse me of being obsessed with number plates, but I noticed today that many Aussie car number plates have inspirational messages about the state they are registered in.

One of them reads "Victoria – the place to be."

I would argue that should read "Victoria – one of the places to be." or possibly "Victoria – one of the many places on planet earth that fulfils all necessary conditions for supporting human life."

But the Australians are unsurprisingly very proud of their country. It is a rather charming patriotism, unlike the more jingoistic and racist English version. I've noticed that whenever an Australian appears in a foreign TV programme, the trails for the show will proudly boast, "starring Australia's Hugh Jackman" (or whoever it is). It reminds me of something a local paper from a small town in England would say, rather than a national TV station.

I'm not saying it's a bad thing. Quite the opposite. I think it's great that the Australians are proud of the citizens that have been successful. It would be great if the UK showed equal support for its own people.

And it's not show-offy in an American way. It seems to be a statement of both pride and humility. There is almost an element of surprise that someone from the little town of Australia has done so well in the big world.

Which is again a good thing. None of the British "so what?" – none of the American "of course". Instead an Australian "Isn't it great? That's quite an achievement. And he or she is one of us."

I truly love it.

As the crowd at the Aussie Rules Football match showed, the pride in the country or the state or the town or the team is not fuelled by hatred or excessive competition. The car number plates are just stating pride in Victoria. The fact that the message is on a car number plate shows that they aren't really crowing about it.

Maybe they just didn't have room to write "Victoria – the place to be...if that's where your house and stuff is."

Wednesday 30th April

I was having a sandwich and a cup of coffee for lunch and reading the excellent *Age* newspaper – an example of its genius was that last year it claimed of my show *Christ on a Bike* "His claims to be the new Messiah don't quite ring true." Well, you don't say.

I had looked at the main news section and had moved on to the tabloid-style A3 bit when a woman came across from another table and said, "Have you finished with the main bit, because it's the only bit I don't have?"

I got the impression she thought I was reading a copy of the paper already left in the café, but I wasn't. I'd bought it myself for $1.20. And although I had had a good browse I felt that I had more to get out of the paper, especially as the A3 section was looking a bit rubbish already.

So I said, "No".

She looked at me slightly askew as if to say, "But you're not reading it, so why can't I read it."

And I looked at her slightly askew (but in the opposite direction) as if to say, "Because I might want to read it again in a minute and anyway it's my own paper and maybe I don't want to give it to you. I believe they may have some more copies in the newsagent. It costs $1.20."

It was quite a complicated concept to get across in a look and I think she assumed I was about to sneeze or something because she went away.

As it happens I did go back to the main section and read some more of it. I got a few anticipatory glances from the penny-pinching woman who couldn't wait to get her hands on my property.

But in all honesty by the time I had finished my lunch I had got everything I was ever going to get out of the *Age* paper of the 30th April 2003.

A voice in my head was saying "Oh go on, leave her the paper she so clearly covets."

But another voice was saying "No. I may want to read some of it later in my room."

A third voice was saying "No you won't. But fuck the bitch anyway. Take it and put it in a bin."

The first voice (who had been responsible for me carrying that suitcase up those stairs all those months ago) was upset by the unnecessary language and sentiments of the third voice and unconvinced by the shilly-shallying of the second voice, but he was out-voted on this occasion and I uncharitably took the paper away with me.

The minute I was gone, the woman was on her feet and at my table, rummaging through the sections I had left behind. I could see her disappointment as she realised the prize she sought, the one ray of light in her dull existence, had gone. Her face fell.

I waved the paper in the air, and then ripped it up in front of her astonished face, shouting, "Don't you understand, this was my own paper? Why should I share it with you?"

OK I didn't do that, but I felt like doing that, as well as being guilty about my lack of charity.

Later in my room I pretended to read a bit of the paper again, so that my second voice felt like he was vindicated in his decision.

But all four of us knew it was a lie.

 It was nearly time to go home and face the music. I had decided to forget about my troubles and drink and party the month away and behaved like the single man that I officially wasn't. Despite there having been some fun distractions my overriding memory of the festival is depression: depression about S and the lack of success of my show. It's a long way to go for a mediocre reception and I felt bad for the promoter who had taken me out there to presumably lose her money. Though I still had some fun and made some good friends and reconnected with some old ones I decided that I wouldn't make the trip to the other side of the world again unless I was better known out there, which would really mean that I'd have to be in a TV show that aired in the country. This has not happened and for the moment this remains my final stint at this Festival. Also, as far as I know, they've never asked me back.

Thursday 1st May

I started packing for my trip home on Saturday.

I brought far too much with me and it's interesting to see the things that I brought that I didn't use and should have left at home.

Mainly I overestimated the number of pairs of shoes I would require for my trip. Really two pairs should have sufficed. I decided I needed five (including running shoes). My boots have been squeaking (but luckily only when I've been wearing them, or I would have checked for mouse squatters). I will probably leave them here. It seems unlikely that they will never walk on English soil again (unless they get found by a tramp who is unlucky enough to get deported). And I didn't even give those boots a chance to say goodbye to the country that they had spent their whole life in. I feel bad.

But fuck them.

Those boots weren't made for packing.

The squeaky boot doesn't only not get the grease. It gets left in Australia.

Wait a minute. I begin to wonder if those boots have been pretending to squeak on purpose in order to get to stay out here. They would rather be on the stinking feet of a tramp than have to return to our useless country. The sneaky footwear.

Well I won't let them get away with it.

I'm going to wear them on the plane back and then give them to a British tramp. Ha ha, that will teach that ungrateful pair of cunts.

I remember debating with myself for some time whether I should include that offensive and gratuitous swear word, mainly because I knew my mum would read it and make a disapproving face. But in my emotionally and physically fragile state, the idea of calling my boots an "ungrateful pair of cunts" seemed irresistibly amusing. Now I am less hung over and confused I am not sure I agree, but it's not my job to censor my idiotic younger self. The boots were indeed left behind.

Friday 2nd May

I was struck with an obvious but nonetheless disappointing truth today.

I will never see my own skull.

I'm not including X-rays of computer simulations on this one. They don't count, obviously.

Nor peeling back the skin and looking in the mirror. I mean an entire disembodied skull with nothing inside or attached.

It is simply not possible for a human being to stare upon the box that contains his brain (and let's try not to imagine the unpleasant picture of someone achieving this... ooops, sorry we have already).

You might argue that it is possible to create some kind of false metal skull and then have some kind of operation which substitutes the cyber skull for the real one. After which you could have the doctors clean up your skull and have a look at it.

But that technology will never exist. For the simple reason that the expense would be prohibitive and there would be no point in developing it, as it would never be useful in any other circumstance than giving people an opportunity to view their own skull. And no one's going to pay for that. It would be a waste of money.

I only thought this because it would be interesting to see how your own skull measured up to all the others and also what the alien archaeologists of the future would find if they dug up your remains.

Skulls are just kind of cool.

I know there was a bloke who was dying and donated his skull to the RSC or somewhere so he could get to play Yorrick after his death. That's an imaginative use of an important resource.

I wonder if it would be possible to have your skull made into a drinking vessel, so people could still enjoy you after you were gone. Perhaps all your friends and family could drink from your skull at your own funeral, as a kind of tribute. I'd like to make it known at this point that that is what I would like to happen in the event of my death. I know it might be a bit unpleasant for my friends and family. But hey, it's really what I would have wanted.

I think it is time for me to go home now. Don't you?

Sunday 4th May

The people I hate on planes are the ones who insist on getting up at the end of the flight before the seat-belt light has been turned off.

You know, you're taxiing up to the arrival gate and the Captain has been very insistent that you stay seated until he gives the signal, but they think that if they can pre-empt the official standing up point that they will be ready to get off the plane first.

This is stupid and selfish for so many reasons. Obviously it's partly a safety thing. If there is an accident as the plane is still moving, those idiots are going to get hurt (and probably hurt other people). But my main problem with it is just how much time are these people going to save?

OK, they might get a bit closer to the front when the doors finally open, but all that will happen is that they will get to the baggage carousel a bit earlier and have to wait there a bit longer instead.

Even if it saved them a couple of minutes, once again (as with the people on the tube I mentioned the other month), what have they got that is so important in their lives that an extra minute or two is going to make any difference. These people have been on a twenty-one-hour flight from Australia and now they are worried that they might waste a hundred seconds by not being ready to get off a plane.

Perhaps these people are all just claustrophobic and have been really holding their fears in for all that time, but now, so close to the end, they can stand it no more and have to be let off.

Or perhaps they are idiots who haven't got over that school-days routine of wanting to be the first off the bus or the first in the canteen queue.

I got home and went to see S and P. I had bought them gifts and we went out for dinner and for a while it almost seemed like we were going to carry on with the facade. That night in bed, we were lying as far apart from each other as we could possibly be, after having been apart for so long and we were forced to acknowledge that this wasn't how things should be. We discussed the situation calmly and maturely and both agreed that things had come to an end. It was sad, of course, though at least some consolation that we were clearly still friends. Nevertheless I was somewhat heartbroken that such a promising relationship had come to nothing and it was a major disappointment to have another failed romance behind me. And this time I would have two people to miss. I had really bonded with P and felt I was letting him down as much as his mother.

Though our friendship endured and I carried on popping down to Hampshire to see them every now and again and I was there when P walked his first proper steps, and within half an hour was staggering, laughing back and forth between the two of us, which is one of the most magical things I have ever witnessed. Ultimately though I was about to move into the big house that I had bought for us all to live in, but on my own. It was to be a symbol both of my financial success and my romantic failure and it took me a long time to get used to it. This depression formed the starting point of my next stage show The Twelve Tasks of Hercules Terrace and took well over a year for me to begin recovering from.

But I am glad to have both S and P as my friends and though I don't see him so much I had a most enjoyable day out on the South Bank with them both towards the end of 2007 and it was so strange to see him as a proper grown up little boy. He's a cracker. I still love them both. In a good way. Not in that bad way that most love is.

Clearly we took the break up in our stride somewhat as unusually for a separating couple we spent the next day together as well. Look –

Monday 5th May

S, P and me went to feed the ducks today. S had packed a few bits of stale bed and we drove to a pond that she'd used to go to as a child.

As we arrived at the pond (more like a lake as it turned out) we could only see a swan by the water's edge, so we went to say hello. I threw a bit of bread in for the swan. P took one look at the swan and began to cry. Poor lamb. He was scared. Of a swan. The baby coward.

The swan gobbled up the bread, but it was not satiated. It swam towards the bank and looked at me expectantly. I threw more bread. The bread was dispatched. P cried more. The swan had tasted bread now and was hungry for more. It proceeded to get out of the water and advance towards us. It could move fast. Even as a thirty-five-year-old man I found this quite frightening. But at least I didn't cry, like P.

The swan would kill us all and eat all our bread. I kept throwing bits of bread in different directions to try and divert it, but it would just pick them up with its swan beak, eat them and then head towards me as I retreated.

We managed to get away and we still had plenty of bread. P stopped crying. I sent S back to get the buggy which we had abandoned close to the water's edge. The swan was still quite close to it. I couldn't go. I had the bread.

We walked round the pond-lake (it was a fair distance) and found a bunch of ducks (that's the correct collective term) swimming by the shore. There was another swan with them. I threw the first piece of bread to it. I hoped that would keep it happy. Plus there was a step up from the water to the land and I figured this swan couldn't get out so readily. P immediately began to cry. "Oh P," I said, "it's only a swan." I shook my head at S. Imagine begin scared of a swan!

The more bread I threw, the more P cried, so S gave him a piece of bread and said, "It's OK. Why don't you throw them some bread?" But instead of throwing the stale bread, P ate it. And stopped crying. He hadn't been scared of the swan at all. He'd been crying because he thought we'd been throwing his lunch to some birds. He had wept through selfish greed, not fear. So it was just me who was scared of the swan. Once again P was close to proving his superiority. Though I thought he'd come off looking a bit childish over the whole 'not sharing the stale bread' incident. As I had largely hidden my own fear (I only screamed about twice) I think I still looked best.

As we threw the last of the bread we noticed a small sign near our feet, sticking out of a flowerbed. It asked us not to feed the ducks and informed us that bread was not particularly good for them. They probably should have made the sign a bit bigger and put it nearer to the ducks (especially as a father and daughter had just arrived with a great big bag of bread).

Then I realised that the reason P had been crying at us giving the birds bread had not been about greed. He was aware that the bread was too refined for their bird stomachs, that it would do them harm. They were tears of empathy and pity. So concerned had this tiny sixteen-month-old child been to protect the ducks that he had been prepared to eat some of the stale bread himself. But how much could one baby do in a world where so much bread is thrown to so many ducks? How much stale bread can one child eat?

As we left the pond a single tear of frustration and hopelessness fell down his rosy cheek.

Tuesday 6th May

Back to my UK tour with a gig rather reminiscent of the Melbourne run. I was in a thousand-seater venue in St Albans with around about 100 people in the audience. This kind of gig is meat and potatoes to me now. How nice of the people of St Albans to stay away so that I would feel at home.

Through bleary-eyed jet lag I performed my little heart out and they weren't a bad crowd. Though my head was thumping and my ears were ringing (and still a bit blocked from the descent of the plane on Sunday) so I couldn't quite work out if it was the sound department that was awry or my own brain that was frazzled (it was the latter).

I battled on, but with the bits I cut for Australia re-instated the show suddenly seemed very long to me. It was fun to suddenly remember bits that I hadn't thought about for nearly two months.

The best and weirdest thing about this show, though, was the shouting out bit at the end.

First I get men to shout out "We love our cocks!" The men of St Albans did this reasonably loudly.

Then I get the women to shout out "We love your cocks!" They really went for it. It was very funny.

Then I get gay and bi-sexual men (and any man who accepts that there is a part of him that is gay) to shout out "We love our cocks and your cocks!"

Quite often no-one shouts out on this one. This happened tonight.

As usual I explained that someone had to shout it out for the show to continue and added the usual incentive of explaining that if you were a straight man and did it, what happens is you get a massive round of applause and nine times out of ten a woman in the audience will have sex with you. I said I would wait.

And I did.

I waited for a long time. There were pockets of giggles from people as they waited for someone to do it. But no-one did. Previously I have had to wait maybe thirty seconds for someone to relent and join in (which is a long time to have nothing happening in a live gig), but it seemed that easily a minute had passed and no-one had chimed in. I chuckled under my breath and now extra tired after seventy-five minutes on stage, the whole experience was made especially surreal because of the effects of jet lag.

But I was determined to win this stand-off. I waited and waited. It was pretty funny. I laughed, laughter smattered round the auditorium. It was actually quite an exciting theatrical experience. I looked at the floor, looked up, made an expectant face, then stared hard into the faces of some of the cowardly men who weren't even prepared to do this simple thing in order to get out of the theatre and into the pub.

It went on even longer. Reluctantly (because I would have loved just to keep the silence going in some ways, but felt the situation needed comment), I remarked "The men of St Albans. So macho, they can't even let the idea of being gay into the public arena" (or words to that effect) and told them that the show was over unless someone shouted it out, which would be a shame.

Eventually (and I wish I'd had a clock in this, because it felt like three minutes or more, but time stands still when a theatre is silent) I heard a bloke tut and make a sort of "all right" noise and he shouted out "We love our cocks and your cocks!"

The audience cheered with relief. He held his arms aloft.

Disingenuously, I broke into his celebration. "Usually I'd let you enjoy that," I said, "but to be honest you waited so long that I think you should be ashamed, rather than proud."

Maybe I was a bit harsh on him. And there was an odd, but slightly exciting atmosphere in the air.

Weirdly as I took my bow the house lights (the lights in the auditorium) came up. This doesn't usually happen and was obviously a mistake on behalf of the lighting technician. But I got to see the faces of everyone in the audience. A ragbag of St Albans' people spread out in clumps in this massive theatre.

I got to look them in the eye and telepathically chastise them for their yellow-bellied behaviour (only the men, of course. The women had been fantastic!).

But I liked them for it too. We had played a game of chicken and I had won.

Though I felt like I'd been hit by a lorry when I came off stage so maybe it was a Pyrrhic victory.

Wednesday 7th May

I completed purchase on my new house just before I went to Australia, so I haven't had time to move yet.

Whilst I was away someone left a dilapidated piano on the path inside my front gate.

It is falling apart and the top has come off and the keys are all wonky.

I don't understand. Is this a bizarre welcoming gift from my new neighbours? Have Laurel and Hardy been working down my street trying to deliver a piano with hilarious consequences? Or have the thieves who stole my shitty bike had a sudden pang of guilt, found out my new address and left me an equally shitty piano to make up for it?

What kind of person decides to dump a piano in someone else's house? It's just the ultimate selfishness isn't it? "Well, I don't want to have to pay the council to take it away, so I'll put it on his property and he'll have to deal with it."

Why not just leave it on the pavement?

Well you can never have too many smashed and rotten pianos, I suppose. At the moment it is the only piece of furniture that I have at my new place.

So I might use it to sit on.

It will be my musical chair.

My next-door neighbours were having a big clear out at the time I arrived home, but later insisted that, as suspicious as this seemed, the piano was nothing to do with them. Yet how far away could this piano have come from? It's not something that I can imagine someone pushing down the street, searching for somewhere to dump it and then just chancing across a pathway and thinking "Ah, that'll do!" Realistically it could only have come from a twenty-yard radius (and I'm being generous with that) and is unlikely to have come from over the road, as that would have meant lifting it over kerbstones and avoiding parked cars. Also I think, you would only push this on to someone's property if you were pretty sure that no-one was living there at the moment. All of these facts would suggest that one of my next-door neighbours was to blame. And were I a detective I would take the simultaneous clear out as definite circumstantial evidence. But I am making no libellous accusations in print, and a couple of years later those neighbours did treat me to a lovely dinner, so I would forgive them even if it was them, not that I am saying it is. But whoever it was they broke several of the tiles on my path in the process, tiles which, in typical Richard Herring fashion, remain unrepaired almost five years later.

Thursday 8th May

So after arranging to pay my not inexpensive council tax, I rang the council to explain my unwanted piano situation. I had to wait a while to get through, of course, but finally I found myself speaking to a woman with a hollow and uninterested voice (and the absence of interest was clear just from the words "Good morning").

I told her about this strange (almost miraculous) appearance of a piano in my front garden. She said, "Sorry we don't take pianos."

I said, "But you see, it isn't my piano."

"It doesn't matter. We'd have to send out a special lorry with lifting equipment. It would cost hundreds of pounds. We don't do it."

"But it was dumped on my property…"

"If it's on your property, then it is your problem."

"What if it was on the street?"

"Then we'd come and collect it."

"So what if I pushed it off of my property on to the street."

"You would be dumping it on council property and be liable to a £1000 fine."

"So essentially what you're saying is I am being punished for being honest. I could have just pushed it into the road and not informed you and you wouldn't know where it had come from."

"If it's on your property, it is your problem."

My voice maybe raised a little in frustration, "So what do you suggest I do with this piano?"

"I'm not interested in having an argument about it. That is how it is."

And she hung up.

No "goodbye". No "thanks for calling your local council". No, "I know this is really stupid and unfair, but there's nothing I can do. I am really sorry."

She just hung up.

That is just rude.

I wish I had found out her name, because I would loved to have paid a removal man to move the piano into her front garden and then seen what she did with it. I could, of course, just shift the piano into the street and see what happens, or I could be like the kind person who decided that they would rather this was my problem who put it in my garden in the first place.

But I think I will just bide my time and wait and formulate my revenge against the council, the anonymous hollow-voiced woman and the anonymous piano dumper.

In the meantime, if anyone wants a broken and rubbish piano (perhaps to perform one of the many Dadaist conceptual arts pieces involving pianos – smashing one to bits or bringing it some hay and seeing if it eats it are two that I've heard of) please do get in touch and you can have it for free!

Friday 9th May

Brighton is a fine town and it's the middle of the Brighton Festival so the streets were filled with people on stilts with fireworks exploding off their heads and men rowing up the road in a boat and massive inflatable spiders. At least I presume that was because of the festival. Maybe it's always like this.

I bought some over-priced chips and soaked them in vinegar and took a walk on the pier (obviously the one that hasn't burnt down and fallen into the sea). It was reminiscent of childhood days spent on the pier in Weston-Super-Mare as I watched the sea crashing beneath me and wondered whether I would be hurt if I attempted to dive in (as the signs warned me).

As I finished the chips a gust of wind caught the polystyrene tray and the pool of excess vinegar spilt all over my T-shirt. That was annoying. I like vinegar a lot, but not enough to wear it as a cologne.

I wandered back through the amusement hall, remembering how much I loved these places as a child. I was hoping to find a pinball machine, though I don't know why as they never work properly in such arcades, but clearly pinball has lost out in the video games revolution. Instead I had a go on a few-decades-old fruit machines.

I was delighted to win £5 on a Monopoly-based fruit machine for landing on Park Lane, until I pressed collect and was greeted with twenty-five twenty pence tokens. All wins of £3 and over were paid in tokens. I had forgotten all about tokens. What a total con. If I had stuck at Leicester Square I would have had £2.80 in cash.

No matter, that was twenty-five free goes on the fruit machines, so I played on. But the tokens didn't even really work properly. I was left with about seven of them that wouldn't work in any of the machines and just clattered out into the pay-out tray.

I went to one of the booths to complain, but the woman said they would not exchange tokens. I said I didn't want to have money,

I would he happy with seven tokens that actually worked in the machines they were designed to go in. She said that if I went to the office they would exchange them for vouchers which I could use to buy snacks in the café.

I had seen the café.

I didn't want to eat there.

Perhaps it was partly because I've run into the brick wall of bureaucracy already this week, but I was really annoyed by this whole turn of events. I thought I'd won £5, only to find I'd won some silver metal discs, £1.40 of which were useless, unless I wanted to buy some more unpleasant chips, which would probably only result in me being covered in even more acetic acid.

I decided to take revenge on this cheating arcade that knowingly filled its machines with tokens that didn't work, aware that its patrons would just lose heart and give up their hard-earned winnings.

I thought that if I could jam these tokens into the coin slots of seven machines, the resulting loss of earnings and maintenance costs would more than outweigh the £1.40 that had been swizzled out of me.

Unfortunately the tokens were too small to get jammed in any machine I tried. Instead they just clattered out into the pay-out tray.

Then I stopped and thought about it. What would this look like if I was caught? I was a thirty-five-year-old man, with a well-paid job and vinegar all over his clothes, failing to sabotage some out-of-date gaming machines in a children's arcade.

I don't think I would have gone down in the annals of legendary avengers against evil.

I decided to go back to the hotel and change my shirt and threw the tokens into a bin.

Saturday 10th May

Had a really cracking second show in Brighton, but with quite a bizarre incident half way through.

I was talking about the various penile injuries that men have suffered, specifically the rather bloody event of having the frenulum (or banjo string) break, when I saw a dark shadowy shape on the aisle seat of the second row slump to the floor.

A young man had collapsed. It was right at the front of the audience and I couldn't have ignored it even if I wanted to. And I didn't want to, because I was slightly concerned that a member of my audience had died. Or worse, fallen asleep. Death I could cope with, but boredom? That would be unforgivable.

Obviously I stopped the show to check that the fella was OK. A few concerned audience members checked him out as others speculated on the cause of this unusual occurrence. Someone thought he might have had an epileptic fit. Another voice reassured me, "Don't worry Rich. It's not your fault." Which was a relief. It would be a grave responsibility to think that my sense of humour was so strong that it could kill people.

Personally I thought he was probably an attention seeker attempting to upstage me.

The house lights came up. The show had come to a definite halt.

Thankfully the slumped figure on the floor stirred. He was helped out of the theatre by some of the staff. I told him that this was the most devastatingly effective heckle I had ever received. How do you come back on that one? How do you recover? How can you follow the mysterious collapse and possible death of a member of your audience?

Correctly as it turned out I figured that he had fainted because of the rather gruesome images of penile injury that I was describing (he had a problem with the idea of blood, so I suppose that mentioning plumes of blood shooting out of still erect penises was a bit much for him) and said "Well it's a good job he's out the room, because I was just about to talk about penises being put in mincing machines and fed to pigs."

Thankfully the audience laughed and they got behind me even more than they had done already. The man came back about five minutes later and seemed to have made a full recovery. I considered cutting off my own arm to see what reaction the ensuing bloodbath would have on him, but felt that such a joke might rebound on me.

Due to the power of this blog I actually ended up
corresponding with the fainting man and his friends over the
next few months, and then in 2006, when I announced that I
was going to be holidaying in Tobago, one of the friends got in
touch to say that the fainting man, Darren, was getting married
in Trinidad the week I was going to be over there and asking me
if I would like to come along as a guest. How could I resist? Isn't
it strange how things work out?

Sunday 11th May

Because I've been spending a lot of time in dressing rooms recently I have had plenty of opportunity to consider my physical appearance. Dressing rooms are full of mirrors, partly because actors need to check they are looking exactly right before a performance and partly because actors are extremely vain and love to look at themselves. A dressing room is nothing more than a budgie cage, though generally the food you get isn't as good in the theatre.

Especially at Swindon Arts Centre.

As I was writing my book (hey, I'm over half way through and I still have nineteen days to finish it) in the roomy (but slightly smelly) dressing room at the Nuffield Theatre in Southampton, I would glance over the top of my laptop at the hung-over face in the mirror. Increasingly this year I have noticed lines and wrinkles and baggy eyes that I haven't been aware of before.

I'm not that bothered. I kind of like them, but they are a telling advertisement for the approach of old age and my inevitable death, so I can't be too fond of them.

Today I also realised how grey my hair is becoming. There is a whole clump of white hair above my right temple. Again, it's supposedly distinguished and, unfairly in men, signs of maturity are considered quite attractive, but it gives you pause for thought because I don't feel any older than I did ten years ago.

The other day I chanced across my first passport. There's a photo of me in there when I was seventeen or eighteen. I was actually surprised at how thin and attractive I was. I always thought I was nothing special and remember thinking I was fat as a teenager (but then I didn't realise how far it would go). But I tell you, I was gorgeous. I'd have done me. And in fact I did. About three times a day. Because no-one else seemed to want to.

The last eighteen years have hardly been cruel, in fact I am probably fitter now than I have almost ever been (at least I was before I went to Australia and behaved like an alcoholic pig at an all-you-can-eat buffet), but it is still quite shocking, or at least sobering, to see the contrast.

I spent the whole of my twenties worrying that I was getting old. Now I'm in my thirties I realise that was a stupid waste of time, as I was in fact really, really young and should have just enjoyed it.

I'm not going to make the same mistake with my late thirties. I am still young. But the wrinkles and the greying hair are the warning signs on the road down the steep mountain pass that leads so quickly to oblivion.

Let us all make love in the streets while there is flesh on our bones, for it will all be over much too soon.

In eight years time I will be old and then I will buy some slippers and take up golf. But for now I'm going to pretend I'm the lad in the passport, without the inferiority complex and I'll just smash every mirror that I come into contact with.

So three years to go now until this arbitrary milestone is reached. I am greyer and more wrinkly now, though still feel like a man in his mid-twenties, which was of course the theme for my 2007 show Oh Fuck, I'm 40, *which even partially used the mountain metaphor I allude to here.*

Monday 12th May

I was in a taxi driving up Chiswick High Road and we passed the VW garage. I was looking at the cars for sale on the forecourt and noticed that on each price tag, beneath the sum required to own the vehicle (averaging around about £12,000), was the single word "Affordable".

And I thought to myself "Well, that pretty much depends on who is looking at the car, doesn't it?" Yes, if Richard Branson happened to pass then £12,000 probably wouldn't be a stretch, but VW are making quite an assumption about most people's incomes to think that kind of sum is something that is universally affordable.

Unless the sign has some kind of computer chip in it, with an iris scanner or something, which can register who is looking at the car, access their bank account and then display an accurate assessment of whether the prospective customer has a chance of owning that particular car. Maybe someone else would look at it and it would say, "A bit pricey for you, mate. Maybe if you sold one of your kidneys."

If that is the case, then the signs were malfunctioning. I have just bought a house and so very little is affordable for me any more.

I wonder if the psychology works on anyone. They look at the car, look at the price and then see the word "Affordable" and think, "Oh look, it's OK. It's affordable. Even though I don't actually have £12,000 I will buy it anyway."

Maybe it works. From now on, I am going to walk around with a badge saying "sexually attractive" on it, just in case.

Tuesday 13th May

I was out for a walk this afternoon, thinking about my book, not paying much attention to anything. A small, excited boy ran past me and shouted to his friend, "A bus has crashed into a building." He grabbed his playmates hand and they ran to look.

Sure enough when I got to the corner there was a crowd of people looking up the road, at the somewhat surreal sight of a double-decker bus, which had for some reason veered off the road at a sharp angle and smashed into the front of a house.

There wasn't a massive amount of damage. Luckily the house had a short drive and presumably the driver had had an opportunity to brake. But the top front windows of the bus were smashed and the roof above the porch of the house was smashed.

That'd spoil your day wouldn't it?

You go out to work, everything is fine. Then you come home and a double-decker bus is embedded in your home.

I don't know if anyone was hurt and I don't know what had

caused the bus to turn so sharply off the road. There was a sharp corner just before the accident, so maybe the bus had taken it too wide and then swerved to avoid a collision.

Or maybe it was a very low rent terrorist attack.

It is weird the way that two everyday objects can become so interesting and bizarre when placed in an unfamiliar arrangement. I couldn't help but join the gawpers, looking at the confusing spectacle. Though none of them quite exhibited the glee of the little boy, they were all standing there because of the same impulse.

If nothing else, it's another indication that you should enjoy life while you're here.

Your house could be hit by a bus tomorrow.

Wednesday 14th May

I finally got to see *Bowling for Columbine* last night. I think Michael Moore is a bit in love with himself, but he does produce some interesting and thought-provoking work and he's always definitely worth having a listen to.

The American pre-occupation with guns and violence is indeed terrifying (especially given their level of control over everything) and I think Moore is right to suggest that a state which promotes so much violence in the world should not be that surprised if its citizens also turn to violence to express themselves, nor indeed if their enemies choose to respond to them in the same way they have been treated.

I also think the South Park guy (who weirdly went to Columbine too) makes some good points about how feelings of teenage alienation and failure seem so important at the time, but are transitory. Certainly we might feel powerless and oppressed as kids and violence might seem like the ultimate revenge for the belittlement that we all experience. But none of it is important in the long run and there are so many better ways of expressing that frustration. Shooting people dead is the easiest way to overcome any problem you have with them in the short term, but I would argue that it is worth searching for a more difficult, but less final solution.

I hope the Americans can see sense and do something about

their obvious gun problem, but think it is extremely unlikely.

Certainly Moore covers the subject of school shootings more sensitively and intelligently than Kelly Rowlands (or as the little black girl from Grange Hill would call her, Kelly Row-lands – and yes I am aware it's actually Kelly Rowland, but regular readers will understand!), whose song about a bloke going off his nut and murdering his class-mates has been increasingly annoying me over the last few months.

When I first heard the song, I quite liked the quirkiness of all the stuff about the girl having the same-sized hands as Marilyn Monroe. It seemed like an unusual thing to sing about. Then one day I listened to the words in the rest of the song and realised what it was about and it is such a trite and superficial way to try and cover such a complicated and tragic issue.

If anything it makes me side with the quiet boy who blows his fuse and guns down his school chums. If nothing else because Kelly Rowlands seems to think he is weird just for enjoying studying books on science. What kind of message is that putting out? She acknowledges that all the smart stuff he likes isn't "cool" and argues that his alienation at being clever is enough for him to kill his more cool peers. Maybe it would be better if Rowlands sang a song that pointed out that studying hard at school might be a good idea for everyone and that possibly being good at science is more important than having the same-sized hands as a dead film star.

Because it is also interesting what she laments about the victims of the murder, and how superficial her feelings are.

Personally if I were killed, I would hope there would be more to say about me than the fact that part of my body shared similar dimensions to that of a long-dead celebrity (although maybe if the body part was different and the movie star was Errol Flynn then I wouldn't mind so much). It's like having the same-sized hands as Marilyn Monroe somehow confers the status of Marilyn Monroe on to you and makes you important. Why would you want to be like Marilyn Monroe anyway? She was a tragic figure. Is that the point of the song? I don't think so. What Rowlands laments is the fact that Mary "could have been a movie star" but "she never got the chance to go that far."

It's as if being a movie star is the most important thing that could happen to anyone. Yet the example of Marilyn Monroe reveals how superficial and stupid being a movie star can be. And to be honest what were the chances of Mary going on to be a movie star? She's presumably quite attractive and has hands the same size as another film actor. But there's quite a lot more to it than that. To be honest any sixteen-year-old girl 'could' be a movie star, but it is something that is extremely unlikely to happen, even if you do get a chance to go that far. More likely she would have been a waitress, trying to be a movie star and failing. Not that that would matter. There is dignity in being a waitress that isn't apparent in all movie stars. Just it's an odd aspiration to bestow on someone. The tragedy surely is that a young person has been senselessly slaughtered, not that they might possibly have one day become something as spiritually unrewarding as a movie star.

The other victim that Rowlands mentions is a bloke who can chuck a ball into a basketball hoop from twenty feet away. That's quite a skill, but is it the most important thing about a young person's life. Again this fella has the chance to become a celebrity because of his skill. He has a try-out for the Sixers (which I'm guessing is some kind of basketball team, rather than something to do with the cub scout movement). The song seems to be bemoaning the fact that we have lost two potential celebrities, rather than two actual young people. That this was all about being cool or not. The priorities are all to cock.

Yet the song doesn't make the link between the increasing importance of celebrity and the disillusionment of those who could never aspire to those virtues of beauty and wealth and coolness.

If society values those things so highly then how will those who are conventionally unattractive and poor and uncool and have no apparent route out of their dead-end lives going to respond?

It is because of these notions that the previously quiet and respectful young man has rebelled against the beautiful, sporty people who mocked him and castigated him. Ironically as a clever bloke he had a much better chance of being a success outside the confines of his school, whereas becoming a top actress or sportsman would most probably have eluded the people he murdered.

He chose a stupid way to show his frustration but you can understand why he might have felt like doing it.

I'm quite a clever bloke who likes reading about science and smart stuff and Kelly Rowlands is an attractive girl who is already a celebrity and has a pretty good shot at being a movie star and I feel like killing her. If only because she insists on singing, "Her life was stole."

No it wasn't. It was stolen! Stolen!

Maybe if you'd read some books about smart stuff you would have realised that. And you could also have written a song which tried to really understand why stuff like this happens. It makes me so cross that I'm not sure I would be responsible for my actions if I met her.

I guess Kelly Rowlands is just lucky that the gun laws are so much stricter in the UK!

All right mate, calm down. It's only a made up story in a rubbish song. Get a grip.

Thursday 15th May

Parents should get much more credit than they do. The problem with having children is that it is a twenty-four hour job, seven days a week for (at least) eighteen years and the wages are terrible. You have to pay for the privilege.

Oh, of course, you get the joy of seeing the course of a new young life and the triumphs and disasters that will ensue. But when you're tired and pissed off and have just done your weekly shop and have been queuing in Sainsbury's for ten minutes, it can be difficult to remember why you wanted to be responsible for another human life in the first place. Not just another human. A really stupid human who doesn't know anything and can't do anything for themselves. What were you thinking?

This is the vibe that I got off the exasperated woman in front of me at the supermarket today. She was frazzled and weary, but was accompanied by her alert and curious (maybe) eight-year-old daughter. Now this girl was very sweet and was well behaved, not making trouble in the slightest, but even so her mum was getting to the end of her tether.

The girl spotted a magazine with Courteney Cox-Arquette on the cover. "Mummy," said the girl, pointing at the picture, but the woman pretended not to hear. "Mummy," she said a bit louder. But Mummy was trying to unload her trolley and again feigned deafness. "Mummy," insisted the girl, quite politely, "It's the lady out of *Friends*."

"Mmmmm," agreed her mother, feebly pretending to be interested. Although the girl was satisfied with this, it was quite clear to the casual observer that the mother's "Mmmmm," was quite clearly intended as a sarcastic "Oh, is it really? I would never have recognised her if you hadn't pointed it out. How incredibly fucking interesting."

It's a shame that as parents we're not allowed just to say that sort of thing occasionally. But no, we have to nurture and reward, so a half-hearted "Mmmmm" which might mean "well done", but could mean "piss off" is a much better option.

The mum just wanted to get her shopping checked through and get out of the shop, so she could get home and make her family dinner, then get the kids to bed and maybe get half an hour to herself before falling into an exhausted sleep, but her child needed stimulation. Shopping is boring. She'd got that right.

She was investigating the empty till next to her and found an advertisement competition scratch card that had fallen out of a magazine. You know, one of the ones that always wins, but you have to ring up and spend £5 to discover you haven't got the £25,000, but instead have a voucher entitling you a trifling sum off the price off a holiday that you don't want.

"Aren't I clever, mum?" opined the girl, seeking the approval that her mother was reluctant to give her, "I've found this."

Again the mother hovered between the parental duty of counterfeiting interest and the temptation to say "And how does that make you clever exactly? It makes you nosy. In a sense it makes you a thief. That promotional leaflet belongs in a magazine that you haven't paid for. At best I might say you were lucky to have found a worthless bit of paper on the floor. But if you were clever then such an item would have no interest for you whatsoever. I, for example, am clever and find your discovery extremely dull."

What came out of her mouth was another "Mmmmm" and then a "let's just try and get out of this shop."

But the girl was excited. She had found a scratch-card which promised her the possibility of wealth beyond her tiny dreams. "Can I have a coin, mummy?"

The mother didn't reply. She carried on putting her shopping on the conveyor belt. The girl was not discouraged, "I can use my finger nail. I'll use my finger nail."

Possibly relieved that this would keep her spawn quiet for a few seconds the mother let her get on with it.

Eventually the shopping was going through the till, and the mum was trying to pack the bags, but the child was excited. Unsurprisingly, she had won. "Look mummy, I've won."

Everything in the woman's demeanour suggested that she was thinking, "Of course you've won. It's a promotional leaflet. They all win. It's a scam to make you ring up an expensive phone line to discover that you haven't won a cocking thing of any value. Why can't you just notice that I am beyond the end of my tether and give me just a second of peace? Just a second. You parasitical, attention-seeking piece of shit."

But instead she mumbled, "That's good!"

She was aware of her motherly duty and I felt was doing the bare minimum required to demonstrate her love and approval of the adorable (though admittedly annoying) child by her side.

Had the child been more alert she may have picked up on the weariness and the insincerity and said, "Listen mum, I never asked to be born. If you didn't want to have to humour me through my difficult childhood days then maybe you shouldn't have let daddy put it in you. Or at least he could have worn a johnny. So get that surly look off your face and look more interested at this wonderful period of curiosity that your child is going through."

But for now the girl was satisfied and totally unaware of the fact that her mum was suffering or of the notion that this woman might be a human being in her own right, who might have a life beyond caring for her and her insignificant concerns.

Tonight, why don't you ring your parents and say "thank you".

Friday 16th May

I have just reached the point in my book where I am writing about Sigurdur Hjartarson and my visit to his Icelandic Phallological Museum. As you may know if you've seen the show last June I flew to Iceland especially to visit with and interview this extraordinary man who has made it his mission in life to collect a severed penis from every species of mammal in his native country. And then to display them in bell jars and charge people to come and look at them.

I admire him for this enterprise. I think it is good.

When I talked to him he mentioned that he was hoping to collect a human penis, once a willing donor had died. His best bet was an octogenarian Icelander and womaniser called Paul Arason. Sig was very adamant that Arason had to be dead, and to have died of natural causes, before he would consider removing the old man's penis. Though I thought he could have helped things along by dressing up in a scary mask (perhaps fashioned from some of the penises in his museum) and jumping out of a bush as the aging lothario passed. But Mr Hjartarson would not be swerved and I suppose if you're not frightened by the idea of living on a small island with a man who covets your severed penis, then you're probably not frightened of anything.

Nearly a year on I was wondering if there had been any developments in the quest for the human penis. Perhaps selfishly I thought it would make a great topper to the story if Mr Arason had (very unfortunately) died.

So I emailed Sigurdur this week asking for some photos for my book, but I also subtly sneaked in the question "And how is the health of Mr Arason?"

You see, cleverly, I made it appear that I was concerned about the old fella's constitution, rather than expressing my wish that he'd snuffed it and had his penis sliced off and put on display. You have to show respect.

Mr Hjartarson got back today to say, "As regards Mr Arason, he seems to be in excellent health!"

How selfish of him! Doesn't he realise that his death would mean that chapter seven of my book would have a slightly better conclusion? Some people simply have no humanity.

Incidentally I have 35,000 more words to write in fifteen days. Stay tuned to this channel to see if I make it. So what if it's taken me five months to write the first 45,000. I can do this. I can!

Saturday 17th May

I had decided to stay in tonight and write. For some reason, instead, I decided it would be a better idea to paint my bathroom.

I am currently still living in my flat, which remains unsold and I had been looking at the peeling paint in the bathroom and bit tub of white paint in my utility room and thinking, "well, maybe if I painted my bathroom with the paint that I have, the bathroom wouldn't look so scuzzy and someone might buy my flat."

Although I'm sure my subconscious was thinking "if I paint my bathroom I don't have to write my book."

This is the curse of the writer. Anything that gets you out of writing, even if it is harder work and more difficult than writing, is better than writing.

I hadn't considered the fact that I only have one very rubbish and small paint-brush, nor the fact that I didn't have anything to cover my bathroom up with, nor that the last time I painted anything was about eighteen years ago. It didn't even bother me that it was 10pm. I was about to add maybe £20,000 to the value of my flat.

Within about five minutes I realised I'd made a mistake. I had no idea what I was doing. Paint was splashing everywhere, the paint itself was old and thin and to begin with I didn't realise that that situation would improve if I stirred it, the state of the brush meant I wasn't getting the hoped for effect. Unfortunately the walls were cream and the paint was white, and that meant that I couldn't just stop now I'd realised I'd made a stupid mistake. I had to press on and do the whole (admittedly small, but now feeling surprisingly big) bathroom.

The white wasn't covering the cream, or the cracks in the paint as I had hoped. It just shrouded them like a light swirling fog. I was covering the black woodwork with splodges of white paint. The whole thing was a disaster.

I painted on and got about three quarters of the walls and ceiling smeared with some weak brush strokes of misty paint before I decided I wanted to stop. I realised that I was going to be painting this bathroom for days, applying coat upon coat of paint until it started to look anything like OK again. And even then it was going to look worse than it did. All I had done was highlight to any potential buyer that the bathroom needed serious redecoration. Not that that needed any advertising. But now it looked like I had made a hasty and unthinking attempt to hide that fact. It looked like that, because that is what had happened.

I don't have time to paint my bathroom. I can't believe now I genuinely thought I could do it in a couple of hours.

I should just concentrate on doing something I can do, which is write my book and just hope that someone who likes doing DIY sees my flat as a challenge and buys it.

Or I could spend today trying and convert the loft into another room. It can't be that difficult.

Yes that is what I shall do.

Sunday 18th May

What I enjoy very much about living on my own is that I can have conversations with myself out loud. This doesn't make me a mental. On the contrary, I do it because I am all too well aware of my own sanity and thus enjoy the 'joke' of appearing to be insane. It is post-modern insanity and thus very amusing to the audience of me. Of course, in reality, anything I have to say to myself can be said silently in my head. But where's the fun in that? It wouldn't be out of the ordinary and thus have not comedy value at all. As long as I don't tell anyone that I talk to myself then what harm can it do? Oh bum.

Yet I have noticed that I do tend to talk to myself out loud more often when I am faced with an issue which I have contradictory opinions about. Almost as if there are two distinct personalities within me, who disagree and have to have it out in the open. As I say this couldn't be defined as mentalness of schizophrenia because I know that I don't have two personalities. Just one personality, that some time doesn't agree with itself. It's an important distinction.

I had been bingeing on snacks all day as a way to get me through my work (and painting the second coat of paint in my bathroom – still looks shit). I put on half a stone in Australia and I want to lose it, so it is annoying to me that I continue to eat rubbish all day, even though I have asked me not to.

Just before I was going to sleep I caught myself heading for the kitchen. I could tell by the way that I was walking that I was going there to make a couple of pieces of toast. Even though I wasn't hungry and even though I was about to go to sleep. I called myself an idiot, but I didn't care. "What do you think you're doing?" I asked.

"I'm making some toast," I replied. I had a surly look on my face and was clearly challenging my authority and I didn't like it.

"But, I thought you wanted to lose some weight," I chided. I found myself judgemental and patronising and I didn't like it. And I told myself so.

"Don't act all high and mighty with me. You're exactly the same as me, so don't pretend you're better than me. I don't care what you think. I just fancy eating some toast," and I laughed openly as I said it. Well you can imagine that I didn't like that. I pushed the bread away from myself and told me that I couldn't have any. But no one tells me what to do. I'm a rebel. I hate all kinds of authority. Even when the authority is me.

So I made the toast and I ate it in front of my own stupid face. And I loved it. And hated it. But I was above having more of an argument. I wanted to show myself how childish I thought I was being, so I just let myself eat the toast, with a slightly smug smile playing on my lips, which meant I ended up spilling a lot of the toast on the floor, which was what I'd wanted. But I just ate the crumbs off the floor with no regard for hygiene. It was a Pyrrhic victory (the epitome of a Pyrrhic victory in fact), but it was still a victory.

"You'll regret eating that in the morning," I informed me.

And when I stepped on the scales to see I had gained another pound, I saw that I had been right all along. And wrong of course. And I was both unhappy.

I decided from now on that me and me weren't talking. And so did I.

I wonder which of me will break first.

Monday 19th May

I had popped over to my new house in the morning to drop a few things off and check it was still there and that no one else had left me a cumbersome musical instrument. A harp perhaps, or a church organ.

I was disappointed to see that they hadn't, but the piano was still there at least, so everything wasn't lost.

I only had twenty minutes to check up on everything as I had a meeting to go to, but just as I was preparing to leave I noticed that the dustman's lorry turning into the road. I had had no idea when the rubbish collection was and so was pleased to discover that I should put my bins out on Monday.

As I was stepping out the front door one of the bin men was putting my bin into the road (I'd chucked out some old yellow pages and other bits of junk that the previous occupants had been thoughtful enough to leave. It was nice, but it was no piano, was it?). He gave me a cheery Dick van Dyke "hullo", tipping his cockney cap (some of this isn't true) and I wished him a good day in return.

Now I know the horrible witch- I mean, woman at the council had said that they would have nothing to do with the removal of my piano, but I thought, "nothing ventured" and said, "Hey mate, someone dumped this piano in my garden. I don't suppose you guys could take it could you?"

He looked very dubious, "I doubt it," he said, "because it's made of metal, we couldn't crush it up...... but you could ask the driver."

So I walked up the road and greeted the driver cordially and appraised him of the situation, explaining that it was a small piano.

"What do you mean, a small piano," he asked, not unreasonably.

"Well, you know, it's not a grand piano," I replied, realising that I was clutching at straws.

He said, "Look, if we can lift it, we'll take it."

Brilliant! There was no "We'll have to send a special lorry with a lifting device!" like I'd got from the council. I had thought at the time, well it's not THAT heavy. Maybe you could just send a normal lorry and maybe three blokes. Unlike the cow at the office this bloke was prepared to listen and be reasonable – "And if not," he added, "I can give you a number." I thought he was trying to hit on me, but then realised he meant the number of someone who would take it.

What a great bloke.

The other three dustmen were soon at my gate. I showed them the piano and they just nodded and two of them started to move it away! The third stood by the gate and said "That'd be £27 plus VAT if you did it officially."

He didn't need to fish. I was planning on giving them money anyway.

"Don't worry. I'll slip you twenty quid."

"Oh no sir, I don't want to rip you off. A fiver would be fine!"

He asked me what I did to have such a nice house and I told him I was a comedian. He didn't even ask me to tell him a joke. I loved these people. "It's a nice road this, mate. You'll like living here."

After all the worries with the council and the fact that one of my neighbours had uncharitably dumped their problem on me, I felt a little glow of the warmth of human kindness. From a humble dustman. Jesus could have made some kind of parable out of it.

I tried to give the fella twenty pounds, but he wouldn't take it. I finally talked him up to ten in a wonderful satire of bartering. I thanked them heartily and waved them off. It was so like something out of a Disney film that I almost expected the dustcart to fly off.

I felt really happy for the rest of the morning.

Then I began to wonder if the dustmen had dumped the piano on me in the first place, in the hope that I would pay them to take it away.

God damn my cynicism. They were just nice blokes. It wouldn't have worked. Unless they were waiting round the corner for about two months until they saw me arrive in return for a tenner. In which case, good luck to them.

But if there's a double bass in the garden next time I get there, then I'll start to get suspicious.

Tuesday 20th May

I first saw *Jerry Springer the Opera* (written by my friends and associates Richard Thomas and Stewart Lee) at the Battersea Arts Centre a couple of years ago. It had minimal set, a cast of maybe ten and (I think) Richard playing the music on a keyboard. The second half was work in progress and a bit of a mess, but still interesting. We were told we could go home at the interval if we didn't want to see it as well. It was a brilliant show already.

Then I saw it at the Assembly Rooms in Edinburgh last summer. I was astonished by how lavish and large it had all become. The cast was bigger, there was video projection. The second half was properly written and rehearsed and was much better, though still not quite right.

Tonight I went to see it at the Royal National Theatre. It was unbelievable. Set, costumes, cast of dozens (well, two dozen maybe), surprises galore. The second half is triumphant. It's like a proper show that would get put on in a real theatre. Only better, because it is actually entertaining: not something you can generally say after watching something at the theatre – you know it wasn't just worthy and clever and made me go "Aaaaah!", I actually had a good time as well.

I remember when we first went on TV, Stew and I couldn't believe that we'd write a sketch and then it was several people's jobs to make our stupid sketch become reality. And also someone was happy to pay thousands of pounds to make a silly idea on a piece of paper turn into an actual thing. It was when I was sitting in a milk float on Richmond Common at six o'clock in the morning, with three stuntmen made up to look like plague ridden demons galloping around on horses around me that I first felt this uneasy wonder. "It was just a joke," I said. But none of the twenty or thirty people who were there heard me. It was their job to make this thing happen. Whether they thought a Milkman of the Apocalypse was funny or not.

With *Jerry Springer the Opera* tonight I got that feeling times a hundred. Because so much work and money had clearly gone into every aspect of the show, which is essentially just a silly idea about an opera based on a TV show with swearing in it (albeit with brilliant and intelligent execution).

This isn't a negative thing. Quite the opposite. It is just amazing to have witnessed the journey of this extraordinary show, from a small fringe theatre, to one of the most prestigious venues in the land. It is joyfully obvious that this is only another beginning and that there is a long way for this to go yet.

I know there is a part of Stew, however proud he is of his work (and I hope he is proud and happy, because he should be) that is still thinking, "It was only a joke."

The minute we stop thinking that, I think all is lost. And we will have become wankers.

Wednesday 21st May

You can judge a person by their shoes.

I haven't really considered that cliché before, but I think it's probably true. You have to make a lot of decisions when buying a shoe, about style, comfort etc. It's a definite statement, though it's sometimes a statement which although bold leaves its audience thinking, "What the fuck does that statement mean?"

There was a girl opposite me on the tube today, who was reasonably attractive, her hair was quite trendy, her clothes were smart, but stylish. You'd probably meet her and think, "She looks nice, maybe we could be friends. Perhaps after a few weeks we may become lovers. Then when the time is right, I will ask her to be my bride and we will buy a place together, have a couple of kids. I might have an affair about six years in. She'd be hurt, but she'd forgive me and in a sense the whole episode would make our relationship stronger. We would become old together and watch our grandchildren grow up in a world that neither one of use really understood any longer. But we would be happy."

That's what you'd probably immediately think.

Unless you looked at her shoes.

Because her shoes told a whole different story. Firstly they were an odd, unpleasant shade of blue. Darker than navy, but kind of dirty. Not that the shoes were dirty, you understand. Just the colour. What was more striking was that on the toe of each shoe was an incredibly unattractive representation of a flower. I suppose it was a rose, with that petal inside a petal effect. But it was more of a kind of blodge on top of another blodge and was too big, and still in the awful blue colour of the rest of the shoe. The shoe itself was clunky and clumsy, seemingly painfully sensible from the front. But then I noticed that at the back it lifted up and was perched on a high and narrow heel. It was wrong. Like two shoes that had been involved in some kind of high-speed shoe accident and had been welded together by an unscrupulous cobbler.

One had to ask why anyone would chose to buy such a shoe, but anyone can make a mistake under the hot lights of a shoe shop, so more importantly what kind of person would actually wear a shoe like that? The kind of person who thought that this was the shoe for them must have something deeply wrong going on in their brain.

Far from forgiving you for that affair, a woman wearing that kind of shoe would take dreadful revenge upon you and the woman (or man) that you had dallied with. But she'd make you stay with her for the sake of the kids and make the rest of your life a living Hell. However much you tried to explain it had been a mid-life crisis, that both of you were to blame because you'd taken each other for granted, old blue rose shoes would screw her face up at you and snarl and call you a bastard. You'd try to complain, but she'd hiss, "Shut up, the kids will hear."

You'd die at fifty having subconsciously deliberately drunk yourself to death. And she would dance on your grave in her blue rose shoes (stumbling slightly due to the structure of the heel).

All because you had been failed to look at her shoes.

She got off at the next stop and I watched her awkwardly waddle off. In fact I watched the shoes. And considered the fatal mistake I had so nearly made. Realising that one day a man would come along who wasn't so observant. The clopping of the sole on the floor was that unfortunate man's death knell.

Could he not hear?

Could he not hear?

There are none so blind as those who don't look at people's shoes. Yet ironically it is the people who constantly look at people's shoes who end up bumping into stuff.

Thursday 22nd May

I used to listen to the News Quiz on Radio 4 as a student, so it was both flattering and slightly strange to be asked to appear on it tonight.

As it turned out I was quite rubbish on it. I hadn't really had time to prepare and as soon as it started I realised the preparation I had done was wrong. I had read the papers and thought of a few vaguely humorous opinions and arrogantly assumed that I could riff through it. I was to be the inevitable victim of my own hubris. But everyone else had fairly solid gags that brought the house down and most of my stuff got a couple of stifled and embarrassed chuckles. Or groans.

And a couple of boos!

Of course once an audience smells the fear you are done for in any case. Much of comedy is about style over content. I am not a comedian with an endless stream of anecdotes and gags primed and ready to go in my mind and the show was strangely competitive. Not that anyone wanted to win, but just everyone was trying to get in with their gag and because I was losing confidence I didn't bother trying to chip in too much (often only to hear one of the others make a similar crack to the one I had had in mind).

It's probably not the best format for me. One of the questions was about scientists proving that ghosts did not exist and I knew that the obvious way to go was to make reference to the *Scooby Doo* gang. But I couldn't bring myself to do the obvious material. Of course one of the others did it (pretty well I have to admit) and it went down a storm.

Yet the others (all fairly seasoned panellists) made the game seem easy and were extremely entertaining. So the show itself was good, despite my floundering performance.

Over an hour of stuff was recorded for a half hour slot, so it will edit down and the producer might be able to make me look vaguely competent and slightly amusing. But I wasn't.

It was like being in an exam that you have failed to revise for. Or probably more like being in an exam that you thought you were clever enough not to have to revise for, only to discover that you aren't.

I apologise to the BBC license payers and vow not to make the same mistake again.

*I don't know why I agreed to do this show when I had
so much else on my plate and I don't know how I thought I
would get away with doing zero preparation, but if you were
unfortunate enough to hear it, then you will know how bad I
was. I had been pencilled in to return to do the show the next
month, but this pencil was silently and hastily erased after
tonight's recording.*

Friday 23rd May

I've had so much on this week that it has been very difficult to get on with the book. The pressure is beginning to tell. However great a job this is the times when it gets stressful are truly, horrifically, nervous breakdown-inducingly awful.

I know I make it appear that I sit around all day wondering what my own skull looks like and prevaricating (and there is a fair amount of that, I have to say) but I do actually work quite hard. If all goes to plan I will have written a book and a film in the first half of this year, as well as having done quite an extensive tour and being on one episode of the News Quiz! Oh and I've also written this bloody, bastard thing you're reading now as well. That's not bad going really is it?

I am a comedian. It is in my interest to pretend my life is easy, partly because my job is to give all you poor fuckers a respite from the drudgery of your own jobs and humdrum lives.[31] You don't want to go out on a weekend and hear me complaining as well – which I'm not incidentally – and that I sit around in my pants all day watching daytime TV.

Again there is quite a lot of that. In fact if I did less of that then I wouldn't end up facing these near-impossible deadlines. But nothing's going to change. I am old enough to realise that the procrastination is all part of it.

I think maybe writing is similar to giving birth – now calm down, I'm not saying it's as painful or difficult or indeed as amazing.

---

[31] *The phrase "humdrum lives" is a quote from the taped voice-over in the first room in Nottingham's Tales of Robin Hood, which greatly amused Stew and me when we were killing time there on one of our tours. "You are about to leave behind your*

I was talking to one of my many friends who have recently spawned progeny and he was affectionately recalling how his girlfriend had been screaming blue murder and vowing she'd never have any more children as she was giving birth (an understandable reaction from all accounts. God bless all the mothers of this world). Yet a few hours later as she held her tiny boy in her arms she was already cooing that it would be nice to have another one. Somehow the brain manages to blank out the memory of the pain and terror (and when you see what you get out of it, many women would think it was all worth it anyway).

So what is similar here (on a much lesser level. I told you calm down) is that I always go through this mini-Hell producing a piece of work and while I do it, wail and moan and decide that I'm going to get a job in a chapeau shop (like Nigel Tufnell[32]). Yet once it's all over, my body floods my brain with that same serum that makes the mothers forget and I look at what I've created and think. "Ah, isn't it cute? I must have another."

So I have written this entry solely for the me of the future. In July I want me to read back over this and remember how unhappy I was on the morning of 23rd May and go to the job centre and see what they've got going in the hat industry. You are happy to start low down and work your way up. Remember how alone and depressed you were, how throwing yourself in front of a tube seemed a valid option…. No, stop looking at the mock up of the book and thinking it's cool. It isn't. The stress has taken five years off your life and it's caused damage to all your human relationships. No don't look at the cheque either. No, you don't want to do another one. Stop it. Will you never learn, you twat?

At least promise me Rich, that you won't write anything else about cocks. Just that. That's all I want.

My problem now is that my brain is bound to make me forget about this entry as well. I am doomed to a life of doing anything I want, sleeping in late and getting well paid for it. Literature's gain (well probably loss actually) is the hat shop's loss (actually probably a gain too).

---

humdrum lives!" We thought that this was presumptuous, believing that our lives are less humdrum than what follows, essentially a lot of waxworks in bad wigs.
[32] *A Spinal Tap reference*

On a positive note I imagined I was still about 25,000 words from the end, but on counting it all up this evening I find I only have 18,000 words to do.

Although the words "only" and "18,000" are somewhat relative.

Saturday 24th May

There is a tramp who has sat on the top step of the stairs leading down to Balham tube station ever since I first moved here (I guess that's eight or nine years ago). He was one of the eccentric men of the street and was always extraordinarily happy (most likely because he was constantly full to the brim with strong lager). As you ascended the steps from the bowels of the Northern Line he would often be sitting there, singing opera in a booming voice which echoed into the chasm beneath him. He was pretty good and it made you wonder what his story was.

I don't think he'd decided, like I did in Melbourne, that it would be cheaper to live on the streets.

I don't really know how old he is. It's difficult to guess the age of a homeless person (though I expect late night Channel 4 will one day turn that challenge into a game-show of some kind).

Anyway I used to like seeing him. He'd make the commuters laugh. I'd usually give him a couple of quid. I'm sure he did pretty well.

Over the years though I have seen his decline (and it's not like he the starting point was very high up), but he now looks thin and much older. He's sunk too far into his drunken stupor to smile now, let alone sing for us. I sometimes still slip him money out of pity now, but it's not like that money is helping him to do anything but get more drunk. I suppose that's all he's got now and all he's likely to have, so it's probably not our place to judge.

I don't know what I'm trying to say. I don't actually think there is any constructive way to help the man. I think you have to want to be helped (which is why the *Big Issue* is such a good idea).

I suppose I am just saying that it is sad.

The opera-singing tramp disappeared from the step over the next few months and I am sad to report that I think he has died. I'd be delighted to hear otherwise and that he had turned his life around and was making his way in the world, but I fear that that is unlikely to be the case.

Sunday 25th May

I have invented a great new way to keep fit and stay ahead with your favourite hobby.

It's called orient-CNPS-ing.

I had heard that cheeky Emma Kennedy[33] was spending half an hour each morning cycling round her local streets looking for number plate numbers, which explains her prodigious CNPS form.

I have been reluctant to get back into exercising (which is the basic reason for my recent slight weight gain), and I am also quite keen to finish doing CNPS at some point before my fortieth birthday. It's a young man's game.

So it struck me, there are thousands of cars parked in the streets around my house. I have occasionally mentally noted one or two of them that are close to the number I need as I've walked to the station. What if every morning I went for a jog around the streets near to my home, took a notebook and made a record of where the cars in the next twenty or so numbers I needed were parked. As they probably belonged to someone in the street they were likely to be there if I return at a later date.

When I had seen the previous number on a jog, I could check my notebook and then sprint to the recorded address and thus get fit and complete my annoying self-imposed and insane task much earlier.

It's amazing what an incentive this was to exercise. Usually when I go running I manage twenty-five minutes and am ready to stop, but with the promise of 129 being just round the corner I found I carried on going much longer than usual.

---

[33] The first mention of my good friend and (now) fellow blogger – www.emmakennedy. net – who would I had met at University and had done comedy shows with. Our lives would overlap on several occasions over the next few years.

Although I haven't seen many numbers that I immediately need, I have already got good leads on most of the numbers in the 140s (and it's going to be fun criss-crossing Balham to go and pick them up – presuming I haven't moved first as I'm only here for another week). I've got four 141s!

More importantly I have run for over half an hour.

I feel an exercise video coming on.

And I think it's ideal, because I think most of the nerds who want to spot number plates are probably couch potatoes whose skin is rarely exposed to the sun and who to be honest could do with losing a bit of weight.

NB Try not to be too obvious noting down the addresses and numbers. If a member of the Mafia sees you looking at his car and making notes then he might think you are some kind of snitch and send you to sleep with the fishes. No-one wants to have to spend the night in a dark aquarium. Spooky!

15,000 words to go now. I think I can have a couple of days off!

Monday 26th May

It's been a stressful bank holiday weekend for me and I've pretty much been stuck in the house or the library working. It's going OK. I have a week to finish two and a half chapters (and just over 11,000 words now).

Tonight I felt the need to go out and at least be around other human beings for a while, so I went to read some of my books in a bar and had a glass of wine. On my way home I was tired and anxious and depressed and my stomach cried out for fried chicken. I had already eaten, and so I tried to resist it, but I somehow convinced myself that just on piece would cheer me up. I don't do drugs and fried chicken is the crack of the thirty-something overweight man who lives on his own.

By the time I'd got to the counter I'd convinced myself I might as well have two pieces of chicken and chips. I am crumbling so easy.

But before me in the queue I saw myself. Not literally myself, but another version of me. A more extreme version of me. He was about my age, a bit more overweight, had more grey hair and was more of a nerd than me. He was such a regular of the Flavas fried chicken shop that he greeted the confused man behind the counter like an old friend. He actually insisted on reaching over the counter and shaking his hand. He was such a chicken addict that he wasn't even ashamed to be here, like me. He ordered the same thing I was about to.

"Anything else," enquired the man behind the counter.

"No!" chirped the outwardly happy man (though I am convinced inside he was screaming in anguish at his loneliness. It's a guess, based on him being an exaggerated version of myself). But he then looked up at the board and um-ed and ah-ed self-consciously as if the thought of having something else had just struck him. "Oh… actually just four chicken wings as well". He chuckled a little awkwardly. Thank God. He was embarrassed to be here, and ashamed of his greed, he just hid it better than me.

I gave my order, quite pointedly not ordering anything extra. It was good to feel superior to the other sad fool who was clearly a proper addict and we waited for our chicken. I wondered how many thirty-something overweight men were spending this glorious bank holiday night eating unpleasant, artery-clogging fried food, before returning to their flats alone.

I thought it was probably twenty-nine.

I wondered about saying to him, "Hey look, we are similar. I am a bit cooler than you, obviously, but we're both doing nothing, why don't we go and have a drink and see if that eases the pain of solitude that fills our hearts".

Then I looked into his eyes and realised he was thinking of saying exactly the same thing. Perhaps he had seen me jogging round Balham this morning with a notebook and looking at car number plates.

In any case, our chicken was ready, so we couldn't have gone to the pub even if we hadn't both been scared about having to talk to a more nerdy version of ourselves.

Instead we both went home to our separate flats. I was glad. The desperation of loneliness clung to him like a lingering fart.

Not me though. No. Because I am cool. Comparatively. The car number plate thing notwithstanding.

It is important to me to feel superior to the man who is essentially the same as me, because unlike most nerds I am not comfortable with my nerd status. I'd like to think that in the kingdom of the nerds I am the king. Realistically though I realise I am more like the junior minister for transport.

Even nerds aren't impressed by that.

And nerds are impressed by anything.

Aren't you?

Wednesday 28th May

A car in Midmoor Rd (also, as you are probably aware, home to numbers 135 and 136) has an amusing bumper sticker on it. It says, "Unless you're a haemorrhoid, GET OFF MY ASS!"

Which is all well and good as far as it goes. I presume he is trying to inform drivers behind him not to come too close (which is sensible advice, as in the event of an emergency stop they might crash into the back of him).

But there is an implicit flaw in the advice. The fact is that haemorrhoids are extremely unpleasant (so I hear) and no one in their right mind would want one of them on his backside. So really the sign should read, "Unless you're a haemorrhoid, GET OFF MY ASS! And actually, also if you are a haemorrhoid, can you also get off my ass, because it's quite painful when you are on there. Thanks."

Actually, even that isn't really sufficient, because why would you have to give that advice to a haemorrhoid on the back of your car. So it should then say, "And if you are a haemorrhoid, what are you doing, sort of disembodied, behind me on the road? How are you able to live independently of a human body? Surely you can't even read, so am I not totally wasting my time in putting this advice to you on the back of my car anyway?"

All right it's not the catchiest of bumper stickers, but it's accurate. It's funny because it's true.

It would probably be better if the bumper sticker just said, "I would appreciate it if you didn't drive too close to the back of my car, because in the event of an emergency your closeness might result in a collision."

No, even that wouldn't be good enough. You'd have to add, "Unless of course we are in a traffic jam or very slow moving traffic in which case it would be ridiculous and annoying for you to maintain a thirty-foot distance. Clearly you should consider the circumstances and the weather conditions carefully and make a common sense judgement as to what would be the safest distance to be at. You probably know this already. I suppose it's slightly arrogant of me to give you advice about your driving. You don't give me advice about my rubbish and ultimately illogical sense of humour, so I should just leave you alone. In the event of you rear-ending me you will take liability for the accident, so you realise that it is in your interests to drive sensibly. To be honest, if you're the kind of idiot who likes to risk everyone's life by driving too close at high speeds, then a humorous sign telling you not to is going to have no effect (except possibly to make you deliberately drive even closer), so I think I'll just shut up. Just pretend I didn't say anything."

Again, maybe bumper sticker that was that long would cause more accidents than it prevented, as drivers struggled to read it.

Of course, there is another possibility. The driver of the car might have a donkey, which he doesn't want anyone to ride. But he doesn't like his donkey. He thinks the donkey is an idiot. The donkey annoys him. So he wants the donkey to get piles.

Of course once again he has failed to realise that haemorrhoids are not conscious creatures. They cannot read, or exist independently and in fact to imagine them getting on to a donkey or an anus is a misunderstanding of all medical fact.

So the bloke or woman who owns that car is a twat whatever the circumstances. Go and stand by his (or her) car and whenever he (or she) comes out to drive it, point out how stupid they are.

Keep doing it until they remove the sticker.

Thanks.

Thursday 29th May

I saw something that slightly baffled me in one of the toilet cubicles at the British Library today.

That's got your attention. Unfortunately it is nothing that interesting.

I was sitting there, minding my own business, quite literally, when I noticed that one of the toilet rolls had something written on it.

It wasn't one of those novelty toilet rolls with poems or gags or the photos of football players from opposing teams printed on it. It was written on in biro and it said this,

"Not studying – I work in IT."

I looked at it, trying to work out what it could mean and why someone had written it there.

I don't think it was an attempt at humorous graffiti. If it was, I don't get the joke.

If anything it seemed like the answer to something someone else had said. Were two patrons of the British Library lavatories having some kind of written conversation between two cubicles? Presumably strangers, one of them had passed a piece of toilet paper under the partition saying "Hi, I'm Ian. What's your name?"

The other bloke rather than being freaked out had written back, "I'm Keith. What are you doing here (not in the toilet, I can hear what you're doing. I mean in the library)?"

It was going well for them. The unusual opening gambit of making friends by passing toilet paper notes under a toilet partition had paid dividends for Ian. Ian is a shy man who finds it difficult to interact in social situations, but with the anonymity of the bathroom he feels happy. He knows that he has something in common with the neighbour, they are both doing a poo. It's a bit like a very low-tech version of the internet chat-room, except you're more likely to meet the other person at the basins after.

Ian writes back, "I am studying the effect of the death of Thomas a Becket on Anglo-Papal relations in the thirteenth century. What are you studying?"

Keith gets the message, chuckles to himself. He is just a visitor to the library. Possibly he's just come in to use the toilet. "Not studying", he writes "- I work in IT."

But before he can rip it off the roll something happens. I don't know what. Perhaps the British Library has a toilet patrol to stop people passing notes to one another under the toilet door. The toilet patrol has spotted Ian passing the note, then timing everything just right, they wait until Keith has written his message then kick open both the doors and drag Keith and Ian off into the bowels of the British Library where they are punished for their dirty correspondence. Ian loses his library privileges. Keith's photo is given to security with the words "Do not allow in. He works in IT and is only coming here to use our toilet facilities."

Ian and Keith never get a chance to exchange numbers. They never meet again.

It's a human tragedy

That's the only thing that makes sense to me.

The only other possibility is that two men were in the same cubicle and one was giving the other a blowjob. The receiver was trying to be chatty to his new friend who was doing him such a favour and said, "So what are you studying?"

The giver of the blowjob did not want to stop half way through to answer and risk breaking the flow, but nor did he want to appear rude. So he took out his biro, being careful to keep the blowjob going, then wrote on the toilet roll, "not studying – I work in IT."

The bloke getting the blowjob said, "Oh right. Interesting." That was pretty much the end of the small talk.

Though that scenario doesn't seem as likely as the first.

Those are the only two possibilities. I challenge you to think of any other chain of events that could have led to this strange missive.

Write them on a postcard and then put them in the bin.

Or pass them under a toilet partition and see what happens.

Friday 30th May

There was a big, fat fly in my dressing room today. He was flying around lazily in the heat, the pitch of the buzzing giving away the fact that even he was too sweaty and tired to really put any effort into his job (which basically involves shitting on bits of food as far as I understand it).

I too was hot and bothered and trying to work and much as I love all the creatures of God's creation I wasn't in the mood to share this limited space with this disease harbouring interloper. I tried to shoo the flying insect out of the door, but he was having none of it.

Another time I may have persisted, but I was tired and sweaty and just not in the mood, so I decided that me and this fly would have to fight this out. It was going to be a battle to the death. Only one of us would leave that dressing room alive. My money was on me, unless the fly could do a spectacularly potent shit on the *Prêt a Manger* sandwich I was half way through eating.

I am afraid it wasn't much of a spectacle. There was a mismatch between the sides reminiscent of the recent Battle for Baghdad (and possibly my reasons for destroying my enemy were similarly tenuous – revolving as they did around similar accusations of weapons of mass destruction, although opponents of Bush and Blair will not be satisfied if only fly shit is found in Iraq). A couple of times I dealt the fly a blow which knocked it to the ground. It was stunned, but shook itself off and resumed its irritating flight. Taking a tip from the gladiators of ancient Rome I grabbed a towel and threw it at the fly. I caught him in my trap and the towel and the fly fell onto the surface of the table. I pressed down on the towel around the spot where I knew the fly to be. My enemy was vanquished. I expected to feel exhilarated, but the ease of my victory left me hollow inside.

I couldn't bear to lift the towel and see the squished form of my nemesis beneath, so I left him there. Literally crushed.

Fifteen minutes later I got a bit disgusted by the idea of a squished fly on my dressing room counter, so I went to move the towel. As I lifted it off the counter and looked for the body of the unfortunate creature I was shocked by the unharmed fly rising like a phoenix and heroically heading for my face. It was like that bit in Carrie where the arm comes out the grave – or that bit that is in all horror films where someone you think is dead turns out to actually be alive. How had he survived my onslaught? One had to admire his tenacity. As he had survived my execution I considered letting him live (commuting his sentence to life imprisonment), but within about two seconds he was annoying me, so I punched him in the face and while he lay stunned on the floor I stepped on him until he be dead.

I felt slightly guilty at the senseless destruction of life (not that I'd been that bothered about the chicken that I'd just eaten in my sandwich) and wondered if the gods would punish me by making me have a bad show.

As I lifted my shoe I was surprised to see the fly had gone. Had he survived again? Had he just been a phantom fly?

No, he was wedged into the bubbles on the sole of my shoe. I tried to shake him off, but he wouldn't go. I rubbed my shoe on the floor. He was still there. Eventually most of his crushed carcass fell to the ground, but some of him remained lodged in the grooves of my shoe.

Even in death he mocked me.

Saturday 31st May

I am finally moving into my new house on Tuesday. After being in my flat for over five-and-a-half years it is deeply strange to be moving out (which is probably partly why I haven't been in a massive rush to get to my new place). Given everything else that is going on at the moment it is a bit of a hassle (but the other reason it's taken so long to move is that I've had so much on and there isn't really an end in sight, so it would be a fag whenever I'd finally chosen to go).

Three more nights in this place.

Today I got a note through from the girls downstairs. You may remember I have previously been critical of them for letting me know about garden parties late and then not inviting me. This note informed me that one of them was having a thirtieth birthday party in the garden that evening and hoped that that would be OK. Of course, it's not like a birthday is something you can plan for in advance, so there's no way they could have let me know before. They always seem to have parties when I have a lot to do and am very tired (but maybe that's just because I always have a lot to do).

This note was different though. Because it closed with the words, "And please do pop down for a drink."

Not exactly a whole-hearted invite – "pop" down for "a" drink. But still, progress has been made. I have to say I wondered if they'd been reading my diary, which I always forget is a possibility and I felt a bit embarrassed by my unwarranted attacks on them.

Then it struck me that if they are reading my diary, then they KNOW I have a lot of work on this weekend and have deliberately decided to have a party, to disrupt my plans. The bitches! Inviting me along is just to let me know that they know. They are insulting me more than ever.

As it happened I couldn't go because of writing and gigging and when I got home the party had mainly broken up and they hardly made any noise at all. That's not the point. It's psychological. They're trying to fuck with my brain. I bet it was them who put the piano at my new house too.

They're good.

I have one chapter (or 3000 words) to do by tomorrow night. It is quite a tricky chapter. Wish me luck!

The deadline for the book was the 1st of this month, but even after all the delays and despite writing about a fifth of it in the last two weeks I still didn't quite make the date. But with just one chapter to go I was close enough. It was a book that I had practically sweated blood over and despite delivering it much later than intended and the last minute rush I had worked very hard on it. It was thus quite galling when at the last minute the publishers seemed to lose faith in it (despite having had the early chapters for several months) and decided it needed more pictures to make it look more like a book you might read on the loo, rather than what it was: an amusing, but still rather academic look at the subject of male genitalia. In the end it was not really pushed in the bookshops (perhaps the title did me no favours and put people off asking for it by name) and did not sell many copies. I have had nice emails from a few of the people who actually got hold of a copy, but it was another knock at a time that I was already rather blue to have done all that hard work, seemingly for nothing. Writing is indeed like pulling teeth!

Sunday 1st June

I saw a programme on TV the other day about a family who had survived a boat trip gone wrong in extremely cold circumstances. The observation was made that they had survived because they had treated the crisis, not as one big situation, but as a series of tasks that needed to be overcome. They didn't get overawed by the scale of what they were going through, merely concentrated on each problem as it arose. People who don't survive such situations generally get over-awed and just give up.

On a less serious scale I realise this is an excellent way of dealing with many things, especially writing. When I started writing the book I found it difficult to get on with it because it seemed so huge and daunting. To be honest, at the start of each chapter I felt the same. There was so much to do, so much to say and often I wouldn't be able to do anything.

I realise now a bit too late that the way to write if you're having trouble getting going is to have a go at one of the bits you know you can do, or to try to do a little bit of something you're not sure about. Gradually it will build up and the work will get done. I suppose this is what I do to some extent, but I waste so much time getting overcome with the difficulties and metaphorically freeze to death in my boat.

I realise this is a bit late as I should have finished the book today. I have got close, but the last chapter still needs some work and annoyingly I have lots of little bits to write which are essentially fillers. If I'd be clued in I could have done these easily at any point in the last six months when I couldn't get on with the chapter I was on.

It's going to be OK. The final draft of the book has to be with my editor on the 9th. I do have to pack and move house this week, but I've got a lot done in the last three weeks and so know I will be able to do the necessary work (because I have to).

I just wish I'd made this obvious realisation a couple of months ago.

Monday 2nd June

My book *Talking Cock* concludes that size of genitalia isn't really all that important, that a man is not defined by his penis and that many of our perceived notions of penis-based masculinity are bogus.

Despite all this, last night, with the book swimming around

in my head as I considered the approaching deadline, I had me a dream.

I had decided to have a penis enlargement operation, because I thought it would impress a woman that I was seeing (who had been holding things back on the sexual front). The process involved me having my penis removed, and then sent away to be worked on by surgeons who would reattach it the next day.

Consequently I had twenty-four hours (though the dream didn't run to scale) of having no penis (or testicles, they'd taken them too) at all. I remember being quite upset about this. I was fearful that the operation might go wrong or that my penis might get lost in the post. I also wondered whether my penis would be recognisable. Would I still be ME? What if I ended up with someone else's penis by mistake? That would be a tragedy. Would it all have been worth it for the sake of a couple of inches of length?

Then by magic my new cock was there, swaddled in bandages and inside my trousers. I didn't want to get it out and I was worried about how it might look. I also wondered if it would burst if I got an erection[34].

Inevitably, I got a hard-on and I could see from the bulge that my knob was substantially bigger. So could a group of women who were passing by, who started taking an interest in me. One of them kissed me. My apparently gargantuan penis naturally made me attractive to all women.

Then the girl who I'd had the op done for turned up and shooed off the girls (though she was understanding that they couldn't help themselves). Together we undid my trousers and unwrapped the bandage and there it was.

It was enormous.

It was slightly bent at the bottom, presumably where the extra inches had been added, but it was still beautiful. Much thicker, much longer and so very hard and virile. I felt fantastic and much more manly than I had before. The girl I was with cooed and touched it and wondered if it was ready to use.

I thought that it might be a bit risky, but within moments I had

---

[34] *Now you know about the fact that I had recently had stitches in my Spurt Reynolds, this revelation makes a lot more sense.*

decided that I just didn't care. That I would use my wonderful new manhood to make love to this beautiful girl.

Then my alarm went off and it was time to get up and finish this sodding book about cocks. So I had to endure all that stupid symbolic rubbish, without even getting to dream about having great sex.

I can't believe that I genuinely had that dream, but I did. So despite all my claims that being a good man was about your heart or your self-respect and that you should learn to love your penis however it looks, my subconscious is still equating my penis, not only with virility and attractiveness, but also with identity itself.

I suppose it shows either that there is a part of us that is supposed to think like this or that the stereotypes are so ground into our brains that it's going to take some kind of miracle to change things.

On the other hand it's given me a good start to my final chapter.

Indeed it did, the dream went into the book pretty much as I had written it above.

Tuesday 3rd June

Being a removal man is a tough job. I would imagine that there aren't many removal men who are also members of a gym. Their job is essentially a weights machine crossed with a step machine. It would be a busman's holiday.

The pay isn't all that good, but what you save on gym membership makes removal men the richest people in the world. Plus unlike most people who are members of gyms they also get regular exercise.

It was hard knowing which firm of removals men to pick, 'cos they don't have a picture in the Yellow Pages. I went for the one whose voice I liked the sound of best.

They turned out to be a bit of a ragbag, a young lad who liked to smoke, an older fella, the boss (the only one who looked like he was fit, who ironically did the least lifting) and a slightly weird one who assembled stuff that had had to be dismantled and if they were to make a film of his life – unlikely, even if they called it *The Dismantler*: those drawn in by the title would be disappointed by the content of the film, which would involve some dismantling, a drive and then some mantling – he would be played by Steve Buscemi in a grey wig (partly because that's what he looked like and partly 'cos Buscemi will do any old shit these days).

It was a clammy day in West London and I got exhausted carrying a few relatively light items up one set of stairs. When the removal men came to lift my widescreen TV up to the second landing, I thought one of the older one was going to die.

Luckily he didn't, because I don't think his mates would have been prepared to act as bearers at his funeral. "More lifting stuff and carrying it around? No thanks, we do that all day."

If I were a removal man I would insist that my work-mates did the honours at my funeral, but then, just for fun, I would buy a plot for my grave which was on the roof of the tallest building in town. All those stairs!

Of course the climb would probably kill a few more of the removal men and more men would have to be drafted in to lift my coffin, as well as the coffins of the other removal men (who, with foresight, I would also have purchased plots for, also at the top of the tall building – I am aware it would cost a lot, not least because there aren't many buildings that would devote a floor to the carcasses of the dead, but every building manager has his price).

Eventually nearly every removal man in the country would be dead, but I tell you my friends, whichever removal men were still standing at the end of all that, they would be the ones to employ for your move.

I think I might institute such a test next time I move and award the contract accordingly. Not that I'll have to die first. I will fill the coffin with a couple of widescreen TVs. That should sort the men out from the smoking boys.

*A*nd so I was now officially in my new house, even if I had not sold my flat in Balham just yet, but it still seems a fitting place to end this first (and last?) volume. I was not overjoyed to be moving into this family home on my own and was inevitably quite unsettled by the change. I had selected this location partly because it would be convenient for S to get out of London to see her parents and partly because it was close to Al Murray's house, which had proved a tricky commute from South London. I had thought I would be working with him again on a quiz show we'd come up with, but on my return from Australia he informed me he had decided to devise it alone. Which he had every right to do. But it meant my two main reasons for upping sticks were now no longer valid. I felt a bit displaced and lonely, as well as overwhelmed by all the work I would need to do in order to furnish a house that was at least three times bigger than my previous flat. I was concerned that I might have overstretched myself. What if the work stopped coming in? What if an orchestra of instruments was left on my path and I had to give the binmen five pounds to take them all away?

Still, as I realise in my more lucid moments, there are worse problems to have than owning a gigantic house and I would soon come to love rough and ready Shepherd's Bush and feel more at home there than the new posh Balham I so distrusted. Life and the blog plodded on. And I was about to experience the delights of the Box Lady. But you'll have to read the second volume to find out about her...

Consecutive Number Plate Spotting

THE RULES

- The aim of CNPS is to spot every number on the conventional old-style UK number plate, in order, from 1 to 999.

- It is very important to realise that you have to spot the exact digit you are looking for. If you see the car Y11RTS, you cannot count that as a 1. It is an 11. If you see the number 223 that can't be counted as a 23 or a 22. If you see the number 234 you can't call it an anagram of 342. Only the exact number you are looking for is acceptable.

- You can only progress to looking for a number 2, when you have spotted a number 1 and so on. You can not hold the 2 in your memory and then when you've seen a 1, say "ah yes, and I saw a 2 yesterday, so now I'll look for a 3." NO! It is called CONSECUTIVE number plate spotting. If you want to play the easy game of spotting all the number plates in any order then that is up to you (and I feel sorry for you). It must run, 1,2,3.... And so on, right up to 999. There are no exceptions. Even if you saw the next number just a second before. You have to clearly see the numbers in order.

- You cannot have two or three chains of CNPs running at a time. That is, you can't be looking for 5 onwards, as well as 45 onwards in the hope of eventually joining the chains up. Each individual number must be seen in its own right, consecutively.

- It can be frustrating when you keep seeing the number after the one you're looking for, or when after days of looking for a 4 and finally spotting one you see 10 more in the next 24 hours. Do not allow this frustration to allow you to cheat or think that you can count any number which isn't the one you are looking for.

- You must be sure that you have had a definite spot of the number. A car travelling quickly in the opposite direction may have looked like a 6. But can you be sure it wasn't a 16? Or a 66? Or even a 5? You must have clear sight of the number and be able to confirm without ANY DOUBT that you have spotted the number you want. Your mind will be so keen to see the next number (especially after hours and hours of failing to do so) that it is easy to be tricked into thinking you might have seen the number. If you collect any number in this way then your achievement is null and void. Think of the shame at the back of your mind when you get to 999, if you are not sure the 123 you saw was genuine. You will only be cheating yourself.

- Be aware that some number plates are spaced in a confusing way by irresponsible car owners. Please ensure you are not excluding a digit that is on the number plate or confusing a letter for a number. I have seen D1 4GAV. That is a 14. Not a 1 or a 4

- Knowing that a number you need is in a particular location is not enough. You actually have to go and look at the number plate for it to be counted. That is why the came is called Consecutive number plate SPOTTING.

- Only numbers on number plates can be included in this game. That is why it is called Consecutive NUMBER PLATE spotting.

- The number plate you see MUST be attached to a motor vehicle of some kind. A number plate lying in the road on its own is not acceptable. To allow number plates to be spotted on their own might encourage unscrupulous players to remove number plates from vehicles and store them for later use (or indeed to pay to have them made up at a shop). Also if you were to spot a number plate on the floor you could pick it up and store it for later. For this reason vehicle and number plate are both required. A number plate attached to a caravan or trailer is acceptable.

- Only UK number plates are acceptable in this version of the game. No use of numbers on foreign plates can be countenanced. Anyone found to have included a foreign number plate number will forfeit their life. If you commit this crime, please turn yourself in to the nearest police station and explain what you have done.

- Diplomatic number plates are not allowed and if you see a number plate with more than three digits then you can not divide those numbers up (even if they are separated by a letter) eg 123T456 is not a 123 and a 456. Nor can you pick and choose numbers as you wish.

- Those red trade number plates used on cars that have not been licensed and by people delivering cars across the country are not acceptable. Only licensed number plates.

- Extreme CNPS players may choose to also ignore obviously personalised number plates TIM 1 for example, or indeed the new style number plates which are at present a good source of 2's and 51s and 52s. In the current climate where old style number plates are slowly dying out, this may be a rule too far. For all but the most obsessed player, personalised and new style number plates are acceptable (make sure it is not a foreign plate though).

- To clarify the new style 02 on a number plate can be counted as a 2. However some new number plates also include the letter 'O'. Do not be tempted to use these 'O's to turn an 02 into a 200.

- You cannot include number plates that you have seen in photographs or on TV. Clearly you could just store or tape the number and look at it again at the appropriate time. Only real, three-dimensional number plates can be counted. Similarly your friend cannot text you a picture of a number plate that they have just seen. However they can ring you and tell you where the vehicle is and you can, if you so choose, go to see it.

- As A CNP Spotter you must abide by the CNPS code:

"I promise to do my best at spotting numbers consecutively, to do my duty no matter how boring and to never, ever cheat in the game or lie about where I've got up to, because I will only be cheating myself in the end."

Say it out loud before you start and at any point when you feel you are tempted to cheat or stop playing because the game is rubbish.

- Remember on average you should be seeing the number you need approximately once every 1000 cars. If you are getting through numbers significantly more quickly than this you are probably not playing the game correctly. Go back and read the rules again and then remember the name of the game is CONSECUTIVE NUMBER PLATE SPOTTING. It's not that hard.

- When you have spotted all the numbers from 1-999 you can stop playing. Please email me if you achieve this feat. Also let me know about the most CNPs you have spotted in twenty-four hours. Make a note of how long it has taken you.

HINTS

- This game is very long and practically impossible to complete. In order to give yourself a fighting chance it is worth familiarising yourself with number plates of cars that are regularly parked in and around your road. Especially if the numbers are within the next twenty or so that you are looking for. Then when your reach that number you can conveniently go and spot it. You can often clear three or four numbers on a good day if you are well prepared.

- Looking for cars on foot is a more efficient way than playing this game in a car. You can be sure of your spots and you can also run back to previous cars if they will help complete your sequence. Playing on a motorway is not as productive as it may appear, because it is hard to be certain of the number plates on the cars on the other side as they go past so fast. You will actually not see that many cars on your own side of the road.

- Be aware that some businesses have bought several vehicles at the same time, and consequently have consecutive number plates on these vehicles. Haulage companies at their base and pizza delivery motor-bikes parked outside a shop might provide you with unexpected riches.

- Please do not play this game whilst driving. Be on the look out for pedestrians and other obstacles. CNPS is a game of boredom and tedium. No-one should die because of CNPS and if they do it should only be through frustration.

- Car parks provide a large number of cars, all parked, in way that makes them easy to return to. A dedicated CNPS will spend his or her weekends and all his or her spare time in their local multi-storey. In such circumstance and with a big enough carpark one would imagine it might even be possible to spot every number (consecutively) in a day. Personally I think this spoils the beauty of the game and would not go to such lengths. But to any CNP spotter the car park is a wonderful source of numbers.

- Make sure you make a note of which number you are up to. Sometimes it is easy to get confused or forget or become bored.

- Be aware that any 1 in a number can be easily missed or ignored. You must make sure that you have definitely spotted the number you require and that there isn't an un-needed 1 in front or after it. 111 can look like 11. 21 can look like a 2 etc. Do not accept any number that you have any doubt about.

- You must know that once you take up the call to be a CNP Spotter you have to see it through to its bitter end. You can't start up the game, decide it's rubbish and impossible and then stop. By agreeing to start you have signed a contract that you will do all in your power to complete the task, even if it takes five or ten years.

Good luck and happy spotting.

Maybe you'd like to set up a CNPS club, with a membership card and – I don't know, a T-shirt or something. Maybe you could even organise club outings to car parks or second hand car dealerships and meet other people who like collecting car number plate consecutively. I won't be coming on those though, because all the people on them will be strange. If you have any questions about the rules or need clarification on any point, then please email me.